NEW YORK BEGINNINGS

NEW YORK BEGINNINGS
THE COMMERCIAL ORIGINS
OF NEW NETHERLAND

Thomas J. Condon

NEW YORK: NEW YORK UNIVERSITY PRESS
LONDON: UNIVERSITY OF LONDON PRESS LIMITED
1968

© 1968 by New York University
Library of Congress Catalog Card Number 68–28003
Manufactured in The United States of America

PREFACE

Throughout seventeenth-century Europe, in guildhall and counting house, in government office and village home, a great many men and women, excited by the accounts of explorers, ship captains, and adventurers, fashioned assumptions as to how the Old World might make use of the New. By far the greater number of these people looked at America with an eye toward its immediate, practical usefulness, and as an opportunity for adventure or financial gain. As circumstances changed over the years of the seventeenth century so, too, did these assumptions.

What, after all, did Europeans know about colonization when the New World was thrust upon them? It can be argued that Spain and Portugal had had some experience in the settlement of the Azores and Madeira. And there had always been Ireland for the English. But for the most part, European discussions of what could be done in the New World were predicated on examples derived from classical antiquity, which were not able to provide very much information on the mechanics of colonization. "Plantations," Sir Francis Bacon wrote, "are amongst ancient, primitive and heroical works." This came to be an expression for the times, repeated with but slight variation by other Europeans as articulate as Bacon, and passionately believed in by countless others who could neither turn nor read such a phrase.

But how begin a plantation or colony? How see a plantation through its early struggling years so that it might one day stand by itself? Classical antiquity was of little help. Thucydides, for

example, only showed Corcyra at its height, not during its beginning years as a colony of Corinth. The answers to these perplex-
ing questions could not be provided by theoreticians such as
Bacon. They were, instead, hammered out by merchants, ship
captains, and ambitious adventurers who were perhaps no less
idealistic than men such as Bacon but who were also intently
interested in present personal gain. It has long been recognized
that colonization and settlement in the New World were intimately connected with the commercial expansion of Europe in
the seventeenth century. But in addition to being driven by
commercial impulses and inspired by classical triumphs, men of
the time also had at hand the more useful example of Spain's
activity in the New World.

At the beginning of the seventeenth century, to sketch broadly,
Spain offered a specific example of a successful approach to the
problem of how the Old World could make use of the New.
The Spanish example, or the Spanish "way," exhibited an articulated colonial policy which rested on tested assumptions as
to what was involved and what could be expected from the New
World. These views found embodiment in a fairly well developed colonial administrative organization. At the end of the
seventeenth century England stood as an example of a different
but also successful approach to the problem posed by the New
World. The efforts of England, France, the Netherlands, and
Sweden throughout the seventeenth century to imitate the Spanish example, to prey on Spanish success, and to fill the interstices between points of Spanish colonial power ultimately
resulted in the creation of an entirely new approach to using
the New World — the English "way." The British Old Colonial
System thus began in imitation of Spain and, after much shifting of assumptions to accommodate itself to acquired experience
and the peculiar conditions of North America, eventually developed a well-defined colonial policy and colonial administrative
organization.

The years of the seventeenth century, then, can be characterized as a period of transition, of groping and experimenting, and
as a period of difficult-to-perceive change. Andrews has suggested
that it was not until the 1660's that people in England began
to recognize that while the situation in North America might
not fit into an acceptable Spanish pattern, still it might in time
prove to be an unexpected source of great profit to England. For
with the settlement of a great number of Europeans in North

America, the possibilities of developing it altered drastically. The English "way" had not been planned by officials in England; rather, it had developed otherwise, for reasons associated with why great numbers emigrated from England and for reasons which many officials could not all approve of at the time. France, too, began to develop its North American possessions through the means of permanent French settlers. The Dutch were never able to emulate the English example, chiefly because Netherlanders seemed not at all anxious to emigrate permanently to the New World in any numbers. The Dutch did manage to derive considerable profit from what might be termed a "transitional form." This was a combination of preying on Spanish colonies and filling the interstices temporarily. The Swedes failed to achieve even this degree of success.

The beginnings of New York, like the beginnings of many another American colony, can be traced to the activities of a commercial company — the West India Company. But unlike the Virginia Company or the Bermuda Company, the history of the West India Company is not primarily the history of its North American colony, New Netherland; for while the Virginia Company or the Bermuda Company aimed at the successful and profitable development of fairly specific geographical areas in the New World associated with these companies' names, the West India Company had half the world for its oyster — the continents of Africa and North and South America, the West Indies, and all the islands stretching from the Cape of Good Hope in the Western Hemisphere to New Guinea in the Eastern. Forming, thus, only a minute part of a more broadly conceived commercial venture, New Netherland was, until 1664, a stepchild of the West India Company.

The implications of this relationship have not been examined by historians in any detail. Instead, the great source collections of New York history have been ransacked to yield answers to such questions as whether New Netherland was more or less democratic, more or less religiously tolerant than her English neighbors in America. The answers obtained have depended for the most part on whether the point of view taken was Dutch or English. The result has been a curious concoction: one part myth, one part fancy, and one part history.

The key question for the years 1609–1664, which has not received the attention it deserves, is, What were the Dutch and the West India Company trying to accomplish in New Netherland? Were they, for example, consciously trying to rear up a peculiarly Dutch society in North America? The answer to this must be in the negative. Indeed an earlier generation of historians has paid lip service to this by dutifully noting in the beginning of works on New Netherland that the area owed its birth to commercial rather than to settlement impulse. However, in filling out the details of New Netherland's history, the same writers have failed to probe the implications of this commercial orientation, preferring instead to substitute for such an analysis the notion that, after all, a Dutch society was really in the making during these years. Thus the question of what the Dutch and the West India Company were trying to accomplish in New Netherland has not really been answered but merely deflected.

This work is an attempt to provide an answer to that question. For it is an understanding of the relationship of the Netherlands and the West India Company to New Netherland which provides the key to making sense out of the Dutch period of New York history. New Netherland's origins were commercial and it was a commercial company which dominated the development of New Netherland throughout its existence as a Dutch province. New Netherland had no breathing spell such as Virginia had between company rule and the tightening of imperial control from afar. Such a breathing spell, provided its population also increased as greatly as Virginia's did between 1624 and the 1660's, might well have given New Netherland a more permanently distinctive Dutch coloring. But as it was, the none too firmly rooted Dutch institutions were extirpated in 1664 and English ones substituted.

Within the brief span of New Netherland history, and despite the thinness of its population, New Netherlanders encountered much the same problems in creating a society in the wilderness as their English neighbors, north and south. Although the Dutch in New Netherland drew up no Mayflower Compact, they nonetheless found themselves involved in questions of organizing society. They approached these questions in much the same way as their neighbors, by attempting to combine remembered institutions with the requirements of an essentially new situation. Despite the commercial origins of New Netherland, the response of its inhabitants to the frontier environment of North America was quite similar to that of Englishmen.

The circumstances of life in the New World created for the immigrant stepping ashore at New Netherland an interest that was separate and distinct from the interest of the West India Company at home. Gradually a new set of assumptions about the development of the area came to be held by those Dutch and other European immigrants, who for one reason or another found themselves remaining in New Netherland. In this they were at one with immigrants to New England or Virginia. Formed in part from European assumptions, influenced greatly by the familiar cultural and institutional values of the Europe they left behind, and formed in part from the realities of North America, this new set of assumptions, these "American" assumptions, also underwent considerable change in the seventeenth century.

It may seem strange to refer to "American" assumptions in the seventeenth century, for certainly an image of America could not then have been conjured up in the same way as could one of England or Holland. Even though America could not have been imaginatively opposed to Europe, still, Boston was compared to Bristol, New Amsterdam to Amsterdam, and Virginia to the West Country. And in an age when local loyalties had as much, if not more meaning than national loyalty, these new loyalties were immensely real in a personal, every day sense.

A new nation was taking shape in seventeenth-century North America — not as brand, spanking new as the patriotic historians of earlier generations have led us to believe, but a mixture of old and new, a blending of old values with the new experience of the frontier. For America, despite the claims of the patriotic historians, did not spring Minerva-like from an aged and decaying Europe; it developed, rather, in fits and starts, caught as it was between the strivings of a dynamic new people in an embryonic new nation and the stirrings of a Europe in one of its most creative ages. It could not be completely new because in external matters it was to be Europeans who would control the leadstrings for many decades: merchants, politicians, and administrators. Finally it could not be completely new because its inhabitants brought with them their old ways, ingrained in habit and thought, and attempted to introduce them willy-nilly to the American scene, until experience suggested that modifications would be necessary.

Thus the significance of the Dutch period lies not in the picturesqueness of a way of life that really developed few permanent roots, but rather in the similarity of reaction of New Netherlander and New Englander alike to the American frontier and the problems of building a society in the wilderness.

CONTENTS

ABBREVIATIONS

Ecclesiastical Records	Edward T. Corwin (ed.), *Ecclesiastical Records of the State of New York.*
Huntington Docs.	A. J. F. van Laer (ed. and tr.), *Documents Relating to New Netherland 1624–1626 in the Henry E. Huntington Library.*
NNN	J. Franklin Jameson (ed.), *Narratives of New Netherland, 1609–1664.*
NYCD	Edmund B. O'Callaghan (ed.), *Documents Relative to the Colonial History of the State of New York.*
Prehistory	Simon Hart, *The Prehistory of the New Netherland Company.*
VRB MSS	A. J. F. van Laer (ed. and tr.), *New York State Library Van Rensselaer Bowier Manuscripts.*

NEW YORK BEGINNINGS

CHAPTER ONE

THE ROLE
OF PRIVATE MERCHANTS
IN THE BEGINNINGS OF
NEW NETHERLAND
1609–1623

As the seventeenth century opened, the geographical area that was to become New Netherland lay a sprawling, undisturbed wilderness of glistening lakes, long, navigable rivers, and a lush, variegated green forest that was only occasionally broken by scattered Indian settlements. To the seventeenth-century Dutchman, or European for that matter, it was a beautiful country. But so too, as surviving accounts tell us, were places like the West Indies, Brazil, or even New Guinea, halfway around the world again. How, then, was a footloose European of the seventeenth century to choose where he would make his voyage, or as the century progressed, where he might even settle and perhaps make a new home? Should he try the Orient or the New World? And even if he could narrow his choice to the New World, there were still many places to choose from. Beauty was hardly a guide — there was simply too much of it. More prosaic factors influenced his choice.

There were, for example, areas to which he could not go because they had already been taken by other nations — particularly, by Spain in the New World. Of course he might, and often did, participate in pirating or privateering ventures against these more established places. Such adventures, however, were not very satisfactory; the risks were great and the opportunity for this type of activity only infrequent. There were, however, other places, the "yet uninvaded countries," to which he might go in an attempt to duplicate the successes of the more established areas.[1] New Netherland was such an area. But why should he not go to Brazil or Curaçao instead? Except perhaps in the most wildly romantic way, no one then could have imagined that this nearly empty land of New Netherland would in time outdistance the wealth and population of the Netherlands, eventually to become known as the "Empire State" in a union of states that would even outstrip Europe itself. Indeed, there were many at the time who thought Brazil or Curaçao a better bet. Of course some dreamed and talked of the grand future that lay in store for New Netherland, and the promotional literature of the day, as might be expected, encouraged this. For the most part, however, the designs and expectations of the individuals actually involved in doing something with New Netherland were much more modest and much more limited.

Like many another remote, near-empty area then and now, New Netherland required only people — people with their plans and their dreams but especially with their physical beings — to transform it into something else. Who were these people? How and in what ways did they hope to transform the wilderness of New Netherland? These questions are difficult to answer because different answers are required over the fifty-five years from 1609 to 1664, during which the Dutch laid claim to the area of New Netherland. Although the period was brief, conditions changed rapidly in both the Netherlands and New Netherland, consequently affecting the kinds of people interested in New Netherland at any one time, their plans, and their expectations. In an attempt to impose some semblance of order on this elusive historical kaleidoscope of New Netherland history, the profile and activities of three major groups will be examined in detail and traced throughout certain arbitrarily defined periods. These three major groups: (1) private merchants, (2) incorporated Dutch West India Company merchants, and (3) inhabitants of New Netherland dominated the history of New Netherland. This first chapter is devoted to a discussion of the first major group, the private merchants, in the years 1609–1621.

Private merchants were responsible for initial attempts to develop the area of New Netherland. The news of Henry Hudson's discovery in 1609 of an uninhabited area of North America aroused the interest of a number of individual merchants in Amsterdam who had in mind certain limited objectives for the area. Until recently these merchants have gone unnoticed by historians, and yet it was their labors which made possible the later exploits of such familiar names in the history of New Netherland as Minuit, Van Rensselaer, and Stuyvesant.[2] Unlike the merchants associated with the Amsterdam Chamber of the Dutch East India Company who had retained Hudson to discover a northeast or northwest passage to the Orient, the interests of these independent merchants faced westward, to the New World and, especially, to the Canadian fur trade. To Hudson's employers the voyage had been a failure. Not so to these independent Amsterdam merchants for whom it represented an unexpected but exceedingly timely windfall. Two pieces of information from Hudson's voyage were of particular importance: First, that a vast area existed between French Canada and English Virginia which was neither fortified nor occupied by the French or English, and, second, that Hudson had traded with the Indians for furs along the river which now bears his name.

Dutchmen, even as the French and English before them, first became interested in the North American continent as a result of the cod fisheries off the shores of Newfoundland, Nova Scotia, and Maine. In search of drying areas and salt to preserve the cod for transshipment to Europe, these fishermen drifted ashore and established contact with the Indians. Out of this contact grew the extremely valuable North American fur trade which figured so prominently in the early histories of New France, New England, and New Netherland. In search of furs and gold, silver, or other precious metals, further explorations of the North American continent were undertaken. Unlike other nations, however, that came to the Grand Banks to fish, the Dutch came to trade — first for codfish but later for furs.[3]

Until the end of the sixteenth century the Dutch showed little interest in the Newfoundland fishery. The Netherlands had its own fishing banks, or "chiefest trade and principal goldmine" as contemporary writers referred to it, much closer to home.[4] During the fif-

teenth and sixteenth centuries, Dutch fishermen had gradually mo-
nopolized the fishing grounds of the North Sea, in the very front yard
of England. The enormous annual herring catch there provided a
food supply for the domestic market and an article of trade for other
lands. It served also as an important mainstay of the Dutch economy
because of the employment opportunities it created not only for fishermen but for the many related industries. In 1603 Sir Walter Ra-
leigh complained bitterly that the Dutch "made £1,759,000 a year
from the sale of fish captured in British waters." In 1615 it was estimated that "2,000 sails of Dutch busses, employing 37,000 hands, were
engaged in this industry." [5]

As a result of the dislocations in the European economy stemming
from the religious wars and the shift of the center of trade from Antwerp to Amsterdam, the Dutch began increasingly to enter the Mediterranean Straits trade in the last decade and a half of the sixteenth
century.[6] An item much in demand in these markets was the great
cod from the Newfoundland fishing grounds. From the beginning of
the sixteenth century and perhaps even earlier, fishermen from Bor-
deaux and Bayonne in France, from Devonshire and Dorset in England, from Portugal, and from San Sebastian and St. Jean de Luz on
the Basque coast of Spain had resorted to these rich fishing grounds
to supply their local needs. Dutch merchants began casting about for
ways of obtaining this much sought after commodity in the Straits
trade.

Circumstances ruled out direct Dutch fishing in those waters. In the
first place, the herring and cod seasons coincided so that it was unlikely that many Dutch fishermen could be lured to a fishery so far
away when such a profitable one existed much closer to home. And in
the second place, the Dutch lacked areas ashore for drying and salting
the cod even if fishermen could be induced to make the journey. The
justly heralded Dutch shipping industry provided a way out of these
difficulties. The first expedient hit upon was to buy cod at Plymouth
and Dartmouth in England for subsequent use in the Straits trade.
Between 1591 and 1602 a number of charter contracts to do just that
were recorded by Dutch merchants.[7] The principal merchants involved in the trade were Frederick Lubiner, Isaac le Maire, and Pieter Wiltbraet. After 1601 an even better solution was found. This was
to buy the codfish from the fishermen at the Newfoundland Banks
and sail directly to the Mediterranean ports with their cargo. Wilt-

braet was one of the first to contract for such a voyage in 1601. There are indications that this became a familiar trade pattern in the years after 1601 even though a regular trade cannot be fully documented until 1623.[8] The availability of shipping, Dutch ship design, and the fact that fewer men were required in their crews enabled Dutch ship captains and merchants to derive a profit from this operation.[9]

Thus it was through the trade in Newfoundland codfish that Dutch merchants at the turn of the seventeenth century became interested in North America. While the merchants undoubtedly knew from their very extensive commercial network in Europe of the existence of the valuable fur trade in North America, it was the codfish trade that pointed the way to Dutch participation in it. Ship captains and crews thereby gained considerable knowledge of North American waters as well as firsthand insight into the peculiar conditions of the North American fur trade. From this information and with their appetites whetted by the trickle of furs incidental to codfish operations, Dutch merchants sought ways of marshaling their capital and trade channels to enter the fur trade on a large scale.

French claims to a monopoly of the northern fur trade posed a serious threat to these ambitious plans, especially when the French began to back up their claims by establishing outposts designed to prevent traffic in furs by any interlopers. The French had been the first to capitalize on the North American fur trade. In 1602 a company of merchants was organized at Rouen to develop this trade. Champlain and Sieur du Pont Gravé, a wealthy St. Malo merchant, were sent out by this company to explore the possibilities of development. The planting of the first permanent settlement in North America is traditionally attributed to the efforts of this company in establishing a fort on the Island of Saint Croix in 1602 by Champlain and De Monts. It was not, of course, a permanent settlement but a base for conducting fur trade operations and a means of excluding other nations from participation. In 1605 this "colony" was moved to Port Royal in Nova Scotia.[10]

Although the French government tried to place a tight monopoly on the Canadian fur trade there was some traffic between the Dutch and French in New France at the beginning of the seventeenth century. Around 1600 there is mention of a trading and privateering voyage to Newfoundland sailing under a letter of marque from the Stadholder, Prince Maurice.[11] In 1605 Jan Munter and Company

applied to the States-General for a six-month monopoly of trade to
New France. Although the petition was denied, Munter and Company and others are known to have traded there before and after this
date.[12] In 1606 the ship "Witte Leeuw," sent out by a company of
eight merchants in Amsterdam, raised such a furor in New France by
its wild privateering activities that the French king registered a sharp
complaint about it to the States-General.[13] Not only had the "Witte
Leeuw" traded for furs with the Indians in defiance of the French
monopoly, but it had also captured two French ships, taken 107 bar-
rels of train oil and seven guns from a Spanish ship, and 24,000 pieces
of cod from a Portuguese ship. This expedition was under the command of Hendrick Cornelisz. Lonck, in later years an admiral in the
service of the Dutch West India Company and involved in both the
seizure of the Spanish silver fleet in 1628 and the capture of Brazil in
1630. Accompanying Lonck as supercargo was a French merchant
from Rouen, Nicolaes de Banquemaire, who had been retained for
the voyage by the Amsterdam company. Rouen was the center of the
Canadian fur trade in France and many of the Amsterdam merchants
had commercial connections there.[14] The stolen ordnance was later
returned; the furs were not — instead they probably yielded a hand-
some profit to the company. As a result of the "Witte Leeuw" inci-
dent, however, the French began to crack down on Dutch trading to
New France, making it increasingly difficult for Dutch merchants to
be involved so directly.

Undaunted, some Dutch merchants devised an ingenious substitute
for this curtailed direct trade. Arnout Vogels of Amsterdam, for one,
entered into a partnership with two French merchants of Rouen:
Lodewicq Vermeulen and Jehan Andries, who could legally trade
with New France for furs.[15] This company was to last for five years,
during which time the partners promised in a legal contract not to
participate privately in any direct or indirect trade to New France.
DuPont Gravé, who had earlier been associated with Champlain,
served as supercargo for the company and was admitted to a fourth
partnership. Hans and Abraham Pelt, brothers-in-law of Vogels and
also merchants in Amsterdam, took part, in this fashion, in the North
American fur trade.

Vogels was a young merchant of about thirty at this time. He had
been born in Antwerp and, like many an other merchant of that town,
moved to Amsterdam after Antwerp fell to the Spanish in 1585. His

father was a merchant and fur trader whose principal connections were in Cologne, where in 1600 he invested 30,000 guilders in a company with four other merchants. The elder Vogels was one of the first deacons of the Lutheran Church established in Amsterdam in 1588. The younger Vogels also had connections in Rouen. In 1610 he granted Jacob Eelkens power of attorney to collect debts owed him there. In July of 1610 he entered into a charter agreement with skipper Symen Lambertsz. Mau of Monnikendam for the voyage of a 200-ton ship to the "West Indies and nearby countries and places." Given Vogels' interest in the fur trade, the ambiguity surrounding the ship's destination may have been deliberate, as a way of disguising a trip to North America. Vogels died in 1620. His heirs were his brothers-in-law, Hans and Abraham Pelt.[16]

Thus, while the Dutch had ignored North America before the turn of the seventeenth century, there was a great deal of activity directed there in the first decade of that century. And undoubtedly beneath this flurry lay a growing and far more widespread interest in this area. It was at this point that Henry Hudson, an English navigator, appeared in Amsterdam with proposals for a voyage of exploration. His discovery of the river which now bears his name and the surrounding territory was to be of the greatest importance to these Dutch merchants and ship captains. Actually Giovanni Verrazzano, a Florentine in the employ of the French monarch Francis I, had "discovered" the area much earlier, but in 1524 the necessary capital, merchants, and trade channels were lacking for its development. This was not to be the case in 1609.

Very little is known about Hudson. The circumstances surrounding his most well known exploratory voyage, particularly his own intentions about the destination of that voyage, are difficult to determine and must be pieced together from scraps of information. His grandfather was probably a London alderman who played a role in the founding of the English Muscovy Company.[17] Hudson himself performed two voyages, in 1607 and 1608, for that company in search of a northeast passage to the Orient by way of the Cape of Norway, Nova Zembla. After the failure of these two voyages his services were sought out by merchants of the Dutch East India Company who were also vitally interested in discovering such a route. For reasons unknown, the negotiations between Hudson and the Dutch East India Company were broken off. Only the directors of the Amsterdam

Chamber of the Dutch East India Company resumed the discussions, and for them, finally, Hudson undertook the voyage.

His instructions, presumably, were to sail north to Nova Zembla, round the cape, and proceed thence in an easterly direction to the Orient. But finding his way blocked by ice, Hudson abandoned this plan and sailed west in search of a northwest passage to the Orient. His reasons for this have not been preserved. Some scholars have suggested that Hudson was interested all along in discovering a northwest route. There are many factors which point to such an interpretation.

In the first place, Hudson was very much in touch with the findings of other navigators of his day involved in voyages of discovery and exploration. Undoubtedly news traveled quickly in such circles in the seventeenth century. He was a friend of Captain John Smith who only recently had established the English settlement of Jamestown, Virginia in 1607. From the evidence available it appears that both Smith and Hudson believed that a passage to the Orient through North America could be found. In the second place, Hudson had been approached in Amsterdam by the Dutch merchant, Isaac le Maire, to undertake his voyage not for the Dutch East India Company but rather for the newly forming French East India Company.[18] Le Maire, it will be remembered, was one of the first Dutch merchants involved in the Newfoundland cod trade. He had also been a director of the Dutch East India Company until 1605 when he had a falling out with some of the other directors.[19] French operations in the East Indies never approached in size or scope those of the Dutch at this time. It may well be that the forming French company was interested in a passage to the Orient, but as a new company it might also have been quite content to settle for whatever might develop out of such a North American voyage. The involvement of the maverick Le Maire, whose prior interest in North America can be documented, in the negotiations with Hudson, adds to the validity of such a supposition. Finally, Hudson, in his negotiations with the Amsterdam Chamber, did discuss the possibility of a northwest passage with Dr. Petrus Plancius, a Protestant minister in Amsterdam. Plancius was not only a distinguished theologian, a participant in the Synod of Dort, but also a scholar, geographer, and promoter of voyages of exploration and trade. In many respects he was the Dutch counterpart of the English Hakluyt. He was, moreover, later a participant in the

Van Tweenhuysen Company, a company formed for the purpose of trading to New Netherland. His heir was the Amsterdam merchant, Claes Jacobs Harencarspel, who was also involved in the New Netherland trade.[20]

In March, 1609, Hudson began his third voyage in the famous "Half Moon," a yacht of eighty tons, with a mixed crew of eighteen to twenty English and Dutch sailors — an international mixture by no means unusual for such voyages. Hudson anchored in the lower bay of New York on September 3 and spent the remainder of the month exploring the river up to a point just below the present city of Albany. Disappointed at not finding the much-sought-after northwest passage and plagued by a near mutinous crew, he retraced his steps and arrived back in England on November 7.[21] Hudson dispatched an account of his voyage to the Amsterdam Chamber but was prevented from going in person by English authorities who claimed he should be in English rather than Dutch service. The Dutch historian Emanuel van Meteren, resident consul in London at the time, found this attitude exceedingly curious — as indeed it was. In 1610 van Meteren wrote:

> Many persons thought it strange that captains should thus be prevented from laying their accounts and reports before their employers, having been sent out for the benefit of navigation in general. This took place in January, and it was thought probable that the English themselves would send ships to Virginia, to explore further the aforesaid river.[22]

Hudson made one more journey to the New World, this time to the place now called Hudson's Bay, in 1610. This venture found him back in English service, sponsored by the combined efforts of the English Muscovy Company, the English East India Company, and other unidentified independent merchants.[23] This fourth voyage proved to be Hudson's last, for he was set adrift by a mutinous crew and presumably he perished.

It is difficult to identify the first voyage to this new area after the return of Hudson from his memorable third voyage. One contemporary source, de Laet, mentions "some merchants" who again sent out a ship in 1610. De Laet's account is not entirely reliable and, at any rate, no other details are contained in it.[24] Another contemporary source, the Dutch historian Wassenaer, writing in 1624, states that the area was "first sailed to by the worthy Hendrick Christiaens. of Cleves" but later adds that Hudson "had been there also." [25] Thus no accurate chronology can be constructed from these accounts.

In 1611, the Commissioners of the Amsterdam Admiralty sent out two ships, the "Craen" and the "Vos," under the command of Jan Cornelisz. May, for the purpose of discovering a northern passage to the Orient. In the winter of 1611–1612, May and his mate, Pieter Fransz., charted the waters and coastal areas of New France in the "Vos" and sailed northeast in search of the passage, while the "Craen," under the command of Symon Willemsz. Cat and Cornelis Jansz. Mes, continued surveying the coast of New France. Both ships were back in Amsterdam by October. Neither had been successful in finding a northern passage so that the 25,000 guilders prize which the States-General had established in 1596 for such a discovery remained uncollected.[26]

Dr. Hart suggests that May's voyage in 1611–1612 may have been a deliberate attempt to follow up Hudson's.

> *What Hudson had too easily given up in 1609, May was to achieve and he had taken a great deal of trouble to attain his object. On his departure he was orally instructed to sail in the winter to Nova Francia and to survey the coast. That this was kept secret until the last moment may indicate that the Directors of the Admiralty did not wish to show their merchant-hearts to the States-General. Hudson's experience on his voyage of discovery in 1609 had of course reached their ears, however, they did not know the exact place of the river he had found.*[27]

The maps of this voyage were never published and they are not known to exist now. It is entirely possible that May charted the area of New Netherland even though the term "Nova Francia" was used. In later voyages to New Netherland, for which more complete documentation exists, a variety of terms continued to be used to describe this area — "Virginia," "the West Indies," "Newfoundland," or "New France."

From the scant information available it cannot be determined whether or not there were any Amsterdam merchants in back of this Admiralty-sponsored voyage. But a strong likelihood exists because in 1613, May's mate, Pieter Fransz., sailed to New Netherland as skipper of the "Vos" for a company composed of the Amsterdam merchants Jonas Witsen and Simon Willemsz. Nooms — a company in which the

Commissioners of the Admiralty also participated through their ownership of the "Vos." [28]

An extremely important charter contract has recently come to light which provides a more direct connection between Amsterdam merchants and the opening up of the New Netherland area after Hudson's discovery. On May 19, 1611, three Amsterdam merchants — Arnout Vogels and Leonard and Francoys Pelgrom — contracted with a skipper Cornelis Rijser of Amsterdam to undertake a voyage to "Newfoundland" in the ship "St. Pieter." [29] Vogels was at the same time a member of a French fur-trading company at Rouen. The Pelgrom brothers were members of a large, wealthy merchant family whose connections reached out to Nuremberg, Frankfort, Strasbourg, Prague, Bergen (Norway), and Antwerp. The Pelgroms were Lutherans; their brother Herman was one of the founders of the Lutheran church in Amsterdam. Their father, Gheeraert Pelgrom, was an expatriate from Bois-le-Duc, whose wanderings had led first to Antwerp and then to Nuremberg. Through Francoys' wife Barbara, the Pelgroms became allied to the Spranger family — a family of equal size and wealth whose network of commercial connections extended throughout Europe.[30]

Because of Vogels' membership in the company which chartered the "St. Pieter," the possibility exists that this voyage to "Newfoundland" was still another example of a disguised voyage to New Netherland. The presence of the Pelgrom brothers' names on this contract adds greatly to the probability of such an hypothesis. For in 1612 and 1613 these three merchants, in association with several others, appear as the sponsors for a voyage of a familiar name in New Netherland history, skipper Adriaen Block. In 1613 Block stated that he was in the Hudson for the third time. The second time can now be exactly dated as the year 1612. In a letter to his wife in 1613, Francoys Pelgrom passed along the news that Block had just returned from a successful voyage and spoke of it as a "good voyage, yes, a better voyage even than last year." [31] It seems, therefore, not unreasonable to conclude, as Hart does, that the first voyage of Block to the Hudson was probably in 1611 aboard the "St. Pieter" as Rijser's supercargo.

Considerable information is available on Block's third voyage in 1613. In addition to Vogels and Leonard and Francoys Pelgrom, the merchants who backed this voyage and the one in 1612 included another Pelgrom brother, Steffen, along with Hans Hunger and Lambert Van Tweenhuysen; Block was probably also a financially interested member of this company.[32] Abraham and Hans Pelt, Vogels' brothers-in-law, participated in the 1613 voyage of this company.[33] Details of the proportion of investment of each member are lacking, but it is probable that Van Tweenhuysen was the leading spirit of the company. For convenience this group of merchants is referred to as the Van Tweenhuysen Company. It was the first company formed specifically to trade to the area of New Netherland.

The biographies of these Van Tweenhuysen Company merchants throw considerable light on the development of trade in a new area — in this case New Netherland. Some of the members were related by blood or by marriage but beyond this there were strong personal ties which bound them all together. In the first place, they were all expatriate merchants who had taken up residence in Amsterdam. In the second place, they were all Lutherans rather than members of the Dutch Reformed Church, the established church of the Netherlands.

Like Vogels, Hunger had long been interested in the North American fur trade. He was a member of the company which sent out the "Witte Leeuw" to New France in 1606. He was a wealthy merchant who traded principally to the German states, Sweden, and Morocco. Born in Nuremberg, Hunger had removed to Antwerp where he married and conducted his trade operations until 1585, when he took up residence in Amsterdam. He was a director of the Brabant Company, as well as the Dutch East India Company, in which he had 49,500 guilders invested in 1612.[34]

Van Tweenhuysen was the wealthiest of the group. His commercial connections were extensive and varied, stretching from "Archangel and Spitsbergen to North America, from Northwest Africa to Istanbul." [35] He owned a soap factory in Haarlem and was one of the largest pearl merchants in Amsterdam. His interest in the fur trade derived from his connections with the La Rochelle firm of Jean Macain and Samuel Georges, who were themselves participants with Sieur de Monts in a Rouen fur trading company. Van Tweenhuysen appears to have been an energetic entrepreneur whose special interest was in opening up new areas of trade and in creating new commercial companies. He showed little interest in participating in the stock offerings of either the Dutch East or West India Companies, even though he had pioneered in trading to both areas. He was an early participant in the Dutch whaling industry off Spitsbergen and forged a combined company, the Northern Company, out of a number of merchants whose ruinous competition was making the trade there unprofitable. Van Tweenhuysen was a dynamo of entrepreneurial energy and a man, as Hart points out, who probably "had little interest in companies in whose direction he was not concerned." [36]

According to Francoys Pelgrom, Block's voyage of 1612 for the Van Tweenhuysen Company was a financial success. To the members of the Van Tweenhuysen Company, and in particular Vogels, Hunger, and the Pelts whose early interest in North America can be specifically documented, the way now seemed clear for their direct participation in the highly lucrative fur trade. Since the Hudson River area was unoccupied and unfortified, French claims to a monopoly of the North American fur trade could now be ignored. The members of the Van Tweenhuysen Company undoubtedly looked forward with great eagerness to leisurely plucking this plum which had finally come within their reach. The attainment of this, however, was not to be so easy. For while the company's voyage in 1613 proved to be even more profitable than the previous year's, any dream of its exclusive development of the Hudson fur trade was shattered by the appearance of a Dutch competitor.

In the spring of 1613, skipper Adriaen Block came upon another Dutch ship in the Hudson, the "Jonge Tobias," under the command of Thijs Volckertsz. Mossel. Serving as supercargo on the "Jonge Tobias" was Han Jorisz. Hontom. Mossel and Hontom appeared to Block not only as unexpected interlopers but also as potentially dangerous competitors because of their attempt to engross the trade for themselves by offering the Indians double the price which Block had set. Unable to drive off this threat, Block came to terms. Negotiations between the two captains resulted in an informal agreement which allowed Block two-thirds and Mossel one-third of the furs during the remainder of their stay. To insure that the agreement would be honestly executed, crew members, whose function was to supervise all transactions with the Indians, were exchanged by the captains.[37]

The "Jonge Tobias" had been sent out by a group of Amsterdam merchants associated in what has been termed the Hans Claesz. Company. Participating merchants in this company were Hans Claesz., Barent Sweers, Arnout van Liebergen, Wessel Schenck, Jan Holscher, and Jacob Bontenos. Claesz. was a native of Amsterdam who traded

to Riga, Spain, France, and Sweden. He was a partner in the trade to
Riga with Sweers for many years. Quite active in the whaling trade
off Spitzbergen, he later became a director of the Northern Company
which was formed to consolidate that trade.[38] Sweers, a brother-in-
law of Bontenos, traded to Riga, was a director of the Northern
Company, and managed a marine insurance company as early as
1610.[39] Van Liebergen was a native of Bois-le-Duc. He had commercial connections in Rouen, where his family lived as resident Dutch
merchants. Van Liebergen traded to Morocco and owned 3,000 guilders of Dutch East India Company stock in 1602.[40] Schenk, Holscher's
uncle, was a wealthy merchant who traded principally to Italy. He
was a large investor in the Dutch East India Company when that
company was formed in 1602, participating to the extent of 30,000
guilders. Holscher was born in Dülmen in Munster and came to Amsterdam in 1601 to work for his uncle, Schenk. He also traded to
Guiana on his own and in 1609 was a member of a company which
sent Mossel to the West Indies. Bontenos was a native Amsterdamer
who was associated with his brother-in-law, Sweers, in a marine insurance company.

Evidence is lacking to state specifically how the Hans Claesz. Company became interested in the trade to New Netherland. Several possible explanations can, however, be advanced. Some of the Hans
Claesz. Company merchants had trading interests in the West Indies.
Mossel arrived in the Hudson in 1613 on his return from a voyage to
the West Indies, so that this may have been merely a planned or ac-
cidental extension of more southerly interests. Very little is known
about Dutch merchants' activity in the West Indies in the decades on
either side of 1600. How the news of Hudson's discovery might have
affected merchants interested in the West Indies can hardly even be
speculated upon. But from the available evidence, continuity of interest in North America on the part of Dutch merchants trading to
the West Indies cannot be traced as it has been for those merchants
interested in the North American fur trade. The southern route to
New Netherland, via the Canary Islands and the West Indies, later
became the course most commonly charted by skippers. But in the
early voyages following Hudson which can be documented, it was the
northern or Hudson's route, via Newfoundland, which was taken. Although Wassenaer states that Hendrick Christiaensen was the first to
sail to New Netherland (no date mentioned) and that he "happened
near there" when he "had been on a voyage to the West Indies," all

the later, more fully documented voyages of Christiaensen were by the northern route.[41] Thus the Hans Claesz. Company's venture to New Netherland may have been a result of the interest in the West Indies of some of its members. But the company's interest may be accounted for in other ways.

In the first place, the merchant community in Amsterdam was a rather close-knit group in which it was probably quite difficult to keep anything a secret for very long. Even if skippers or supercargoes were careful in not divulging the business of their employers, there were still many crew members who might easily spill such trade secrets, especially for higher wages and the prospect of an outgoing voyage. Moreover, things like charter contracts and ship sales were matters of public record which would immediately alert an astute merchant that something was in the wind. Nor were merchants easily put off if they scented a profitable venture. The Amsterdam merchant Simon Willemsz. Nooms, for example:

> . . . in the month of August of last year 1613 . . . met captain Adriaen Block on the Exchange. He spoke to him, gave him a hearty welcome back from his voyage and asked him how he had fared. He [Block] said, that it did not amount to much and was poor work. The deponent then replied that he was astonished that he [Block] had made two ships ready to sail there again as one ship would be sufficient to take in the cargo.[42]

Many of these same merchants were also associated together in other ventures. In the Northern whaling trade, for example, the following merchants were associated: Van Tweenhuysen, Claesz., Block, Sweers, Nooms, Jacques Nicquet, Thymon Jacobsz. Hinlopen, Claes Jacobs van Harencarspel, and Samuel Godyn.[43]

And in the second place, it is quite possible that the Hans Claesz. Company's entry into the New Netherland trade was prompted by information obtained by certain of its members whose special interest lay in marine insurance underwriting. Both Sweers and Bontenos were connected with marine insurance and may, as Hart suggests, have either themselves underwritten the voyages of Block in 1612 and 1613 for the Van Tweenhuysen Company or obtained detailed knowledge of it from fellow underwriters.[44]

When Block returned in the summer of 1613, the Van Tweenhuysen Company attempted to eliminate its unwelcome competitor for Hudson River furs. The first step taken was to obtain an exclusive patent for the trade to New Netherland from the Stadholder, Prince Maurice. The company knew full well that such a patent, unlike one from the States-General, carried little real weight since there was no way in which those who chose to defy it could be effectively restrained. Nonetheless they apparently tried to pass it off as a patent from the States-General, threatening with serious injury anyone who would not honor it. When Block was told that *several* companies were interested in the new trade he warned that "he would force those who wanted to go thence with his guns." [45] Six of these guns were subsequently obtained on loan from the Amsterdam Admiralty. [46]

The Hans Claesz. Company was just as busy during the months of August and September trying through negotiations and legal procedures to maintain its precarious foothold in the New Netherland trade. The company protested to Prince Maurice about his grant of exclusive trade to the Van Tweenhuysen Company. In rescinding it on September 23, 1613, the Prince urged both companies to settle the matter amicably. The Hans Claesz. Company then employed the good offices of the Reverend Petrus Plancius in negotiations with the Van Tweenhuysen Company. They offered three proposals for dividing up the trade but no agreement could be reached. [47]

The first proposal, that each group should be allowed to trade "freely and peacefully," was obviously unacceptable to the Van Tweenhuysen Company. The second proposal was for a merger of the two companies but was "probably not accepted for lack of confidence." [48] The third proposal indicated that the Hans Claesz. Company's first venture to New Netherland in the spring of 1613 had been unprofitable. The Hans Claesz. Company offered to sell its ship, already fully equipped for the second voyage, to the Van Tweenhuysen Company and also demanded:

> . . . *in recompense for their trouble and in subsidy for their previous damage and loss, the lump sum of one thousand Flemish pounds, and at the same time they are willing to quit sailing or trading in the . . . regions.*[49]

Since there was no guarantee that other companies might not also attempt to hold up the Van Tweenhuysen Company in the same way, this proposal also had to be rejected.

The result was that both companies again sent out ships to New Netherland in the fall of 1613. The Hans Claesz. Company sent out Mossel in the "Nachtegael" and legally notified members of the Van Tweenhuysen Company that they would be held "jointly and severally liable for all loss, damage and interest which may result" from any interference by their skippers with Mossel's mission.[49a] The Van Tweenhuysen Company sent out skipper Hendrick Christiaensen in the "Fortuyn" and Adriaen Block in the "Tijger." They, too, filed a legal notice, warning the Hans Claesz. Company that interlopers would not be tolerated in the Hudson.[50]

When Block, who was in overall command of the Van Tweenhuysen Company's expedition, arrived in the Hudson in January 1614, an informal, on-station agreement was worked out between the two companies. Block was to have three-fifths and Mossel two-fifths of all the skins traded. A series of incidents followed which altered this arrangement.[51]

Block intended to leave Christiaensen and Mossel in the Hudson while he went off to explore the area further — probably looking for an even better source of furs. However the "Tijger" caught fire before this scheme could be acted upon. Mossel and Hontom, who was again supercargo for the Hans Claesz. Company, thereupon offered to take on half or all of the burned ship's crew if the trade proportions were changed in their favor. Block found this hard to agree to and instead proceeded to build the famous "Onrust," the first yacht constructed in New Netherland.

Further complications arose when Hontom, over the vigorous protest of Block, set out with two sloops and seventeen men to explore the fur trade possibilities in the East River and around Long Island. Eight members of Block's burned ship overpowered the few remaining crew members of the "Nachtegael" and took it over. Although Block and Christiaensen, together with their crew members, assisted Mossel in efforts to quell the mutineers, the "Nachtegael" got away and went pirating. The mutineers took it first to the West Indies and finally to Ireland, from which place word of the mutiny filtered back to Amsterdam. The crew of the stolen "Nachtegael" was made up from the malcontents of both companies: ten belonged to Block, four to Christiaensen, and two to Mossel.[52]

To make matters worse, shortly after the departure of the "Nachtegael" the ships of two other Dutch companies boldly sailed into the Hudson to compete with the much harassed skippers of the Hans

Claesz. and Van Tweenhuysen companies. One of these ships, also called the "Fortuyn," was sent out by a company of Hoorn merchants and was captained by Cornelis Jacobsz. May. The other ship was the "Vos," and Pieter Fransz. was the skipper, sailing for the Amsterdam merchants Jonas Witsen and Simon Willemsz. Nooms but owned by the Commissioners of the Amsterdam Admiralty.[53] Fransz. was later killed by the Indians, and his mate, Jan de Wit, took over as skipper of the "Vos." [54]

Both Nooms and Witsen were wealthy merchants and public officials in Amsterdam. Witsen was many times a councillor and burgomaster of Amsterdam; Nooms a commissioner of that city. Both men were directors of the Guinea Company. Witsen was a director of the Dutch East India Company and at one point (1602) held stock in the amount of 12,000 guilders; in the same year Nooms had 10,200 guilders invested in the Dutch East India Company. Witsen's cousin, Gerrit Jacobz. Witsen, was a merchant and public official of Amsterdam and probably also a participant in this venture to New Netherland in 1614.[55] The "Vos" was sent out to look for a northwest passage through Davis Strait, but it seems quite clear that the owners also intended it to participate in the New Netherland fur trade. We know that Nooms was aware of the Hudson area because of his conversation with Block in 1613, recorded in a deposition made in 1614.[56] And in the negotiations by which the company received permission in August of 1614 to re-export duty free those goods which it had been unable to trade in the spring of 1614, the Hudson was specifically mentioned as the ship's intended destination.[57]

The company of merchants from Hoorn included Pieter Clementsz. Brouwer, Jan Clementsz. Kies, and Cornelis Volckertsen. They were among the founders of the New Netherland Company, chartered later in 1614 by the States-General for three years.

The appearance of these two ships in the Hudson, combined with the misfortune which had already taken place there, forced a change in the fur trade agreement which had earlier been worked out between Block and Mossel. The new on-station agreement provided that each of the four companies was to enjoy one-fourth of the furs traded. Just how many furs were traded before the ships departed for home sometime in June is not known. One crew member of Mossel's reported that he had "understood from the crew of Adrian Block and Hendrick Carstiaenss [sic] that two thousand five hundred skins had been traded." [58] In any event, from the suits and countersuits that began as soon as the ships arrived home, it appears likely that none of the four companies involved derived any profit from this venture.

While the various ship captains were actually scrapping for on-station control of the Hudson fur trade during the winter and spring of 1613–1614, the merchants behind these ventures had been far from idle at home. They were engaged in highly intricate maneuvers of their own in an attempt to bring order to the chaotic condition of this trade. Block had been delayed in sailing from Amsterdam in September, 1613, because of last minute negotiations between the Hans Claesz. Company and the Van Tweenhuysen Company. If an agreement was reached before Block finally sailed in October to join Christiaensen and Mossel, the details of it are not known. Block did conclude an agreement on-station with Mossel shortly after he arrived in the Hudson, either of his own devising or on instructions from home. However, the discussions between the two companies undoubtedly continued during the absence of their skippers.

On March 20, 1614, the States-General considered a petition it had received from "divers Merchants wishing to discover New unknown Rivers, Countries and Places not sought for (nor resorted to) heretofore from these parts." [59] The petition asked that an exclusive grant for four voyages be given to such discoverers. The petition also made a point of wanting it clearly understood that "whosoever shall find, discover and explore *the same Countries and Places about the same time* or season, shall be admitted, at the discretion and on the decision of the Lords States General, *to prosecute the aforesaid voyage in company.*" [60] After additional discussion, a General Charter for this purpose was formally promulgated by the States-General a week later on March 27. A fine of 50,000 Netherlands Ducats was to be imposed for any violations against special grants given under its authority. [61] Although no names were mentioned in the petition it seems quite clear that the merchants of the Van Tweenhuysen and Hans Claesz. companies were its sponsors.

The members of the Witsen Company were probably also involved in the negotiations which led to the adoption of this General Charter. Whereas the earlier petition merely mentioned "whosoever shall find . . . the same Countries," the resolution of the States-General on March 27 especially stated "in case two or more companies shall find out such lands or passage in one year, they shall then enjoy this ben-

efit and privilege in common." [62] The Witsen Company's ship, the
"Vos," was already in New Netherland by this date. In addition, one
of the members of the Witsen Company, Simon Willemsz. Nooms, in
August of 1613, had informed Block that unless the Van Tweenhuysen Company had a patent from the States-General there was
little he could do about competition from other companies. Block,
trying to pass off the Prince's patent as a States-General patent, said
he had one. But Nooms replied that "that was impossible, since the
towns had to consent to it, which . . . he knew they would not do."
Nooms also cautioned Block that if he had interfered with him "he
would make the streets of Amsterdam too hot for him." [63] Both
Nooms and the Witsens were politically influential and it seemed improbable that such a grant could have been established without their
support or over their opposition.

The "General Charter for Those who Discover any New Passages, Havens, Countries or Places" seems to have been established
through the pressures of those Amsterdam merchants interested in the
New Netherland trade rather than as the result of a disinterested
policy decision suddenly published by the States-General of the Netherlands. The merchants trading to New Netherland followed this up
on the return of their ships from the Hudson by applying for a special grant under the terms of the General Charter in October, 1614. It
is not known that any special grants for other areas were ever issued
under it.

The misfortunes and difficulties which had beset the ship captains
in the Hudson began to plague their owners once they returned
home. The summer of 1614 was spent in filing law suits, making
appearances, and swearing out charges. The notary's office in Amsterdam was swamped by all this paper work — one of the clerks spent
much of his time rowing back and forth to Christiaensen's ship in an
attempt to keep up with the taking of deposition from crew men-
bers.[64] This legal tangle probably delayed the merchants from taking
any immediate action under the General Charter. The matter was, of
course, further complicated by the Hoorn merchants' ship having also
been in the Hudson and a party to the on-station agreement about
the division of furs. The Hoorn merchants probably used this for lev-
erage to be sure that they would be included in any privileges accorded by a special grant. They certainly qualified for inclusion under the terms of the General Grant even though it seems unlikely

that the Amsterdam merchants were aware of their presence in the Hudson when they pushed through its passage in the States-General. Had they not been included, however, the Hoorn merchants might have been able to prevent passage of a special grant by the States-General.

On October 11, 1614, the "United Company of Merchants who have discovered and found New Netherland, situate in America between New France and Virginia, the sea coasts whereof lie in the Latitude of forty to forty five degrees" were given a special grant by the States-General under the provisions of the General Grant of March 27, 1614.[65] The more commonly used named for this association of merchants was the New Netherland Company. By the terms of this patent it was to have the right to make four voyages to the exclusion of all competitors, during a three-year period commencing January 1, 1615, to the area of New Netherland. This is the first known use of the term "New Netherland."

The New Netherland Company was a composite one, formed from the principals of the four separate companies that had been involved in the trade to New Netherland — the Van Tweenhuysen Company, the Hans Claesz. Company, the Witsen Company, and the Hoorn Company. All the names specifically mentioned in the grant can be identified as participants in these earlier companies. The new company was a monopoly, created to eliminate the ruinous competition which had made the voyages of 1613 and 1614 so unprofitable for these merchants. A further aim was to prevent any other company — and there were many eagerly standing by — from entering the trade. Through bitter experience the principals knew that a patent from the States-General was essential for accomplishing the latter.

The General Grant of March and the special patent to the New Netherland Company in October, 1614, were unquestionably connected. Both were part of a scheme to monopolize the New Netherland trade and both were carefully steered through the States-General by a group of wealthy merchants with great political influence — particularly the Witsens, Van Tweenhuysen, and Nooms. The legal grounds for such a grant to the New Netherland Company were, of course, specious. In 1614 New Netherland was hardly in the category of "New unknown Rivers, Countries and Places." [66] Not only had Hudson sailed there in 1609 for the Amsterdam Chamber of the Dutch East India Company, but some of these same merchants had ships there at least two and probably three years earlier. The voyage of 1614, by which the New Netherland Company laid claim to the area, had not been for the purpose of discovery but was quite openly to participate in the known Indian fur trade there.

The merchants of the New Netherland Company were able to push both measures through so deftly because of the lack of opposition by delegates from the other provinces to the States-General. The General Charter and the special patent appear to have passed quickly and with little public fanfare. This can be explained by the fact that the trade to New Netherland was at this time exclusively in the hands of Amsterdam merchants — with the exception of the Hoorn merchants of North Holland. And since Amsterdam dominated the politics of the province of Holland, it was relatively easy for these prominent Amsterdamers to drown out the clamours of lesser merchants who might also have been interested in entering the New Netherland trade. A factor for some of these lesser merchants, Albert Gerritsz. Ruyl, contemptuously referred to the New Netherland Company's "pretended charter" and the way in which it had been "cunningly obtained." [67]

There seems to be little doubt that it was "cunningly obtained." But then this comment was made not by a disinterested watchdog of public morality but rather by a spokesman for the less-cunning losers. Apparently Ruyl's company eventually concluded an agreement with the New Netherland Company.

In seeking a monopoly of this trade the merchants of the New Netherland Company were merely adhering to a well established pattern of the times. It was quite the usual practice in opening up a new area of trade for competition to proliferate to such a degree that only through some form of merger could the merchants involved hope to derive any profit. The experiences of two other companies in the early years of the seventeenth century — the Dutch East India Company and the Northern Company — illustrate this pattern.

Seven years of intense competition or "tramp navigation," as one writer has described it, preceded the chartering of the Dutch East India Company in March 1602.[68] From 1595 to 1601 some sixty-five ships were sent out to the East Indies, principally to Java and Moluccas, by Dutch merchants interested in pepper and spice. This kind of rivalry, on top of the hazards encountered on such long voyages, made it clear that the trade had to be better organized in order to reduce the heavy risks.

> *Some ship-owners sustained heavy losses, others made big profits,*
> *but only such as were backed by considerable capital could sup-*
> *port the cut-throat competition which was dangerously near com-*
> *pletely wiping out all trade to the Indies. Moreover, the estab-*
> *lishment of the English East India Company . . . did not make*
> *it desirable to put off the amalgamation any longer.*[69]

Like the later New Netherland Company the Dutch East India
Company in 1602 sprang from the "amalgamation of earlier and
independent bodies. It consisted of several 'chambers,' having their
seat in the various trading Towns which had taken part in the earlier
voyages." [70]

The Northern Company (Noordse Compagnie) came into being on
January 27, 1614, in exactly the same way. The whale industry off
Spitsbergen was begun only in 1612 and yet within two years it was
obvious that a combined company was necessary in order to protect
the investment of the merchants interested in the trade. It should be
noted that many of these merchants were also participants in the New
Netherland trade. Both the New Netherland Company and the
Northern Company were formed in 1614. The pivotal figure in both
undertakings appears to have been Lambert Van Tweenhuysen. Hart
suggests that the reconciliation of conflicting interests which resulted
in the formation of the Northern Company made it possible for many
of these same merchants to agree later on how to handle the New
Netherland situation.[71]

Once formed, the New Netherland Company's day-to-day operations
dropped out of sight. From the few details that are known it can be
assumed that the company made full use of its limited monopoly by
sending out at least the four voyages guaranteed by its charter before
it expired on December 31, 1617. There is mention that by August of
1616 the second voyage under the charter had already returned.[72]
During these three years the company's skippers and supercargoes devoted their efforts to consolidating the known fur trade along the
Hudson, particularly in the area of the present site of Albany. But
they also sought ways of increasing their measure of profit by a syste-
matic exploration of the entire area covered in the patent. Although
they certainly did not neglect to look for other sources of wealth —
such as gold, other precious minerals, salt, fishing possibilities, or agricultural products — still, their greatest hope of profit continued to
center on an expansion of the fur trade. And it was this expectation

that accounts for the path of their explorations in the years 1615–
1618. Rivers were the avenues of the fur trade in North America, and
the Hudson (or North) and the Delaware (or South) Rivers became
the focal points of this scrutiny. The skipper-explorers for the New
Netherland Company were Hendrick Christiaensen, Cornelis Hendricksen, and Jacob Eelkens.[73]

The most publicized activities of the New Netherland Company
during its three year existence were the attempts it made to maintain
its privileged position. In 1616, it sought once more to utilize the
terms of the General Grant of March 27, 1614 for its own advantage.
On the basis of skipper Cornelis Hendricksen's exploration of the
Delaware River area in the years 1614–1616, the company petitioned
the States-General for a special grant of exclusive traffic to this "newly
discovered" area for three years.[74] The Delaware area was, of course,
included within the area of the special grant which it had already obtained — that is within the latitudes of 40–45 degrees north. But this
petition was not as ridiculous as it might at first appear.

After all, the area of New Netherland was not a "newly discovered"
area in 1614 and yet the company had experienced no difficulty in
obtaining a special grant to make four voyages there to the exclusion
of all other competitors. Probably the petition for the Delaware patent was finally pigeonholed in November of 1616 not because the
facts were incorrect but rather because the situation in the Netherlands had changed considerably during the intervening years, making
such a grant impossible. In 1614, interest revived in forming a chartered Dutch West India Company to conduct operations in the New
World on a scale comparable to the Dutch East India Company's activities in the Orient. New Netherland would, of course, in this even-
tuality fall under such a company. Secondly, the dissatisfaction, which
later erupted, of some of the members within New Netherland
Company, probably began to be manifest by 1616. Such members
would not be anxious to see the New Netherland Company more
firmly entrenched in its position of monopoly. And in the third place,
it seems likely that other merchants desiring to trade to New Netherland also added their support to the growing opposition to a grant by
the States-General of any additional favors to the company.

Under these circumstances the States-General, in characteristic fashion, procrastinated. As long as no agreement could be reached by the
interested merchants, the States-General was simply unable to act.

Other attempts by the New Netherland Company to renew or extend its charter were also unsuccessful for the same reasons.[75] Thus the limited monopoly of the New Netherland trade came to an end, and in 1618 the trade was once again thrown open to all.

The New Netherland Company continued trading to New Netherland in the years following the expiration of its charter in order, as one of its petitions states, "to preserve the reputation of said trade." [76] The company after 1617 was sometimes referred to by its chartered name but at other times called the Van Tweenhuysen Company.[77] This "second" Van Tweenhuysen Company included the hard core of merchants whose interest in North America and in furs can be traced back to 1591.[78] Over the years these merchants had continually run up against difficulties when complete control of the trade seemed to be just within their grasp. The charter of 1614 proved to be only a temporary victory, not an end to their difficulties. But the merchants of the Van Tweenhuysen Company were not easily discouraged. None of them relied exclusively on the New Netherland trade for his wealth. Their interests were spread over a wide portion of the globe. The fact that they doggedly persisted in their efforts to dominate the trade to New Netherland suggests how profitable it must have appeared to them, both actually and potentially. Thus far the obstacles they encountered had not been such as to induce them to abandon voluntarily their plans for deriving profit from New Netherland. Indeed, the limited monopoly for three years represented some measure of success. Although the difficulties intensified, their efforts to dominate the trade continued unabated in the years 1618–1623.

The first difficulty they had to face was an old one — competition. On October 9, 1618, the States-General took note of a petition it had received from Hendrik Eelkens, Adriaen Jansz. Engel and Company. This company intended to send its ship, the "Schilt," to New Netherland and applied to the States-General for explicit permission to do this "in order that they may perform the . . . voyage without any opposition from their former partners." [79] The former partners referred to were the members of the New Netherland Company. Permission was granted the same day by the States-General.

In the years 1618–1623 a number of such petitions were filed by various companies interested in the New Netherland trade.[80] Because they were the first to open up the trade, the members of the New Netherland Company continued to regard all others as interlopers.

But since their special grant had run out, there was nothing the New Netherland Company could legally do to prevent traffic to New Netherland. When the States-General's permission was granted to a rival this served to put the New Netherland Company on warning that interference would not be tolerated. The principal competitor during these years was the Eelkens Company.

This must have been particularly grating to the members of the New Netherland or second Van Tweenhuysen Company. The petitions suggest that some of the merchants of the Eelkens Company had been former members of the New Netherland Company. Hendrik Eelkens was an Amsterdam merchant born in Bois-le-Duc. Engel was a merchant and had been a ship captain earlier. Both Engel and Eelkens had close connections with merchants in Rouen, France.[81] Still another source of irritation must have been the way in which the Eelkens Company raided the ranks of the Van Tweenhuysen Company for its skippers, mates, and supercargoes. The experienced Hans Jorisz. Hontom, who had earlier been Mossel's supercargo on the voyage of 1613 and 1614 to New Netherland for the Hans Claesz. Company, became one of the most energetic skippers for this new company. Hontom's brother, William Jorisz. Hontom, was also associated. Mossel, perhaps in disgrace for having lost the "Nachtegael" in 1614, was employed as a supercargo or mate to William Jorisz. Hontom on his voyages to New Netherland for the Eelkens Company. Eelkens' nephew, Jacob Jacobsz. Eelkens, was also a member of the company and a skipper of some of the ships it sent out. He had formerly been Hendrick Christiaensen's supercargo on the "Fortuyn" in 1614. He remained behind that year in charge of the New Netherland Company's Fort Nassau.[82]

The problem of competition was at least a matter which the second Van Tweenhuysen Company could deal with. The terms of the problem were essentially the same as they had been in 1614 before the grant of limited monopoly had been obtained for the combined company. And the ways in which the second Van Tweenhuysen Company now approached the matter were quite similar. At home it resorted to threats and various forms of intimidation to discourage competitors. While this may have worked against fainthearted rivals, it was obviously unsuccessful when applied to the Eelkens Company, which reacted to this kind of pressure in much the same way as the Van Tweenhuysen Company's competitors in 1613–1614 had. They countered by filing notices which threatened the Van Tweenhuysen Company with legal action if their right to free trade to New Netherland was interfered with.[83] Seeking explicit permission from the States-General to make voyages to New Netherland merely carried their counter-offensive one step further. This latter action, however, probably indicates just how active the Van Tweenhuysen Company's program of threats and intimidation was.

The Van Tweenhuysen Company continued to nourish the hope of monopolizing the trade. In 1620 it tried once again to obtain a special grant for the Delaware area.[84] This time it advanced the more recent findings of its new skipper-explorer, Cornelis Jacobsen May, as the basis of its claim to be entitled to the provisions of the General Charter of 1614. The Eelkens Company was not taken in by this maneuver. It appeared to them quite clearly as a measure designed to cut them out of the trade and, therefore, they urged the States-General:

> . . . to reject and refuse all grants that may have been demanded, or still will be demanded of them, regarding the Trade on the Coasts, or any of the Rivers of New Netherland, and to allow the petitioners and other merchants of this Country to continue in the free trade they are pursuing there . . .[85]

Up against such a rival as the Eelkens Company there was little the Van Tweenhuysen Company could do in the Netherlands to achieve their goal of dominating the trade to New Netherland. In New Netherland itself, however, the company tried in other ways to accomplish the same end. The company apparently continued to make on-station agreements with any rivals that happened to be there at the same time, in the interest of holding down prices and thereby preventing the loss of profit which they knew from experience was the certain result of over-competition.[86] While sharing the known fur trade along the Hudson with its competitors, the Van Tweenhuysen Company pursued its former policy of exploring the greater area of New Netherland in the hope of discovering even richer sources of furs which it might then monopolize. In exploring the Delaware, Chesapeake Bay, and James River, May was following the example of Block in the years before the patent for New Netherland was granted, and the examples of Christiaensen and Hendricksen in the years during which the patent was in effect.[87]

The second Van Tweenhuysen Company employed one other device which it had inherited from its precharter days as a means of eliminating, or at least minimizing, its competition in New Netherland. This was to leave people behind to organize the trade between voyages. Jan Rodrigues, a mulatto from San Domingo, appears to have been the first one retained for this purpose by Block in 1613. Rodrigues was formerly in Mossel's hire but allegedly refused to return to the Netherlands with him. He was thereupon taken into the service of the Van Tweenhuysen Company and when Christiaensen returned to the Hudson late in 1613 he immediately made contact with Rodrigues.[88] Some months later Christiaensen constructed what is recognized as the first trading post and fort in New Netherland — Fort Nassau on Castle Island. On Block's departure in 1614, Cornelis Hendricksen was left behind in the Hudson to explore the area more thoroughly in the "Onrust." And Jacob Eelkens remained behind at Fort Nassau for the New Netherland Company.[89] Efforts along these lines were expanded during the years 1618–1623.[90]

The building of a trading post in New Netherland was really only a question of time. But it was the competition in 1613–1614 which hastened its establishment in 1614. Dutch traders were long familiar in the Guiana trade with the usefulness of having such a place from which to conduct operations.[91] And certainly the fur merchants of Amsterdam were not blind to its importance since it was the French possession of such fortified trading posts which had prevented them from participating in the direct trade for furs in New France. Given the circumstances of the New Netherland trade, to establish a trading post was to establish a very real monopoly of the trade. Other benefits might of course result — more and better quality furs or a decrease in the time that ships would have to spend in the area — but considerations of monopoly were uppermost in the minds of the merchants of the first and second Van Tweenhuysen Companies.

Since the merchants of the Van Tweenhuysen Company were very much aware of the value of trading posts as a means of establishing a *de facto* monopoly of the trade, it is not surprising that they seriously entertained the petition of the English Pilgrims of Leyden to settle in New Netherland.[92] The presence of additional people in New Netherland, properly indebted to the Van Tweenhuysen Company, could be used to enhance the position of the company in New Netherland and thereby exclude rivals. In their petition to the Prince of Orange on February 12, 1620, they also pointed out how useful such a settlement might be to the state if a timber and shipbuilding industry could be developed in New Netherland. This was the first time that the "timber and shipbuilding argument," inherently so logical and appealing, was advanced to cover over a variety of other, more compelling motives. But the petition was denied by the States-General in order not to disturb Anglo-Dutch relations. And the Pilgrims, therefore, entered upon their "starving times" not dependent upon fur-trade merchants in Amsterdam but rather on fur-trade merchants in England.[93]

Thus both at home and in New Netherland the second Van Tweenhuysen Company tried to face up resolutely to the problem of competition and vigorously attacked it in many ways. There were, however, other difficulties in the path of the company — difficulties that were ultimately to prove insurmountable. Beginning in 1614, seven years before the uneasy truce with Spain was to expire, pressures steadily increased in the Netherlands for the creation of a vehicle that would be able to inflict great injury on Spain once war was resumed.[94] Since the great wealth of Spain came from its New World possessions, Dutch attention focused most intently on ways of cutting this off. The vehicle seized upon was grandiose in design — an incorporated West India Company which, through subsidization, would become a partner of the state in the war against Spain. Ranging over the vast sweep of the New World, its functions would be to choke off the life strength of Spain at its roots. To do this the efforts of the company were to be directed into the twin channels of war and trade — in that order and with no fine line drawn between the two.

New Netherland would of course come under such a company by virtue of its geographical position. In the face of this rising colossus, decked out in appeals to patriotism, nationalism, and profit, there was little the Van Tweenhuysen Company could do except hold on in the vain hope that the great design would never crystalize. But by the winter of 1620 it was already clear to the Van Tweenhuysen Company that it was only a matter of time before a West India Company would be chartered.[95] The shadow of this forming West India Company hovered darkly behind all the activities of the Van Tweenhuysen Company and its competitors in the years 1618–1621. When time was known to be so short, the necessity for compromise or merger seemed hardly a pressing reality. Had there been no West India Company in the process of formation, the Van Tweenhuysen

Company might have been able to create, through absorption of or merger with its competitors, a company sufficiently powerful to develop the trade to New Netherland. But it was neither large enough nor influential enough to resist the kinds of pressures brought to bear on it. When the Dutch West India Company finally received its charter on June 3, 1621, the Van Tweenhuysen Company's only course was to bow graciously to the inevitable.[96]

The ineffectualness of the States-General in regulating the trade to New Netherland proved in the end also to be an insuperable difficulty for the Van Tweenhuysen Company. Committed neither to monopoly nor to free trade for the area, its "policy" was simply whatever the political pressures of the moment dictated. In 1614, conditions had been such that the combined New Netherland Company, created by the merger of the Van Tweenhuysen Company with its major competitors, was able to procure a limited monopoly grant from the States-General. In the following years any suggestion of monopoly for the area encountered so much opposition that free trade became the order of the day by necessity. Unless an agreement could be privately worked out by the merchants concerned, the States-General was virtually powerless. It attempted to reconcile parties, to urge agreement, and to placate interests. Time and again in the New Netherland situation the "resolve" of the States-General was "that parties should consult together and see if they cannot agree in a friendly manner." [97]

When no agreement could be reached, as in the trade to New Netherland, the States-General could only turn down those petitions that requested a change in the *status quo*. This was a serious structural weakness in the system of government adopted by the United Provinces. It served to perpetuate the dominance of provincial interests and to impede the emergence of truly national considerations. This weakness became evident at crucial moments in the later history of New Netherland, greatly influencing as a result the course of its development.

Although the West India Company received its charter in June of 1621, circumstances delayed the start of actual operations until two years later.[98] Subscription lists were not closed until October 31, 1623. In the meantime the ban on private trading to the area covered in the West India Company's patent was postponed from July 1, 1621, to July 1, 1622.[99] And it was not until the fall of 1623 that this phase of New Netherland history finally came to an end. By that time the last ships of the Van Tweenhuysen Company and its tenacious rival, the Eelkens Company, had arrived back in Amsterdam.[100] Once operating, the West India Company immediately asserted its right of exclusive navigation to the areas detailed in its charter. When it became known that David Pietersz. de Vries intended to sail to New Netherland under a French commission, the company quickly and effectively squelched this attempted infraction of its monopoly. For as the West India Company's governing body emphasized in a note to the States-General, it was of

> . . . *paramount necessity, for the maintenance of the . . . charter and its subsequent amplification, also for the promotion of the Company's affairs, and especially for the removal and prevention of such evil designs and malversations, that provision be made, and such example at once determined, as will deter others from attempting the like for the future. . . .*[101]

The sense of confidence and vitality conveyed by this action of the West India Company symbolized the changed condition of the trade to New Netherland. It stood in marked contrast to the fumbling record of the Van Tweenhuysen Company in the previous seven years as it had unsuccessfully wrestled with the problem of imposing order on the trade. Only the cautious position of the States-General on the de Vries matter cast a shadow over this generally optimistic atmosphere, suggesting that things had not really changed as much as might appear. It intoned its usual counsel of compromise: "The incorporated *West India Company* ought not to enter, in the beginning, into a dispute with the subjects of neighboring Kings and Princes, but much rather observe good correspondence and friendship towards them." It therefore recommended that "some other amicable arrangement may be discovered whereby both sides may be satisfied."[102]

Down to 1664 when it passed from Dutch into English hands, New Netherland remained a possession of the West India Company. Private trading to New Netherland as it had been conducted since 1611 became impossible once the West India Company assumed active control in 1623. This did not mean, however, that private merchants in the Netherlands would no longer be interested in the area of New Netherland. On the contrary, throughout its history they remained

interested and very active. The peculiar relationship of New Netherland to the Netherlands actually encouraged this. But the monopoly
of the West India Company did mean that their interest would have
to find different forms of expression after 1623. The resurgence of interest in New Netherland on the part of private merchants will be
examined in Chapter Five.

In 1623, then, the West India Company came into a not inconsiderable commercial inheritance from those private merchants whose
interest in New Netherland extended back well over a decade. The
principal lakes and rivers of the area had been explored in the
process of developing a profitable trade in the area's furs. Many of
the problems peculiar to developing that trade and the area of New
Netherland had come to light during these early years and some ex-
pedients had been devised for meeting them. Not the least of its inheritance was the pool of experienced ship captains, crews, and fur
traders that was at hand, available for immediate employment in the
service of the West India Company. A real foundation had been
poured by these private merchants in the years 1609–1623. It remained only for the West India Company to build on this; to fit what
already existed into its own plans for New Netherland.

What plans for New Netherland did the private merchants have
during the years of their predominance? With the exception of
wanting to extract the greatest possible profit from the area, they had
no plans as such. Schooled in the principles of general European and
East Indian trade, these private merchants trading to New Netherland had only commercial aims in mind. They were neither colonizers
nor empire builders.

But if they did not actively promote colonization, neither were they
opposed to it per se. The proposition of the Pilgrims to the Van
Tweenhuysen Company in 1620, for example, appeared to them as a
practical undertaking which might prove commercially useful to
them. On these grounds the Van Tweenhuysen Company did what it
could to forward the scheme. The maneuvers of these merchants both
at home and in New Netherland in the years 1613–1623 suggest that
they were intensely aware of the peculiarities of the trade and alive to
the necessity of taking advantage of whatever might be presented to
them. The building of Fort Nassau, therefore, was not to establish a
beachhead for future settlement but rather to create and defend a *de
facto* monopoly of the trade.

The role of these private merchants in the beginnings of New Netherland should not be underestimated. Without their practical efforts to wrest profit from New Netherland there would have been nothing for the West India Company to inherit beyond a chunk of worthless real estate.

CHAPTER TWO

ORIGINS OF
THE WEST INDIA COMPANY

For better or worse, the charter of 1621 irrevocably linked the fate of New Netherland to the West India Company. For the next forty-three years, until the English conquest in 1664, the company — not the States-General — shaped the development of New Netherland. An understanding of what the company represented and what it hoped to accomplish in the New World is, therefore, essential in approaching the history of New Netherland.

The analysis in the previous chapter of the group of private merchants associated with the fur trade provides insights not only into the early history of New Netherland but also into seventeenth-century Dutch mercantile operations. The latter is of great importance in examining the peculiar nature of the West India Company. Many historians have described the West India Company but none have attempted to probe such questions as why the West India Company was formed, how it was formed, and what it hoped to do. And yet these are precisely the questions which bear most directly on the history of New Netherland.

The reasons for this neglect can be traced to the view which nineteenth-century historians took of the West India Company. They pictured the company as an oppressive organization which, throughout the period of its connection with New Netherland, consistently and unalterably opposed the interests of the colonists — interests which were presented as well-defined and unselfishly devoted to the task of creating a democratic society in New Netherland. As Brodhead expressed it: "The province had been unwisely intrusted to the government of a close commerical corporation, than which no government can be less favorable to popular liberty. In its scheme of political administration, the West India Company exhibited too often a mercantile and selfish spirit. . . ." [1] Such a view has cast the history of New Netherland in terms of the clash between stereotypical heroes and villains. Labels have been substituted for rigorous analysis, resulting in an oversimplified description of the company. Lost also in this view has been any conception of what men on either side of the Atlantic were trying to do.[2]

The lack of knowledge about the origins and purposes of the West India Company is striking. Here was a company which, only five years after beginning operations, presented a balance sheet listing over twelve and one-half million guilders in assets and enumerating over eighty ships and yachts in service in the New World.[3] Despite this, no single individual or group of individuals has ever been identified as being instrumental in its formation!

The source materials presently available for a study of the West India Company are, unfortunately, meagre. They do not begin to compare with even the limited materials which exist for the New Netherland Company. And yet from scattered bits of evidence, a profile of the nature of the company can be fashioned. In sketching this profile, the detailed account of the North American fur merchants before 1621 affords useful points of contrast.

The development of the North American fur trade conformed to a quite traditional mercantile pattern. The Amsterdam merchants engaged in the trade were primarily interested in furs and profits. And they never lost sight of these objectives whether operating in New Netherland or maneuvering at home. Competition was the greatest problem because, in their eyes, it threatened to ruin the profitability of the trade and hence, ultimately, the entire trade itself. They vigorously attacked this danger by efforts to merge together into one company those merchants then engaged in the trade and also by attempts to establish a legal monopoly in the future. Out of these labors the New Netherland Company was born. The circumstances surrounding the creation of other companies of the period were quite similar — particularly the Northern Company and the East India Company. Against this background the markedly different origins of the West India Company stand out quite clearly.

In the first place, the company was not the result of competitive pressures. Before 1621 no merchants had traded throughout the whole of the vast area which fell under the West India Company's charter. Instead, the merchants concentrated their efforts in some specific area or pocket of the New World. Four such pockets of trade existed: New Netherland, the west coast of Africa (Guinea), the area along the coast of Brazil (Guiana), and the salt trade area of Punta del Rey. Competition may have been a factor within any one specific area — as it was in the case of New Netherland. But since the products of the areas were different, there was no threat of competition between areas, which in the economic theory of the times might have led the rival merchants to consider strongly the formation of a monopoly company. The West India Company simply swallowed up these known areas of trade. In the West India Company's scheme of things, these known areas were to provide a base — a financial base because of the assured profits they would produce and an operating base from which to develop a much larger commercial or colonial empire for the Netherlands.

Nor, in the second place, did the West India Company come into being through a merger of the various merchants trading to the specific areas of the New World. Although no group biographical study has been done of the original directors of the West India Company, all evidence points away from their having been intimately involved in New World trade before the issuance of the charter. Only two of the members of the Van Tweenhuysen Company, for example, became directors of the Amsterdam chamber of the company. And these two — Samuel Godyn and J. C. Witsen — were more political figures than working merchants. Moreover, both the second Van Tweenhuysen Company and the merchants trading to Punta del Rey resisted the formation of the West India Company. Although the latter area had been specifically exempted from the limits of the original charter granted to the company, an amplification of the charter, passed by the States-General on June 10, 1622, placed it under the control of the company.[4]

An explanation of the origins of the West India Company, therefore, must be sought outside the pattern generally followed by merchants in the Netherlands in opening up a new area of trade. The influences responsible for the chartering and the formation of the company in 1621 were many and extended back over the previous three decades. Since 1590, Dutch merchants and sea captains had been acquiring experience in the ways of trade peculiar to the Orient and the New World. The projectors of the company were the heirs of that experience. They hoped to make use of it not only for their own personal profit but also to enhance the greatness of their new nation. Although their scheme was a radical departure from the tried and true mercantile pattern, it failed not because it was ill conceived, but rather because the reality of the New World was different than reason and limited experience had led them to expect. Two influences, in particular, stand out as having contributed most directly to the formation of the West India Company that was ultimately chartered in 1621: (1) the idea of a West India Company and, (2) the example of the East India Company.

In point of time the idea of a West India Company came first. It existed before the East India Company was actually established, long before New Netherland was "discovered," and before there was even very much in the way of Dutch trading activity in either the Orient or the New World. The first known mention of a West India Company in print occurred around 1600 in the writings of one of the most curious figures in the history of the Netherlands or New Netherland — Willem Usselinx. His biographer, J. Franklin Jameson, has pictured him as a great "colonial projector" on a par with Hakluyt who was, "though not directly the founder, at any rate the originator of two of our colonies." [5] More recent historians have, with good sense, taken exception to this description, preferring to see Usselinx as a "rather disagreeable bachelor who was easily offended and believed his compatriots were all in league against his wonderful ideals." [6]

Born in Antwerp in 1567, Usselinx came from a merchant family whose roots were in the southern provinces of the Netherlands. As a young man he spent several years in Spain, Portugal, and the Azores as a factor for one of the Antwerp mercantile firms. Few details of his early life are known, but it is assumed that Usselinx became ac-

quainted with the trade to the East and West Indies because he resided for a few years in the Azores — a stopping off point for ships returning from both areas. He returned to the Netherlands around
1590 at the age of twenty-three, at which time his biographer has suggested he was "already apparently a wealthy man" and that the
"grand project of his life, that of founding a West India Company
was already formed." His activities until 1600, when his first published tracts on the subject appeared, are unknown, but he appears to
have settled in the northern provinces rather than to have returned
to his native Antwerp.[7]

In 1600, when Usselinx first began urging the formation of a West
India Company, the Netherlanders were in the fortieth year of their
war for independence from Spain. The lines of the new political
order that would emerge in the lowlands of Europe from this struggle
had virtually been drawn. The northern provinces — Holland, Zeeland, Guelderland, Friesland, Stad en Landen (Groningen), Utrecht,
and Overijssel — joined together in the Union of Utrecht to form the
Republic of the United Netherlands, independent of Spain and Protestant in religion. The southern provinces — which did not become
known as Belgium until 1830 — lost their battle for political freedom
and remained Spanish and Catholic.

The war dragged on, however, until a twelve years' truce was finally negotiated in 1609. From this the northern provinces won a *de
facto* recognition of political independence. This was unquestionably
a great victory, tenaciously wrung from a far more powerful adver-
sary. But the northern provinces did not emerge from the war as a
truly unified nation. Victory had been achieved by a precariously
balanced coalition of groups and interests which, once the external
threat had been removed, then faced the far more difficult task of re-
solving their differences in the interest of creating a viable political
order. In the succeeding years tensions between the House of Orange
and the merchant aristocrats, between province and province, and between provincial loyalties and the necessity for effective organs of central administration, threatened more than once to tear apart the none
too tightly woven fabric of national unity.[8]

In 1600, too, few Netherlanders had had much experience in the
trade to either the East or West Indies. The first ship to the East
Indies on behalf of merchants in the Netherlands was only sent out
in 1595. Indeed not until two years after Usselinx began urging his

ideas, in 1602, was the Dutch East India Company granted a charter by the States-General of the Netherlands. The condition of the trade in the west was not very much different. Although Dutch capital had long backed some of the Portuguese ventures in the West Indies, and Dutch seamen had found berths aboard Portuguese ships in this trade, no Dutch merchants or skippers became involved there on their own until 1590.[9]

In view of such limited experience it seems unlikely that Usselinx, or anyone for that matter, could in 1600 have devised the comprehensive scheme for the development of the New World which many writers have suggested or implied. Usselinx could not even claim that his ideas were based on firsthand experience since he had never visited the New World. At bottom Usselinx's vague idea of a West India Company was grounded on hatred of Spain and jealousy of Spain's success in the New World. His ideas, charged as they were with overtones of intense Protestant zeal, were more conducive to fitting out a crusade against everything Spanish than to laying the foundation of a commercial company.

The mastery of Spain in the New World grated on all European nations but on none more intimately than the Netherlands. Spain was not only a commercial rival to the Netherlanders but a hated political enemy. Resentment always ran high. "To catch a fish," the term used to describe a Spanish treasure galleon, was a familiar pastime of Dutch and other European privateers. But for all that, Spain's activities in the New World also constituted a model of colonial success, a model to be emulated if at all possible. And men dreamed of duplicating this success as much as they did of catching Spanish "fish."

Usselinx's "plan" was, therefore, a curious compound of such dreams and of the limited Dutch experience in the New World and the Orient. Between 1600 and 1609 he wrote many pamphlets and presented oral arguments in support of his ideas before committees of the States-General and the various provincial assemblies. Notions of war, trade, and religion were so fused together as to make it impossible to deduce any clearly defined plan for a West India Company. Jameson has summarized the labors of these years:

> . . . *on the one hand a Dutch West India Company would directly increase the wealth and power of the Dutch through the*

interchange of their manufactures with the raw materials of the
vast regions thus thrown open as a market. On the other hand,
it would, also indirectly, give opportunities for undermining the
power of the king of Spain in those regions, and, if he sought to
expel the intruders, transferring the war thither, diverting it
from the Low Countries themselves, and impairing or cutting off
at its source the stream of wealth which flowed thence to his mil-
itary treasury.[10]

How such a scheme was to be organized and executed was never touched on in the flow of Usselinx's rhetoric. No one could deny that the vast area of the New World offered unlimited possibilities for Dutch enterprise, but something more was required beyond the clamor of Usselinx that a great commercial company, publicly subscribed to, could provide the vehicle for such a grand undertaking. His views, therefore, while listened to respectfully by the merchant-dominated assemblies, encountered only caution and skepticism. Not until negotiations for a truce with Spain were begun in earnest in 1606 did Usselinx's project for a West India Company attract any prominent notice.

The question of concluding a peace or truce with Spain raised serious difficulties within the Netherlands, north and south. In general the southern provinces were inclined to peace even though this meant abandoning independence. The States-General at Brussels had expressed this as a majority sentiment as early as 1600. There were extremists in the south, however, religious and nationalistic, who opposed all efforts to terminate the war. Among many of the émigrés from the south then residing in the north, opposition to the peace negotiations was intensely vocal.[11] Their position was that the war should be continued until Spanish rule had been eliminated from all the provinces of the Low Countries, south as well as north. Usselinx was, of course, one of these exiles. In the north the peace party was led by the Advocate of Holland, John of Oldenbarnevelt, whose counsel finally prevailed. The war party formed around the Stadtholder and head of the House of Orange, Prince Maurice of Nassau.[12]

Spaniards and Netherlanders alike were exhausted by the more than four decades of war. Although a respite seems to have been desired by both sides, there were still serious obstacles to be overcome which required skillful handling. The northern provinces wanted to secure an explicit recognition from Spain of their independence. In exchange for this, Spain sought to extract a guarantee of religious freedom for Catholics in the north for the duration of any truce. Both sides were adamant on the question of trade to the East and West Indies. The Netherlanders argued for the freedom of the Indies trade. Spain stood by its traditional policy of refusing to recognize in a formal manner the right of any nation to participate in areas she deemed exclusively hers.[13] The negotiators for the Netherlands were hampered by the general distrust of Spanish intentions which prevailed and which, as might be expected, was fanned at every opportunity by the various opponents of the negotiations.

The position of Oldenbarnevelt and the peace party was that the condition of the northern provinces made a truce absolutely necessary. Internal bickerings were placing severe strains on the none too stable elements of central government of the Republic. Moreover, war expenditures were at the point of precipitating a serious financial crisis that might negate the gains already made in the struggle.[14]

The scheme of Usselinx for a West India Company was drawn into the debate which raged over these truce negotiations. Haphazardly, the plan came to be discussed not on its own merits but as part of the larger question of war or peace. In such a controversy the very vagueness of his plan became its greatest virtue. It could and did mean all things to all men. War enthusiasts added the plan to their arsenal of arguments on the futility of conducting any negotiations with the Spanish. They argued that if such a company were formed it would harass Spain so much that a truce would be unnecessary. Those in favor of the negotiations attempted to use Usselinx's plan as a club or secret weapon to be employed if Spain refused to treat with their requests. The southern expatriates seized upon it as an argument to break up the negotiations and thus continue the war. And Usselinx undoubtedly tried to take advantage of this unexpected show of interest to further the establishment of his ideas and, consequently, his own personal interests since he expected a substantial commission from the States-General for the use of his ideas.[15]

Of course the flaw in all of this was that a West India Company of any description simply did not exist. Claims as to what it might do or what it might become were pyramided to the sky, but the most significant question of whether it could in fact be established was never seriously raised at this time. The essential requirement for converting

Usselinx's ideas into actuality was capital. Since the Dutch East India Company, after its establishment in 1602, was frequently cited as a model for the West, this meant a great deal of capital. Where was it to come from? Only two potential sources were available — public subscription or state subsidization. But the merchants controlling both sources wanted more than the assurances of an Usselinx that such a scheme would work. Thus in the years 1600–1609 Usselinx's plan for a West India Company was exploited for polemical reasons, but there appears to be no evidence to support assertions that its establishment received serious consideration or that a charter for such a company was at any time imminent.

Its treatment in Holland bears out this interpretation. When the States of Holland heard the arguments of Usselinx in June of 1606 they noted that the plan was "laudable, honorable, and very useful." [16] A committee was formed to determine whether public subscriptions could be raised for the capitalization of such a company. In August the committee reported that "while many of the merchants are well disposed toward the company, they prefer to wait until the States-General have decided on the patent." [17] This was asking to have the cart placed before the horse. And because of the position of Holland in the States-General this was tantamount to a rejection of the plan. An attempt was made to sweeten the proposal by including a provision that the States-General should subsidize the company to the extent of one million florins over the first five years, or longer if required. But even then the States of Holland finally agreed early in 1607 after many delays merely to *urge* the States-General to issue such a charter. It seems clear from this that there was no strong sentiment among the merchants of Holland for forming such a company at this time. The merchants of Holland remained unconvinced and without their active support any such proposal was unlikely to clear the States-General.

Article 5 and a secret codicil of the treaty establishing the Twelve Years' Truce, signed June 17, 1609, tacitly guaranteed the Netherlands freedom of trade to the Indies.[18] In characteristic fashion Usselinx attempted to take credit for the truce claiming that it was Spanish fears that his West India Company would actually be formed that induced them to agree.[19] Such an argument cannot be accepted. The fact is that once the question of war or peace had been decided, interest in Usselinx's scheme for a West India Company, despite the favorable terms of the truce dealing with the Indies, declined sharply. Seemingly, Netherlanders remained perversely indifferent to the great design. Actually, the reaction after 1609 attests to the artificiality of the interest during the truce discussions.

Thus Usselinx's agitation in the years 1600–1609 for the establishment of a West India Company was so much tempest in a teapot. As far as the merchants and politicians of the Netherlands were concerned, Usselinx was a dreamer with an impractical scheme. Only when it was joined with the debate over the truce negotiations did it attract any widespread attention — and then for the wrong reasons. Usselinx alone seems to have believed that his scheme might have resulted in something concrete during those years. It never did. The writings of Usselinx are filled with statements suggesting that his scheme was on the verge of acceptance; repeated failures seem never to have dampened his capacity for overly sanguine prediction.

The remainder of this pathetic man's life was devoted to more and more fantastic attempts to establish his dream of a West India Company as a reality. His misguided zeal carried him as far as Sweden, where many years of labor brought only one disappointment after the other.[20] To be the leading figure in the establishment of a West India Company became an obsession with him, and he began to see his constant failures as the result of various plots against him and his great design. Even his sympathetic biographer is forced to conclude that his behavior at times reflected "a mind which, however strong and acute, had allowed one matter to occupy too large a part of its horizon." [21] But it was more than this; it was truly paranoiac behavior.

Usselinx pictured himself as a Columbus figure, performing the same pathbreaking service for the Netherlands that the Genoese admiral had for Isabella and Ferdinand of Spain.[22] The price he placed on such an important service to the state was high. At one point he asked for:

> First, two per cent, of all the conditional subscriptions he might obtain, and four per cent. of the subscriptions secured unconditionally . . . Second he desired to have ten per cent of the net revenue to the state from the West Indies, otherwise than from the State subsidy . . . He desired, thirdly, to be assured of one half of all the brokerage of the company's business; and finally, to have suitable employment as their agent.[23]

These were extraordinary demands made by a man who had no first-hand knowledge of the West Indies, and more important, a man who had no capital of his own to invest in such a project. These demands were undoubtedly considered outrageous by his contemporaries. His lack of experience he brushed aside by observing that "he had gathered information which others, *even if they had visited those countries, did not possess.*" [24] Just what that information might have been was, of course, never disclosed.

His lack of capital proved to be a more serious disadvantage. His reputation as a shrewd merchant was irreparably damaged by the one venture he is known to have participated in — the draining of Lake Beemster in North Holland, near Hoorn. He invested around 130,000 florins in a company which was formed to reclaim some 7,000 acres of land. After six years he was reduced to the state of bankruptcy and plagued by creditors on all sides.[25] This failure in 1617 made him a poor advocate for the grandiose schemes he continued to speak of for the West Indies. Oldenbarnevelt, for example, testified in 1618 that he had paid little attention to Usselinx and his plans because he "could not think either the person proposing or the thing proposed acceptable, the person owing many thousands more than he could pay, and the trade being very uncertain." [26]

When it became clear that Usselinx would not be a leading figure in the West India Company that was eventually formed, indeed that he would be ignored by it, his memorials began to intimate that he had "secrets to reveal of the highest importance to the success of the company, which will be divulged only when his claims are settled." [27] Again, just before leaving the Netherlands in 1623, "he resolved to give them no more advice, still less reveal any secrets; for though he had presented to them more than a hundred memorials and had as many conferences with them, he had not told them in full where it was best to begin the operations of the company." [28]

There were no secrets to which Usselinx alone was privy. Rather, he was more committed to the *idea* of a West India Company than to any company actually formed. If there was any plan, it was a plan of placing himself in control of any West India Company that might have been formed. He tailored his statements to fit the desires and interests of any individual or group — whether their interests ran to war or trade — provided they held out the hope of investing him with the leadership of such an enterprise. Details of organization and opera-

tion, therefore, were really of little importance to him.[29] This attitude is even more readily identifiable in his later efforts in Sweden
and France. His only stock in trade, then, was the appeal of his general ideas which, in an age of tremendous movement and adventure,
stirred men's imagination until a closer scrutiny revealed to them the
utter lack of any practical plan underneath. His idealism, too, was no
different from that of any other merchant who frankly admitted that
his was mixed with profit seeking.

Usselinx's biographer and others have erred in describing him as a
great "colonial projector." Certainly his connection with the history
of New Netherland is extremely dubious. He never expressed any interest in New Netherland, or for that matter in North America, because he felt there was "little to be gained there but furs, skins, and
tobacco and the filthiness of it is, to honorable people, a great detrac-
tion, seeing how injurious it is to the health." [30] He would have
exempted New Netherland from any monopoly given to the West
India Company in the New World. This was based on his belief that
the climate was too cold to produce any valuable commodities for export to Europe. And the distance was so great for transporting the
things that might grow — foodstuffs such as grain and fruit — that the
settlement of North America was, therefore, impractical.

His disinterest in North America has been variously explained
away by his champions who have held him up as a man nonetheless
of great vision, who saw the possibility of creating then the kind of
colonial system which later grew up in the English and French colonies in North America. Had his views on a West India Company only
prevailed, the argument goes, the basis might have been created for
quickly developing what only slowly evolved in the course of great
struggle: a society composed of transplanted European freemen based
on an agricultural economy. That such a society ultimately emerged
in North America — an area of no interest to Usselinx — was the result
of complex historical factors, not the result of the working out of any
early ideal plan such as a Hakluyt or an Usselinx might have
imagined.

In one pamphlet in particular, the "Vertoogh" ("Exposition"),
written as early as 1608, Usselinx made fleeting reference to such a
structure for society in the West Indies. Despite a great number of
other, widely differing statements about what should be done in the
West Indies, his biographer has hailed this tract as "being more

exactly in the line in which the principal efforts of his life and those which gave him importance in history were directed." This, his biographer and others have suggested, should have been the purpose of a West India Company and might have been if Usselinx had been in control. But surely this is reading history backwards, creating a plan which hindsight shows would have been a statesmanlike approach and then, despite the wealth of evidence which indicates no consistency of thought on his part, attributing it to Usselinx as his great work in life — a great work which, in this view, failed because of the opposition and lack of vision of crass, profit-seeking merchants.

In the same pamphlet cited, Usselinx went so far as to suggest that instead of a West India Company "the Lords States should themselves take this matter in hand, which in my judgment, would be the best, and that everyone in these provinces should be allowed to trade thither with passports." [31] Usselinx's capacity for shifting his position thus led him even to the point of repudiating what has been called the "grand project" of his life, a West India Company. Certainly it would have been impossible under the circumstances for the States-General itself to have taken on such a venture. Even much more unified countries such as England or France could not have taken such a statesmanlike approach at the time.

Usselinx's place in history is quite otherwise. His activities in the Netherlands, indeed, his entire career which took him to Sweden, France, and other parts of Europe as an advocate for establishing some kind of a West India Company, dramatically represent the enormous appeal which the West Indies, the New World, held at this time. The New World became an obsession with Usselinx but even for most men it was a powerful attraction. On the basis of an idea alone, Usselinx gained easy admission to the seats of power across Europe. He brought his ideas before kings and princes, presented innumerable memorials to ministers and legislators, talked to burgomasters and bishops, and at first they all listened with great interest. In the end Usselinx failed because he had no actual plans to realize the glorious future he so readily conjured up. Surfeited by wonderful images, his listeners soon became frustrated by his inability to match words with practical deeds. Men grew tired of Usselinx and his welcome was quickly worn out. The appeal was nonetheless there; it needed only to be served up in a remotely convincing form to elicit widespread response. A man such as Usselinx was probably incapable of doing this but there were others who tried later and succeeded. The idea of a West India Company, the notion that surely the Dutch could in some way derive profit and glory from the unlimited opportunities which the New World seemed to hold out, can thus be seen as a major influence leading to the creation of the company actually formed in 1621.

For some twenty years, then, before the company was actually even formed, the idea of a West India Company had been in existence. As a result of its innate appeal and of its having received some attention during these years, a number of individuals were predisposed to participate in such a company when an effort to form a West India Company began in earnest around 1618.

In the eyes of Usselinx and those who were at first most attracted to his scheme, the West India Company was not so much a commercial company as it was a political organization, an arm of the state. The commercial form was an expedient, necessitated by the inability of the state to launch such a venture on its own. In soliciting subscriptions to the company Usselinx constantly appealed to the public spirit of his fellow citizens to forward a scheme that was so manifestly intended to enhance the power of the Netherlands as a whole. He dangled before their eyes the vision of a Dutch colonial empire in the New World rather than trade statistics or balance sheets. It was an emotional appeal, resting fundamentally on the expectation that Netherlanders could forge for themselves in the New World a colonial empire fashioned after Spain's example or, if necessary, carved out of Spain's possessions there. The response it elicited came chiefly from war enthusiasts and from politicians throughout the Netherlands. But this political idea of a West India Company gained little support in merchant circles. There it was looked upon as a rather dubious scheme, holding out little chance of profit or success.

The merchants were slowly won over to supporting a West India Company on quite different grounds. A far greater influence for them than the example of Spain's colonial success in the New World was the example of their own East India Company. In the years following its establishment, the East India Company had developed into a powerful commercial and political organization. Although subsidized by the state and engaged in warlike operations such as those the West India Company would later become involved in, the East India Company nonetheless rested on a quite solid commercial base. Trade was

its *raison d'être*. It was, as one writer has phrased it, "a business concern, not intended for the creation of an Asiatic empire." [32] The
success of the East India Company had been phenomenal. In 1612 it
paid a dividend of 162.5 per cent and in 1620 "the Amsterdam board
of the East India Company called attention to the fact that within
eighteen years it had repaid its stockholders twice their capital investment." [33] Over the years the company in the East became increasingly more attractive to the merchants of the Netherlands as a model
of what might also be done in the West if a great commercial company could be formed for that area.

Over the years, too, many more merchants had become involved in
trading operations in the New World, especially during the period of
the truce with Spain from 1609 to 1621. The fur trade in New
Netherland, for example, developed after 1609. A number of ship
captains ventured to the wild coast of Guiana and to Essequibo in
northern Brazil on behalf of Holland and Zeeland merchants. The
west coast of Africa came under closer scrutiny by merchants seeking
slaves for the West Indian trade and salt for the fishing industry.
This increased activity on the part of Dutch merchants after 1609
added to their knowledge of the New World and served to heighten
their interest in it.[34]

The merchants began to flirt mildly with the notion of establishing
a general West India Company to pursue their commercial interests
in the New World. Before 1618 there were two abortive attempts to
form such a commercially oriented company as opposed to the type
suggested by Usselinx. What "some merchants from the provinces of
Holland and West Friesland" had in mind was a company exclusively
for trade to the West Indies.[35] From June to September of 1614 the
matter was considered by the States-General. Two difficulties were encountered in bringing this to a successful conclusion. The merchants
trading to Guinea wanted assurances in writing that if the proposed
company failed they would be permitted to resume free trade there
once again. What they feared was that under the guise of doing something greater in the West Indies, the proposed general company
might serve as a pretext for taking over their trade to Guinea. In the
second place, there was the difficulty of raising the initial capital for
such a company. The States-General hinted that a charter might be
forthcoming if "the sum of four, five, or six Millions of guilders" was
subscribed by May 1, 1615. Presumably it never was, for nothing further appears in the records on this matter.

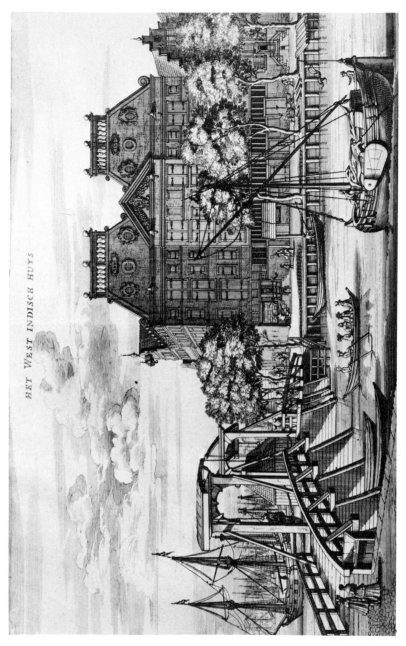

HET WEST INDISCH HUYS

The West Indian House as Seen from the Oude Schans, Amsterdam, Holland. This view shows the head office and warehouse of the Dutch West Indian Company in Amsterdam built in 1641. Copper engraving by Jacob van Meurs from Beschreibung der Stadt Amsterdam und derselben Fegebnisse, 1664. Courtesy of the Museum of the City of New York.

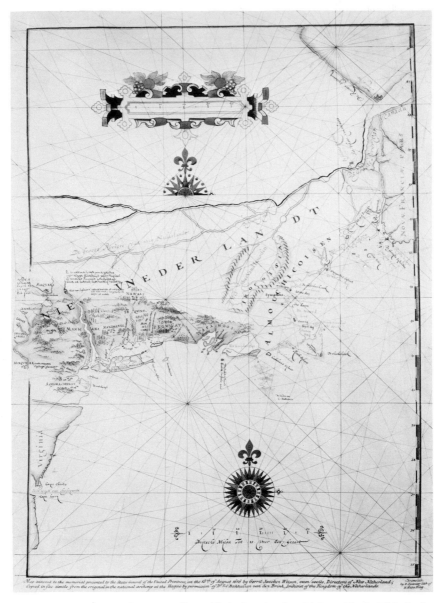

Drawn in gold and colors on vellum. Made in 1614 by Adriaen Block. This is the first map to show Manhattan as an island and the first to employ the term Nieu Netherlandt. Courtesy of the Museum of the City of New York.

The merchants of Zeeland had also expressed some interest in forming a commercial West India Company. Much of the commercial activity to the West Indies centered in Zeeland and after 1614 the States of Zeeland suggested to Usselinx that they might be willing to issue a charter of their own if the States-General failed to act. This seems to have been in the nature of a trial balloon — an attempt to assess the degree of financial support such a company might command in Zeeland. On the basis of this Usselinx went around the province soliciting subscriptions. Jameson notes that some 300,000 florins were "subscribed or promised" but since these subscriptions were undoubtedly conditional subscriptions, rather than paid-in capital, they do not reveal very much.[36] Of greater significance than these figures is the fact that no such company was formed in Zeeland, which suggests that sufficient support could not be obtained. That such a charter would have been effective seems unlikely since the province could not really prosecute violators from other provinces. It would have been very much like the Van Tweenhuysen Company's charter from Prince Maurice which was found to be not at all helpful.[37]

For a variety of reasons, then, merchants throughout the Netherlands began seriously to consider the commercial possibilities of the New World and to fashion ideas about a commercial West India Company. Superficial similarities between the two new areas of trade — the Orient and the New World — induced them to structure their ideas for the West around the available model in the East. They believed "they could build up a commercial system in the Atlantic like that of their colleagues in Asia"; indeed, that the West India Company would be "an improved edition of its East Indian model."[38] As East Indian skippers had ranged the seas of the Orient in search of new areas of trade, so too would West Indian skippers seek out new areas of trade in the New World — areas "not so exposed to the attacks of our enemies the Spaniards and Portuguese." They argued that a West India Company would be able to cultivate trade relations with "those nations and people, who still remain independent of the King of Spain."[39] They seemed to have no doubt that such areas existed and that Dutch skippers would find them. The merchants, too, had their dream of empire — but of a commercial rather than colonial empire.

Thus two conceptions of the nature of a West India Company had emerged by 1618. They had developed from quite different and distinct influences. There were a number of obvious points of coincidence between the merchants' desire to create a commercial empire through a commercial West India Company and the politicians' desire to carve out a colonial empire through a political West India Company. Indeed, the arguments of one were sometimes used to counter or deflect criticisms raised against the other.

But there were great differences between the two views as well. These became more apparent later when policy decisions had to be taken on the course of action to be followed by the company. Policy decisions invariably reflected one view or the other of this fundamental cleavage existing within the company as to its aims and purpose. Which view prevailed depended on whether the politicians or the merchants were in control of the company — and this altered as directors of the company periodically changed. The West India Company can by no means be seen, as it so often has in the past, as a monolithic organization single-mindedly devoted over the years to obtaining certain set aims.

Around 1618 a concerted effort began which brought together into one organization both of these different conceptions of a West India Company. A charter was granted by the States-General in June of 1621 but two additional years were required before there was sufficient capital to commence actual operations. Success attended the efforts during these years for three important reasons. First, a number of the most influential merchants and politicians of the Netherlands now actively supported the formation of a West India Company. Secondly, a comprehensive plan, based on a practical approach which the merchant group found attractive, could now be presented. And, finally, the necessary capital for such an enterprise could be raised.

The schemes of Usselinx and others before 1618 had foundered because they failed to obtain the support of leading Netherlanders. After 1618 this ceased to be a problem; indeed, the principal supporters came from within Holland, the most powerful province in the republic. In September of 1618 a proposal for a West India Company came before the legislative assembly of Holland. By November of that year a charter for such a company was reported out of committee in the States-General — much to the dislike of Usselinx who was away in Zeeland at the time and who, therefore, played absolutely no role in its drafting.[40] Holland continued to dominate the proceedings on this matter and sent the proposed charter off to the provinces for further consideration. The delegates from Holland arranged the mem-

bership of the committee which heard the subsequent provincial reports in July of 1619 and which afterwards steered the charter
through the States-General.[41]

Usselinx opposed these efforts because they departed from the more
idealistic and political conception of the West India Company which
he envisioned. "The variations sprang," as he himself said, "from a
difference of purpose." As Usselinx saw it, the proposed company was
based on "a mistaken view of the work to be done in America, which
was not like the task set before those who had to do with the king-
doms of the East." [42] But it was obvious from the proposed charter
that there were many in the Netherlands who disagreed with him.
The more commercial orientation of the proposed charter was undoubtedly necessary to obtain the much needed support of the merchant group.

Who were the originators of this proposed charter for a West India
Company in 1618? As we have seen in the case of the chartering of
the New Netherland Company in 1614, the impetus could not have
come on high from the States-General.[43] The States-General of the
Netherlands was simply incapable of projecting on its own such a vast
undertaking. The repository of the symbols rather than the real
powers of national sovereignty, it was more an assemblage of provincial ambassadors than of national legislators. The initiative, therefore, had to come from outside.

The evidence available is too sketchy to identify specific individuals
in this effort. But it does suggest that the leadership was drawn from
among the wealthiest and most politically prominent figures in the
Netherlands. These individuals were politically influential enough to
obtain a subsidy of one million guilders from the States-General.[44]
They were, moreover, able to exert such political pressure within the
Netherlands that the Dutch East India Company was literally forced
to subscribe one million guilders as the price for the renewal of its
own charter.[45] They were commercially well connected enough to
impose a monopoly on the vast area of the New World and to absorb
every pocket of Dutch mercantile activity that existed there over the
protests of merchants long identified with these individual areas of
trade.[46] They were obviously men of a much different stripe than
Usselinx.

Some of them were extremely wealthy merchants, active in a
number of other companies including the East India Company.

Others were merchants more interested in politics than in mercantile pursuits. Some of them held high political office in the leading cities and provinces of the Netherlands — particularly in Holland and Zeeland where the greatest interest in the New World centered. All of them undoubtedly had access to the politically influential people throughout the Netherlands. For convenience they may be referred to collectively as the politico-merchants of the new republic.

The role they sought to play at this junction in the Netherlands' history was a political or at least not a narrowly conceived commercial one. Now that the Netherlands had come of age in the international community of states, these men meant to exercise some control over the new state's destiny. Their wealth commanded respect in social and economic circles and because of this they were able either to control or greatly influence their own local political areas and thus the state at large. They were, of course, interested in increasing their own wealth but at bottom lay an urge to political participation so strong that it would at times even prejudice their better commercial judgments.

Many of these politico-merchants were probably not involved in the day-to-day operations of the companies in which they had large financial interests. Their energies were devoted more to commercial policy formulation and to politics than to execution. Their interest, too, tended to diverge from traditional merchant activities and to run more toward the newer areas of finance, banking, and stock speculation. These were the early years of a trend that was ultimately to change the Netherlands from a nation of traders and carriers into a nation of bankers. And these were some of the early figures involved in this transition.

Given the general mercantile cast of society in the Netherlands and the weak, tenuously balanced political stability of the new republic, a commercial company endowed with far ranging political powers was not an unlikely development. In fact it was probably easier to permit such a company to exercise attributes of sovereignty than to submit the question of the proper exercise of national sovereignty to a more formal, constitutional discussion and perhaps thereby risk upsetting the none too firmly established union of the provinces.

The probability that war with Spain would be resumed on the expiration of the truce in 1621 was intimately bound up with the formation of the West India Company. However, even though the company became increasingly involved in the task of waging war once it was chartered, the war itself would not have led to its creation. The war served rather as a catalyst which blended together the two conflicting views of a West India Company.

The expectation of profit from the war seemed to offer a solution to the financial difficulties involved in launching either conception of a West India Company. The war also tended to push into the background the fundamental differences in concept which were undoubtedly known to exist. All could hope that once it was formed it would realize all of their expectations. The important thing, therefore, was to make a beginning. Hope prevailed over disturbing fact — somehow the war would be able to resolve the differences. It never did. In part, the war blurred over these opposing views and, in part, it pushed them aside, forcing men to concentrate on something that could be agreed upon — the prosecution of the war.

To those who led the way in forming it — and who would later direct it — and to those who were asked merely to invest in it, the purpose and aims of the West India Company chartered in 1621 were pretty much whatever they chose to read into it. Since it could appeal on so many grounds, the job of soliciting subscriptions was obviously made much easier. The more politically oriented hoped it would lay the foundation of a Dutch colonial empire in the West that would rival Spain's. Either by discovering new areas — the "yet uninvaded countries" as they referred to them — which would be as profitable as Peru, Mexico, or the Greater Antilles, or by dislodging Spain from some of her possessions, a Dutch colonial empire could be carved out in the New World. The more commercially oriented hoped to discover places outside the existing Spanish sphere of control with sufficient native development so that a profitable trade could be conducted. In this they were following the example of the East India Company which had discovered such places where a thriving trade could be carried on.

Those who were violently anti-Spanish could support such a venture because of its potential for inflicting great damage on the traditional enemy. Many of the southern émigrés undoubtedly supported it on these grounds. But it would be a mistake to claim, as some have, that the émigrés were primarily responsible for the formation of the West India Company.[47] Many of the émigrés were certainly opposed to it. The members of the Van Tweenhuysen Company were mainly

Southern exiles and would hardly have welcomed a scheme which drove them out of a trade which they had pioneered.

One other group found the proposed company most attractive — the stock speculators. Indeed, many of these were probably involved in the efforts to form the West India Company. With the building of the Amsterdam Bourse in 1609 speculation in both commodities and stocks reached such scandalous proportions as to constitute a serious problem for the company's directors.[48] The possibility of having another company's stock to trade — such as a West India Company's — may have been of great interest to speculators and financiers in the Netherlands. How much of a role speculators played in urging the formation of the West India Company cannot be determined. That the company was somewhat of a stock venture can be inferred from the fact that, "Announcement of a West India Company in 1621 was a signal for excited trading in the actions of that company *even before subscription had opened."* [49]

Nearly everyone hoped that the activities of the West India Company in the New World — whether of a war, trade, or empire building nature — would greatly stimulate the internal economy of the Netherlands through the employment opportunities it would create. Sailors and soldiers would be provided with jobs, and shipbuilding, the munitions industry, and all the related trades would be greatly encouraged. This, as some pointed out, was the real benefit which Spain reaped from her colonies, far more important than even the gold and silver she annually obtained from that source. There was general agreement, therefore, that a West India Company would "increase Trade and Commerce, without which the great multitude of seamen bestowed by God on this Country cannot be employed and all occupations maintained in continual action and prosperity." [50]

The plan that the politico-merchants offered to potential subscribers and in which they themselves invested reflected the mixed influences responsible for the formation of the company. The influence of the merchants was most clearly discernible in the original charter of June 3, 1621, and in the subsequent amendments to it. It followed very closely the charter of the East India Company. In justifying the taking over of all existing trade in the vast reaches of its charter, it was not maintained that competition was ruining the trade — the traditional justification — but rather that it was found "by experience that without the common help, aid and means of a general company,

no profitable business can be carried on, protected and maintained
. . . on account of the great risk from pirates, extortions and the like,
which are incurred on such long and distant voyages." [51] Such inconveniences to the trade had not been loudly complained of in the past
by the merchants. Monopoly sprang from other reasons.

The preamble referred to "many other and different pregnant reasons and considerations" which had far more to do with it. Monopoly
was necessary in order to establish the aims of the merchants — the
creation of a trading empire in the West comparable to the East
India Company's. As the merchants saw it, the profits of the existing
trade would help to defray the expense of opening up new areas — areas which they hoped existed and to which a trade could be started.
The promoters of the West India Company apparently found it useful, indeed necessary, to point to the trade already there. It gave the
appearance that the scheme was grounded on a firm commercial base.
While eliciting the interest of non-mercantile potential investors in
the stock of the company, the presence of some trade served the further purpose of reassuring cautious merchants. As the amplification of
the charter in June of 1622, which rescinded the exemption from
monopoly previously granted the salt trade at Punta del Rey, states:
"The majority of the participants largely counted on this as essential
for assured profit." [52] Thus the known trade was used as a form of
insurance to investors because "in case of delay or ill success, it was
expected to make good a portion of the loss." [53]

The hand of the merchants can also be seen in their attempts to
assure themselves adequate representation among the directors of the
company who were originally drawn largely from the politicians and
war enthusiasts. From the various amplifications of the charter between 1621 and 1623 two conflicting interests emerged: the interest of
the war enthusiasts and those inclined toward a politically oriented
company, on the one hand, and the interest of those inclined toward
a trade oriented company, on the other. The former were represented
by the directors of the company and the latter by the "chief participants" in the company. In an "Agreement between the directors and
the chief participants of the West India Company," drawn up in
June of 1623, the chief participants insisted "that the first two vacant
places among the directors at Amsterdam, the first two of Zeeland,
and the first in the Chamber of the Mase shall successively be supplied and filled by the chief participants of the respective Chambers,

absolutely by plurality of votes . . . to preserve their rights in the said meetings of the directors." [54] The trading interest or chief participants also insisted that they be represented in meetings of the Nineteen, the general governing body of the West India Company. A committee was created which would have the power to examine "the books, invoices, and other documents" for the benefit of the chief participants.[55]

In the "Agreement of 1623" the chief participants also attacked the political interest by imposing restrictions on the election of directors. Close relatives could not be elected directors of the same chamber at the same time. Nor could a director of the East India Company also serve concurrently as a director of the West India Company. Perhaps an even greater blow to the political interest was the threat that "directors shall receive no commissions unless they properly attend to the business of the Company." [56]

All these measures, designed to strengthen the commercial or trading interest, were undoubtedly necessary in order to obtain the support of the working merchants. "Desirous of promoting unity and concord between the directors and the chief participants as well as the advancement of the West India Company," the States-General formally approved these changes in the charter.[57]

The influence of the war enthusiasts and those in favor of carving out a colonial empire in the New World is less easy to define. That a separate interest, centering around the directors, existed has already been shown. The charter itself does not clearly reflect their influence. It did, however, insure the predominance of their interest by delegating to the individual assemblies of the provinces the right to set up procedures for the election of directors.[58] The only restriction on this was that a director must himself be a chief participant — in this more general sense of the term, one who had invested at least 6,000 guilders on his own in the company. Nonetheless, this placed the election of directors in the hands of those most politically influential in the provinces.

The charter also made reference to the political side of the company in the requirement that two sets of books be kept — "one relating to trade and one relating to war, each separate." [59] It further specified that profit from captured prizes "shall be kept separate and distinct from the account of trade and commerce, that the net proceeds of the said prizes shall be employed in fitting out ships, paying the troops, fortifications, garrisons and like matters of war and defense." [60] Though veiled, these references do attest to the noncommercial interests of the company.

The influence of these noncommercial interests in the formation of the West India Company can more clearly be seen in the kind of activities which the company initially undertook. Nearly the first operation of the company was an expedition against Bahia in 1623–1624.[61] Quite large in scale, it was made up of twenty-three ships and over three thousand men. Its purpose was not only to wage war with Spain but to take over an area which could become the nucleus of a Dutch colonial empire.

The influence of the speculators was not unrepresented in the charter. The division of the company into five chambers did not necessarily correspond to centers of trade — as it had in the formation of the East India Company — but rather to financial subscription centers. Moreover, places outside of these centers might appoint a director to any chamber of the company if their subscriptions exceeded 100,000 guilders. Foreign subscription was also permitted under the terms of the charter and indeed actively encouraged.[62]

The rift between merchants and war enthusiasts or imperialists was specifically acknowledged in the original charter: "And if it should happen that in the aforesaid general Assembly any weighty matter came before them, wherein they could not agree, or even in which one side should scruple to impose its decision on the other, the same shall be left to our decision; and whatever shall be determined upon shall be followed and carried into execution." [63] In practice, however, one side or the other would prevail. In the first years of operation it was the politically oriented directors who dominated the shaping of company policy.

Thus two distinct interests can be seen both in the emergence of attitudes which led to the formation of a West India Company and in the composition of the company actually chartered in 1621. They were fused together into one organization largely as a result of pressures from the expected resumption of the war and exertions on the part of stock speculators. This struggle between trading interest and colonial interest continued throughout the history of the West India Company and forms the background against which policy decisions were taken affecting the development of New Netherland.

The ambitions which traders and colonialists alike had for the

West India Company were not based on balance sheets or hard facts but rather on assumptions as to what the New World was like and what a massive effort might be able to accomplish there. Although the directors were largely politically oriented during the first years of the company's operations, it really would have made very little difference for the history of New Netherland if the trading interest had held the reins of power. In neither view of the goals to be sought by the company did New Netherland figure very prominently. From the experience of private traders it was known that New Netherland offered little beyond furs and timber. Both the colonialists and incorporated merchants were after much bigger game.

The early years of the company would, under either view, be devoted to examining intensely the tropical regions of the New World, where the basis for either a colonial or trading empire could be established. No one was so foolish as to suggest that New Netherland had the slightest hope of becoming a pivot point of empire. Exotic spices or other products could not be cultivated in the cold expanse of North America. Nor was there any highly developed, indigenous population there with which a lucrative trade might be begun. The role of New Netherland would instead be a supporting one. The fur trade would be pursued vigorously. The profits from this could be used to open up newer areas which were presumed to have a far greater potential.

What chance for success did the West India Company have in 1621? It all depended on whether the reality of the New World in any way corresponded to the assumptions which were made about it. What ever mistakes might have entered into the calculation of the risks involved, the West India Company was hardly a wildcat scheme. Its assumptions, after all, rested on the best experience available at the time. Its two models were the Spanish empire and the Dutch East India Company — the only examples of success in such activities then known. The starving Pilgrims on the shores of Cape Cod or the bickering, disgruntled employees of the Virginia Company could not have then held out an alternate example of success in such overseas ventures.

Conditions in the New World, of course, turned out to be quite otherwise. The commercial expectations of the company in the New World were initially frustrated because trade proved to be "very meager and indifferent with the people and nations who are still in-

dependent of the King of Spain." And hopes for a colonial empire
were dashed when it was painfully learned that "the countries still
unoccupied, are for the most part unproductive and of little value." [64]
But all this was yet to come in 1621.

The history of the origins of the West India Company reveals most
clearly the complex nature of the company. It also provides a frame
of reference for examining the activities of the company with respect
to New Netherland during the years 1623–1629. From the first mention in print in 1600 down to the States-General's charter in 1621, the
term West India Company meant many things to many people. But
at no time did it correspond to any well defined body of ideas or
clearly articulated views on organization and operation. In the early
years of the West India Company its commercial side was subordi-
nated to political considerations. When it later attempted to redirect
its energies in a more commercial direction, it was hampered by the
political tone which it had acquired over the years. Caught by the
need to pursue simultaneously commercial and political aims, and
managed by directors whose personal interest leaned in one direction
or the other, West India Company policy either fluctuated wildly or
else ground to a standstill because no compromise could be reached.
The effects of this on the development of New Netherland were
great; indeed, crucial.

CHAPTER THREE

THE PLAN FOR
NEW NETHERLAND

Launched for a variety of reasons and with great, albeit vague expectations envisioned for it, the West India Company finally embarked on its career in 1623. In the ensuing six years the assumptions upon which the West India Company had been founded were put to the test of experience by the company's skippers, admirals, and commercial agents. The result was that an impressive body of knowledge about the vast reaches of the West India Company's grant in the New World was gathered together in a relatively short period of time. Out of this encounter with reality during the years 1623–1629, new assumptions had to be fashioned about the ways in which the Old World could make use of the New.

In all areas of the charter during its first six years of operation, the emphasis of the company was on exploration and experimentation. A surviving balance sheet shows that in 1626 the company had over eighty ships and yachts deployed throughout its patent, in such places as Brazil, Guiana, New Netherland, and along the coast of Africa.[1]

The company was richer in many ways as a result of this intensive activity. The same balance sheet noted in conclusion that the experience which the company had gained from this was by no means to be counted the least of its assets, for it "has given it more knowledge as to the condition of the places situate in the West Indies and the Brazils; what are useful or useless to the Company in that country; what can, and what cannot, be defended; all of which is of great advantage to the Company and the country." [2]

Experience, for example, exploded the assumption of those who were most inclined to the notion of using the West India Company as a means of establishing a purely colonial empire modeled on Spain's success. They painfully discovered that there was no other Mexico or Peru waiting to be exploited by Dutch masters. Rather did they find "that the countries still unoccupied, are for the most part unproductive and of little value." [3] Equally frustrating for the would-be empire builders were the somewhat productive areas that were found since they were:

> . . . greatly encumbered by timber, &c., and very difficult of cultivation, especially for our nation, who being unaccustomed to so hot a climate, find it difficult to apply themselves to labor, and being unprovided with slaves and also not in the habit of making use of them, cannot easily supply their own inefficiency by the labor of others, as the Spaniards and Portuguese, easily do by that of the Blacks and Indians.[4]

Those who sought to forge a Dutch colonial empire were, however, in control of the company's affairs during the first years of its existence. And in addition to surveying the "yet uninvaded countries" for the potential building blocks of an empire to rival Spain's they cast covetous eyes on Spanish and Portuguese possessions in the New World and undertook a number of costly expeditions to dislodge the hated enemy from these settled regions. Some success attended these efforts though it must be pointed out that greater gains were registered against the Portuguese than the Spaniards. Puerto Rico and Pernambuco were sacked and held for short periods; various areas of Brazil passed under Dutch rule and remained so until 1654.[5]

The hope of displacing Spain in her overseas possessions continued to burn brightly despite the lack of any spectacular conquests. While plans for even more ambitious expeditions were being laid, the pro-colonial empire directors, who dominated the early years of the West India Company, consoled themselves by reciting the damages they had inflicted on the King of Spain or the costs they had put him to by their sniping presence in the New World. In the eyes of these directors, the humbling of Spanish power and the creation of a Dutch colonial empire were the only truly worthy tasks for a great West India Company. They disdained the pleas of their more commercial colleagues who urged a policy of trade for the company, pointing out that:

> . . . from the commencement of our administration, we preferred to proceed in a warlike manner against the common enemy . . . principally because we found that the expected service, for the welfare of our Fatherland and the destruction of our hereditary enemy, could not be accomplished by the trifling trade with the Indians, or the tardy cultivation of uninhabited regions.[6]

The political directors continually observed that the heavy capitalization of the company demanded that its policy be formulated along vigorous political lines rather than narrow commercial ones. They referred to the trade to Africa as "trifling in comparison with the Company's large Capital." [7] As for the products that might ultimately be developed from the Brazilian trade, they inquired: "What of them? Those people are so barbarous, and have so few wants (inasmuch as they feel no desire for clothing and require no necessaries for their subsistence) that all the trade which exists there, can easily be carried on with two or three ships a year, and be maintained with trifling Capital." To settle for trade only, in their opinion, would merely leave the company "a meager scum of a well fed body." [8]

Thus those who had initially seen the West India Company as a vehicle for establishing a colonial empire and who were themselves anxious to play a political role, found themselves more and more driven into the arms of the war enthusiasts. Holding fast to their vision of raising up a great Dutch empire in the New World and aware now that it would have to be carved out of the existing Spanish possessions, they advocated greatly increased subsidies to the company and the continuation of the war as the only possible means to their much desired end.

Subsidies to the West India Company, they argued, should be seen in the same terms as subsidies to foreign nations or princes. The latter had long been an accepted practice in the Netherlands. The essential difference, however, was that such subsidies paid to the West India Company would greatly stimulate the internal economy of the Netherlands by providing employment for its own citizens and by building a merchant marine that would also be able to serve the national interest in times of emergency. As the directors of the Amsterdam chamber of the company presented it to the States-General: "This State hath paid and still pays to foreign princes, heavy yearly subsidies, the money whereof goes and remains out of the country; and nothing was obtained in return except what was effected this last year by the Company, who expend the subsidies in this country." [9] They artfully pointed out that there was less hazard involved in subsidies granted to the West India Company than to "Foreign princes, whose good successes were both to be desired and feared." The company, they concluded, "nestles here under your Great Mightinesses' wings, and cannot be dreaded except by its enemies." [10]

And so, as the terms of some of the first directors of the company were about to expire in 1629, the Assembly of the Nineteen cautioned the States-General about entering into negotiations with Spain for a truce, fearing that "the utter ruin and dissolution of said Company will be the consequence." [11] In the succeeding years the position of the politically oriented directors of the West India Company was that although "the condition of the Company was such, that it improved from day to day," still the company "could not exist, except by war." [12]

Though looked down upon by the political directors, who caustically referred to them as "those who supposed themselves most conversant with this trade," the merchant directors who favored a policy of trade for the company had actually accomplished a great deal during these first six years.[13] Impressive amounts of gold, elephants' teeth, and pepper had been obtained from Guinea.[14] It was estimated that New Netherland shipped home annually furs valued at 50,000 guilders, in addition to oak and hickory timber, whose value, while unspecified, was referred to as "considerable." [15] Other reports mentioned as return cargos from the Caribbean such products as salt, sugar, rawhides, cochineal, tobacco, and "all sorts of precious stones, silk and silk goods, amber, all sorts of drugs, Brazil and Log Wood and other wares, too numerous to mention." [16]

But the experience of the first six years also demonstrated to the merchants of the company that their initial assumptions about what could be expected in the New World would have to be sharply modified. The unoccupied areas remaining in the West Indies turned out to be not at all like the areas which the merchants of the East India Company had stumbled upon. Instead of finding highly developed Indian societies they encountered only an indigenous population of the most primitive sort which cared little for and, indeed, required little from Dutch traders. Still some products were obtained and countless others were diligently sought after.

No unexpected windfalls or spectacular successes fell to the lot of the trading interest within the West India Company which could in any way compare to the conquest of Brazil or the much heralded capture of the Spanish silver fleet for which the political interest within the company took credit. The New World was not the Far East. Success, if it were to come, would have to be the result of the application of different techniques and would assuredly be a long range proposition. Forced to abandon their more ambitious aims as a result of the experience gained in the years 1623–1629, members of the political interest could only throw their support behind measures designed to prosecute the war. Thus whatever victories they might claim were necessarily ephemeral ones since the war could not last forever. However much the political interest might despise it, success for the West India Company in the New World ultimately lay in working out some approach to the "trifling trade with the Indians or the tardy cultivation of uninhabited regions."

New Netherland, too, during the first six years of the charter, came under the company's general policy of exploration and experimentation. The responsibility for directing this activity devolved upon the Amsterdam chamber of the company, which in turn established a committee, usually styled the "Commissioners for New Netherland." [17] The principal Commissioners were Albert Coenraets Burgh, Samuel Godyn, Johannes de Laet, Kiliaen van Rensselaer, Cars Bicker, and Commer Spranges.[18] All six were directors of the Amsterdam chamber of the company and wealthy merchants. De Laet was also an historian of sorts and his writings provide one of the main sources for this period.

It has long been the fashion for historians to treat the early years of New Netherland under West India Company rule as a period of neglect.[19] Although originally cast in the role of a supporting activity, an assured source of profit to the company, New Netherland was far from neglected in the years 1623–1629. On the contrary, from all indications, the Commissioners performed their duty with great fidelity, submitting New Netherland to a rigorous examination in an attempt to determine its potential value.

The notion of neglect in these years derives from a mistaken view of what the company was attempting to do in New Netherland. It involves as well a complete misunderstanding of the term colonization and of the relationship of the process of colonization to the development of society in New Netherland.

The issuance of the West India Company's charter in 1621 was not the signal for the beginning of any massive attempt to settle inhabitants of the Netherlands permanently abroad either in New Netherland or in any other area of the New World for the purpose of developing a new society. As demonstrated in the previous chapter, the two leading ideas in the minds of the supporters of the West India Company were: (1) the creation of a colonial empire similar to Spain's through the discovery of new, profitable areas whose indigenous population could be exploited; or (2) the establishment of a commercial empire modeled after the East India Company's success in the Far East if the new areas possessed highly developed Indian societies.

Indeed, the charter itself made only passing reference to the matter of transplanting Europeans to areas within the control of the West India Company. And, as J. Franklin Jameson has ably demonstrated, this reference should be translated, "Moreover, they *may* advance the peopling of fruitful and unsettled parts" rather than in the imperative sense conveyed by O'Callaghan's translation of the same as "Moreover, they *must* advance the peopling of fruitful and unsettled parts." [20]

Not until years later did the company make any statements about settlement having been an intended purpose. In 1664, in connection with a boundary dispute in America with the English and after men's view of the possibilities of North America had been dramatically altered by the experience gained in the intervening forty years, the States-General defensively articulated what the vague reference in their charter of 1621 meant. They asserted then that the company was empowered forty years earlier to do anything:

> . . . *especially as it may best promote the peopling of fruitful and uninhabited countries; and the aforesaid company having from the beginning, by virtue of the aforesaid charter, in con-*

*formity with Our sincere intention, established their population
and colonists on the coast of America, in the country called New
Netherland, notwithstanding which some persons evil disposed
towards our State and the said company, endeavour to misrepre-
sent Our good and honest meaning, as the same is contained in
the said charter, as if We had privileged the said company only
to trade within the said limits, and not to colonize nor to plant
settlements, nor take possession of lands. . . .*[21]

The implications of O'Callaghan's translation have had important
effects on the way in which the history of the Dutch period of New
York has been conceived and written. For despite overwhelming evidence to the contrary, historians have insisted that the early efforts of
the West India Company in New Netherland were directed and
ought to have been directed toward the transplantation of a truly
Dutch society to these shores. In fact, they were not; and, in terms of
the times, neither could they have been. This was not because the
directors of the West India Company were shortsighted or inordi-
nately absorbed in profit-making tasks. They were as idealistic as an
Usselinx; indeed, they were as idealistic as the nineteenth-century historians who have taken them so to task for their feeble efforts at
colonization.

It was not a question of idealism but rather of the inability of individuals in 1621, based on the experience at hand, to conceive of
North America, especially New Netherland, in any other terms than
its potential for trade. The "persons evil disposed" were probably
correct for it seems quite clear that no extensive program of settlement was either planned or even envisioned for New Netherland during the years 1623–1629. New Netherland was a "known" area and,
according to the best information of the times, certainly seemed an
unlikely site for the launching of a great imperialistic scheme. The
more tropical areas of the New World afforded far better prospects
for great accomplishments than, as the directors noted in 1629:

This district, which we have named New Netherland, *although
it ought to be, in point of climate, as warm and as well adapted
for the cultivation of fruits at least, as the furthest frontiers of
France towards Spain, yet it has been found much colder, and
as much subject to frost and other inconveniences as these; nay,
as more northern countries. The people conveyed by us thither,*

have, therefore, found but scanty means of livelihood up to the
present; and have not been any profit, but a drawback, to this
Company.[22]

The settlement of New Netherland in the years 1623–1629 was, therefore, neglected because it had not really been intended. Instead, an examination of the commercial potentialities of this area was vigorously undertaken by the company. The West India Company was, after all, in part a commercial venture and its directors, unlike later critics, did not consider profit an unworthy aim or even incompatible with the achievement of idealistic objectives. Idealism and the expectation of profit were closely linked together in this age — a view by no means peculiar to the Dutch. The Englishman, too, in initially approaching North America:

> . . . *was a trader first, a colonizer afterwards* . . . *those inter-*
> *ested in a project for Virginia insisted that the investment would*
> *redound to the glory of God, but they expected to convert the*
> *savage by trading with him; they urged the advancement of the*
> *kingdom, but they meant to secure dividends on their adventure*
> *by bringing back to England the supplies she needed most — the*
> *materials for shipbuilding; they insisted on the immense gain to*
> *come from the new country, but they expected the lion's share*
> *for the stockholders.*[23]

And very much like the early adventurers to Virginia, the directors of the West India Company, in pursuing commercial aims and profits in New Netherland, made frequent allusions to other considerations as also being mainsprings to their activity. A variety of motives were combined with no apparent difficulty. As Craven has written of the Virginia Company investors:

> *Their motives were not entirely selfish; their desire to render a*
> *public service is unquestionable. They intended to aid England*
> *in the solution of her economic and social problems by increas-*
> *ing her trade, by relieving her of a dependence upon other coun-*
> *tries for certain necessary commodities, and by relieving her*
> *congested state of population. Yet even these considerations of*
> *public welfare were not wholly divorced from the idea that in*
> *fulfilling its higher purposes there was to be found the best guar-*

antee of financial reward for the company, and hence the best
guarantee of financial profit for each individual adventurer.[24]

For the West India Company, as for the Virginia Company: "To make the business pay was the first aim of all . . . and other matters were of but secondary interest." Commercial rather than political matters, the enhancement of trade rather than the transplantation of a Dutch society, became the first order of business for the West India Company in New Netherland during the years 1623–1629.

From the labors of the private traders before 1623, the Commissioners for New Netherland had inherited a not inconsiderable legacy of commercial experience about the area which now fell to their charge. Amsterdam had been the center of private trading to New Netherland in the pre-company days. And for as long as New Netherland remained under the control of the West India Company, it was the Amsterdam chamber of the company which exercised the greatest influence on the course of its development.

There was, therefore, no sharp break with the past as a result of the transition from the era of private trading to the era of company monopoly in New Netherland. Two members of the Van Tweenhuysen Company became directors of the Amsterdam chamber — Witsen and Godyn. Several skippers and supercargoes, and undoubtedly many crew members, who had sailed between Amsterdam and New Netherland for the private merchants, now entered the service of the company and continued in their familiar ways. Although death had removed from the scene some of the early merchants in the trade to New Netherland — Hunger, Francoys Pelgrom, Vogels, Plancius, and Nooms — before the company commenced actual operations, there were still many merchants left in Amsterdam who could render valuable assistance to the Commissioners — merchants such as Schenck, Nicquet, Hinlopen, Van Tweenhuysen, and Harencarspel.[25]

The paucity of surviving source material has cast a veil of obscurity over the initial activities of the West India Company in New Netherland. De Laet, writing in 1630, stated that "several colonies have been sent by the Directors of the chartered West India Company, from the very commencement of that Company, to wit, from the year 1623, in order to continue the possession of those quarters, and to maintain the trade in peltries."[26] Supporting this, Kiliaen van Rensselaer, writing in 1633, noted, "Sundry colonists, as early as 1623, had been conveyed thither with instructions to dwell there as free persons and to carry on trade." [27] However, no names of ships can be identified with either of these statements.

The first West India Company ship known to have visited New Netherland was the "Mackreel," which arrived there in December of 1623. The supercargo aboard, Daniel van Krieckebeeck, traded with the Indians for furs near the present site of Albany. In the account of this which survives, no mention is made of whether any personnel of the West India Company were left behind in New Netherland.[28] The ship "Nieu Nederland," which arrived in the Hudson in May of 1624, brought, in the words of Wassenaer, "thirty families, mostly Walloons, to plant a colony there." [29] This, according to many authorities, was the beginning of the "permanent settlement" of New Netherland.

Over the years, much time and many words have been spent in defending or attacking the date of May, 1624, as marking the point at which permanent settlement can be said to have been begun in New Netherland.[30] Nearly as many words have been expended on trying to establish whether Albany or New York City should be accorded the distinction of the oldest, permanently settled area of New York. But these questions, around which such heated controversy has raged and endless speculation developed, really have no significance for the history of New Netherland. Any date which might be definitively identified would mark only the establishment of a trading post and not the conscious introduction of any seed of permanent settlement out of which it was expected that a highly organized society would develop. Such trading posts of course became in fact the nucleus of settlement in these areas but the point is that at the time their reason for existing was seen in commercial terms rather than in terms of a first step toward the erection of a new society. From the experience acquired by men and families stationed at these trading posts over the years a new view of the possibilities of New Netherland slowly evolved — a view which saw New Netherland less in purely commercial dimensions and more as a place to set down roots permanently and begin the task of creating a political society. This shift in attitudes towards New Netherland was a slow, imperceptible one so that no formal date can be assigned to mark the beginning of permanent settlement. Society in New Netherland did not grow out of a single planting which eventually flowered, as earlier historians have suggested. Instead of having been born at any one moment in time, society in New Netherland was made over the years.

Much of the confusion about this has resulted from a failure to define what is meant by "permanent settlement." Generally, the participants in the controversy have accepted the presence of women or of families as incontrovertible evidence that a permanent settlement was being launched. But this is an assumption which needs to be examined. Women are accustomed to being with men, wives with husbands, whatever the conditions of the world around them. Their mere presence in New Netherland is not sufficient proof that they intended to stay. The presence of families, too, need not mean that a plan of permanent settlement was undertaken. Many families left soon after they arrived and either returned to the Netherlands or else tried their luck elsewhere in the New World. In fact the presence of women may only attest to the fact that agriculture was contemplated and that women were required to perform their traditional tasks in farming operations. In terms of the plan devised by the Commissioners for New Netherland at least, the notion of a permanent, agricultural settlement is not at all clear.

Writers have also seized upon the term "colony" in the accounts of these years in order to substantiate their contention. They have assumed that this meant an embryonic political and social organization — a society, that is, rather than a commercial organization which seems more likely the case. The connotation of society and presumption of permanent settlement have thus been read into the term colony and automatically substituted for it wherever encountered. While it is perfectly true that, in the most basic sense, any collection of people can be regarded as forming some kind of society, still this simple sense of the term society is not the interpretation which writers on this period have placed on the word colony. In the view of those who have with great pains attempted to determine the precise date for the beginning of settlement, a colony represented a group of individuals with well defined ideas on establishing a political and social order and who were devoted to extending gradually these ideas over the entire area before them. It involved, too, a conscious awareness on the part of the participants that they were forming a new society, with a distinguishable political and social structure, and with which their interests would henceforth be primarily identified. But no such consciousness of a distinct society can be discovered among those who ventured to New Netherland during the years 1623–1629.

Colonies were hardly an innovation at this point; they had a rather long history, especially in the Far East, Africa, and the Caribbean. In the Far East they were usually referred to as factories or garrisons instead of colonies. They were essentially groups of people left behind by ship captains for a variety of reasons but chiefly to maintain the trade between voyages. Different areas required different kinds of colonies or factories, and modifications or refinements were added as experience dictated.

"Colonies for trade" were frequently established in the New World.[31] It was even not uncommon for a colony to be left ashore by a ship's captain so that crops could be raised for a food supply, thus obviating the necessity of returning home for supplies. Sir Henry Colt, on a voyage to the West Indies in 1631, reported: "My men weer ther busied at work in cleering of ground for peace, potatos & wheat agaynst next years journy." [32] As an historian of seventeenth-century migration has pointed out:

> It was impracticable to transport all supplies. . . . The nature
> of these new outposts had to be broadened. Successful trade must
> involve settlement and settlement could not be left to chance.
> The transportation of colonists became a vital part of every proj-
> ect of Western planting.[33]

It was precisely in this manner that the Amsterdam chamber of the West India Company approached New Netherland. The beginnings of settlement in New Netherland arose not out of any great desire to transplant a distinctive Dutch society to the shores of North America but rather as a means of protecting the fur trade. Thus, the colonies sent out to New Netherland during these years were of a commercial rather than political or social nature. The individuals of these colonies regarded themselves not as pathbreakers of a new society but as employees of the company, which in point of fact most of them were.

As noted earlier, in the days of private trading it had been quickly learned that it was useful to leave people behind in New Netherland between voyages. The impetus for this had originally come from the competitive situation resulting from the presence in the Hudson of skippers representing several different Amsterdam firms. It was an attempt to monopolize the trade on-station. Later, under the limited monopoly operations of the New Netherland Company, it was also found more efficient for the conduct of the fur trade to leave a small colony of traders behind.

The Commissioners for New Netherland were well acquainted with this earlier experience and with conditions in New Netherland. Opinion, however, was sharply divided on how best to proceed with respect to operations in New Netherland. The fur trade was indeed a source of profit to the company, but two difficulties stood in the way of extending it. In the first place, the trade for furs in New Netherland centered mainly along the Delaware River and the upper Hudson River — both areas widely separated geographically. To send ships periodically to these areas for a direct ship-to-shore trade would be expensive since it would tie them up for long periods of time. The yield from such a mode of operations was uncetain because the Indians could not be relied on to have a supply of furs waiting for the arrival of company ships. Delays from unpredictable weather only added to the risks. A ship could thus spend many months in New Netherland without any assurance of a profitable return cargo. With such wide geographical separation, there was also the constant danger to this type of trade from interlopers between voyages.[34]

The second difficulty was that New Netherland lay between Virginia and New England and was thus exposed to attack by Englishmen from either area. Unless the Dutch were able to maintain a toehold in New Netherland, the entire fur trade could be lost to the English. An occasional ship trading to New Netherland would be of little use against this difficulty. A fort, garrisoned by soldiers and backed up by some resident population, might serve as a more effective bar against English incursions. Amsterdam fur merchants were well aware from their experience in New France of the importance of maintaining possession of an area in conducting trade of this sort.[35]

From the deliberations of the Commissioners for New Netherland over these difficulties of the fur trade, two potential courses of action were projected. One group, termed the "contrary minded" by the opposition, favored extracting a quick profit from New Netherland. They proposed to run the risks involved and would merely send over ships from time to time to gather up as many skins as could be obtained. The second group, which may be termed the pro-settlement faction, formed around one of the most energetic of the Commissioners — Kiliaen van Rensselaer. The "contrary minded" of the Commissioners, along with a number of other directors, were reluctantly won over to the position of van Rensselaer and the pro-settlement faction.[36]

This second group felt that the protection and the extension of the fur trade could only be accomplished through the creation of a company establishment in New Netherland. Such an establishment would provide a base of stability for the area and would also guarantee an annual profit yield which would enable New Netherland to play its role in the overall scheme of the company. In broad outline they planned a company establishment, or colony, of resident traders, supported by bookkeepers, clerks, artisans, soldiers, and farmers. This would, of course, require a large initial investment, but the proponents of this course of action felt that the increased profits which would result would more than cover the costs. They argued, too, that once launched the company establishment in New Netherland could become entirely self-sufficient within a few years.

A description of this plan for a company establishment in New Netherland can be pieced together from three sets of instructions issued in the years 1624–1625 by the company, from the special instructions given to the engineer Cryn Fredericksz. for building a fort in New Netherland dated 1625, and from the later observations of Kiliaen van Rensselaer, one of the Commissioners at the time. The details are not as complete as one would desire, nevertheless they do show that the projected company establishment was primarily conceived of in commercial rather than political terms.

The establishment was to be in charge of the chief resident trader, who, in the Instructions of 1625, was also the supercargo aboard the ship carrying the colony to New Netherland — Willem Verhulst.[37] This chief officer of the company in New Netherland was variously referred to as Commander, Director, or Commissary. He was to be assisted in the management of the establishment by the leading members of the company who at any time resided in the colony or who happened to be there aboard company ships. These advisors of the Director, a quite informal group at this time who occupied key mercantile posts, were termed his Council.[38]

The Director and his Council were specifically charged "to increase the trade in skins, and other articles that are obtained in the country."[39] Similarly, all residents in New Netherland were ordered to "use all diligence to fortify" the area assigned to them "by common effort, likewise erecting in common the necessary public buildings and establishing trade relations as far as possible."[40] Everyone in New Netherland was to be subject to the instructions of the company and all were exhorted "to conduct themselves in all obedience, fidelity, and diligence in taking up their abode on the South or North river, or at such other place as may be most advantageous to the Company and the management of the Colony." [41] And, whether company employee or free colonist,

> . . . one and all are most strongly enjoined and charged, in addition to performing their ordinary work, to make faithful inquiry whether near their dwelling place, there is no suitable location for planting vineyards, for making salt-pans, for burning charcoal, for burning brick for building houses, for making staves, or for planting tobacco; also, what fisheries there are in the vicinity, or any other resources that might be developed in that country, advising us thereof at the first opportunity.[42]

The commercial exploitation of New Netherland was unquestionably to be the purpose of the company establishment there. As projected in these instructions, the fur trade was now to become highly organized. The peculiar nature of the trade made it not only desirable to have fixed places, such as forts, to conduct barter operations but also to have traders comb the area minutely since "the furs are not all to be found at these places but are scattered about among many rivers and brooks, which must be sailed up and down, sometimes 10 or 20 leagues."

Forts were to be erected at the principal places of trade — on the Delaware, the Hudson, and wherever else might prove feasible. These would serve as trading posts, the primary contact points with the Indian trappers. They would provide as well a station for personnel, yachts, sloops, and supplies which could be defended against hostile Indian attacks or from threats to the trade by foreign interlopers.[43]

The presence of people in New Netherland year round was seen as adding great flexibility to the conduct of the trade and hence as providing the possibility for greater profit. It meant, for example, that the trade could be worked during the winter months, "when most fur-bearing animals are caught." [44] It meant also that the friendship of the Indians could be intensively cultivated. And many advantages to the trade might well arise from the goodwill of the Indians. The Director was, therefore, urged:

> . . . to consider whether it would not be practicable so to contract with the native of the country in various districts as would

> make them promise us to trade with no one but those of the
> Company, provided that we on our part should bind ourselves
> to take all the skins which they could bring us upon such terms
> as would be considered reasonable, or at such price as we have
> hitherto bought them.[45]

Indeed, if the Director could successfully woo the Indians, he might even be able "to learn from them the secrets of that region and the condition of the interior." [46]

To maintain such a network of traders as envisioned by this plan it was proposed that agriculture be undertaken in New Netherland. The raising of provisions in New Netherland would make the commercial establishment self-reliant, increase the flexibility of operations, and eliminate the necessity of obtaining supplies from home. It was estimated that the importation of foodstuffs from the Netherlands was "ten times the expense" of growing them in New Netherland.[47] The development of agriculture was thus seen as a means of reducing the overhead expense involved in the expansion of the fur trade in New Netherland.

It was hoped that the people engaged for agricultural tasks would be useful in other ways to the company. Their mere presence would add to the size of the establishment and perhaps thereby deter the English in Virginia or New England from launching any ambitious designs for the area of New Netherland. They would also increase the military strength of the company establishment in the event of an attack on it by the Indians or the English. The "Provisional Regulations for the Colonists" of 1624 specified that the officers of the company in New Netherland:

> . . . have power to make alliances and treaties with foreign
> princes and potentates in that country residing near their col-
> onies, upon such conditions as shall be deemed most advan-
> tageous to the service of the Company, without paying heed in
> such treaties to any one's private interests. Which conditions the
> colonists collectively, and each of them individually, shall be in-
> volved in war with others, their neighbors, and even be obliged
> to take the field.[48]

In addition to provisioning the company establishment, it was also hoped that the farmers would assist in the more commercial operations of the company in New Netherland. They were at first authorized to participate in the fur trade, particularly in inland areas not being worked by company traders.[49] And they were encouraged to search for surface mineral wealth. As an inducement, the company promised to grant one-tenth of the net proceeds for the first six years to any farmer who "discovered mines of gold, silver, copper, or any other metals, as well as of precious stones, such as diamonds, rubies, and the like, together with the pearl fishery." [50]

Whether in the service of the company or as free colonists, farmers resident in New Netherland would also be able to experiment with the development of an agricultural staple for New Netherland. The quest for an agricultural product which would be highly prized and marketable in Europe was as eagerly pursued in New Netherland as sugar and tobacco were in the Caribbean. Native products such as grapes, hazelnuts, walnuts, and timber were to be examined carefully in terms of their potential for the export market. "Divers trees, vines, and all sorts of seeds" were sent from the Netherlands for experimental purposes. The Director was even required "to see whether he can procure some vines from Spain, the Canary Islands, or other places." [51]

Van Rensselaer favored experimenting with "all kinds of grain and animals which could thence be sent here or at least within other limits of the charter, as Cape Verde, Guinea, and Brazil." [52]

To implement their plans and accomplish their aims in New Netherland, the Commissioners needed people. The recruitment of people for New Netherland thus became one of their greatest problems. And it was by no means an easy one to solve. In fact, the task of peopling New Netherland plagued the directors of the company down to the loss of the colony in 1664. The official explanation, enunciated as early as 1629 and reiterated by the directors over the years, was that

> . . . the peopling of such wild and uncleared lands, demands
> more inhabitants than our country can supply; not so much for
> want of population, with which our provinces swarm, as because
> all those who will labor in any way here, can easily obtain sup-
> port, and therefore, are disinclined to go far from home on an
> uncertainty.
>
> To which can be added, the uncertainty of being able to pro-
> tect themselves, unless at a greater expence than the apparent
> gains to be derived therefrom, seem to justify.[53]

The Commissioners in Amsterdam were interested in the labor rather than in the motives or even the nationalities of the colonists they recruited for New Netherland. In the era of private trading, too, the merchants had cared little for these other considerations, as evidenced by their support of the petition of the English Pilgrims residing in Leyden to the States-General for permission to settle in the area of New Netherland.[54] Had there been any plan to create a thoroughly Dutch society in New Netherland, such criteria would have been of the utmost importance. But, as it was, the procurement of any colonists in the years 1623–1629 proved to be difficult enough.

Whatever other motives the immigrant to New Netherland in these years may have had, the advancement of his own economic self-interest was certainly high on the list. And the company was obliged to satisfy this self-interest seeking in order to obtain the immigrant's much needed services. In attempting to deal with this — since self-interest was by no means construed in the same fashion by all potential colonists — and because of the difficulties in general of recruiting personnel for service in New Netherland, a variety of terms had to be offered by the company. As a result, it was necessary to introduce distinctions among those who did take up residence in New Netherland.

There were, in the first place, employees of the company. Included in this category were the skippers of the company ships, the Director, and those whose primary duties related to the fur trade — the traders themselves, the chief officials or commissaries at the various forts, along with a number of clerks, bookkeepers, soldiers, and artisans. Many of those engaged for agricultural purposes, the "company's farmers" or the "hired farmers" as they were called, were also employees of the company. All employees, regardless of their assigned task, entered into some form of contract with the company and were, therefore, considered servants of the company.[55]

There were a number of advantages to be gained from having a contract with the company. Whatever the conditions in New Netherland turned out to be, those immigrants under contract to the company were assured of daily subsistence and a salary. There was, therefore, very little personal risk involved in holding the status of a company employee. The disadvantage, of course, was that an employee was theoretically always at the service of the company and could not devote any of his labor to his own private gain. Still, for some, the security which employee status conveyed far outweighed the hope of great personal gain from a country about which the immigrant in all probability had very little firsthand knowledge. Besides,

at the expiration of his contract, an employee could continue on in
New Netherland as a free colonist if conditions proved to be so per-
sonally advantageous.

In the second category of immigrants coming to New Netherland
during the early years of West India Company rule were the "colonists and other free persons." [56] Free, in this sense, meant a non-
employee. For the most part such colonists were farmers. However, a
servant of the company, whose indenture had expired but who chose
to remain in New Netherland would be free even though he might
not have become a farmer. The primary distinction between a company farmer and a free farmer was that the latter resided in New
Netherland at a much greater personal risk. The main advantage of
going to New Netherland with free status was the opportunity to participate in the fur trade by bartering or trapping. Such persons also
enjoyed the privileges of hunting, fowling, and fishing in New Netherland for their own profit and could exercise the rights associated
with the first discovery of precious minerals or mines. They could sell
their agricultural products to the company for their own profit even
though the choice of crops to be grown was at first left to the determination of the company officials in New Netherland. The lack of
daily subsistence and of a fixed salary provided the elements of risk
associated with such free status.[57]

In many other ways there was little to distinguish a free farmer
from a company farmer. Both were transported to New Netherland
free of charge by the company. As the "Provisional Regulations" of
1624 stated:

> The colonists shall without paying any recognition therefor re-
> ceive from the company the costs of transportation, as well as the
> places and lands to be cultivated by them, which according to the
> size of their families and their industry shall be allotted to them
> by the Commander and his Council.[58]

Whereas the company farmer was to be supplied with necessities and
clothes from the company storehouse, the free colonist was to be
charged for the same at "a reasonable price." They could, however,
obtain supplies on long-term credit from the company.[59]

While the colonists were free of the company with respect to personal servitude, they were, nonetheless, subject to its authority in
New Netherland. They were required to take an "oath of allegiance

and obedience to the High and Mighty Lords the States General and
to this Company and shall in all things comport themselves as good
and loyal subjects are bound to do." [60] In addition, they were
obliged to take a special oath "to keep secret all transactions and
affairs of the company which in any way come to their knowledge." [61]
The colonists were referred to as within "the jursidiction of the
Company or its commissaries" and were forbidden to conduct any
trade with strangers or even to "hold any intercourse with them
whereby they in any way may learn the profits, needs, or situation of
the place, on pain of being punished therefor according to the circumstances of the case." [62]

Thus the principal difference between company farmer and free
farmer was the degree of personal risk and the opportunity for personal profit involved. And it seems probable that the necessity for this
distinction arose from the difficulty of recruiting people to venture to
New Netherland. The company was forced to make whatever terms it
could in order to obtain people for the colony and, therefore, ad-
justed its conditions to the interests and motivations of prospective
immigrants.

The difference in status by no means turned on the question of the
presence or absence of families. The families of both the free farmer
and the company farmer accompanied him to New Netherland.[63]
Nor did the status of free colonists imply that they therefore intended
to reside permanently in New Netherland. All indications in the
"Provisional Regulations" of 1624 suggest that people in this category, too, were thought of as temporary residents in New Netherland.
They, too, were under a contract to the company which required
them, as the "Provisional Regulations" specifically mentioned, "to
remain at the place of their destination with their families for the
space of six consecutive years, unless a change be made herein by
order of the Company." [64] It was also noted that

> . . . at the expiration of their bounden time, or sooner, in case
> of removal by order of the Directors of their honorable agents,
> they shall be permitted to trade or sell their houses, planted
> fields, and cattle to some one else among the remaining col-
> onists.[65]

Another point in the "Provisional Regulations" referred to "any one
of the colonists during his sojurn there." [66] Part of the special oath,

moreover, enjoined them not to divulge any company secrets "after they have withdrawn themselves from the authority of the company; likewise, they promise that they shall at no time hereafter associate themselves with any but those of the Company to come within the limits of the charter, wherever it may be." [67] Thus any attribution of intended permanency to this group of free colonists seems unwarranted by the facts.

In 1625 an engineer and surveyor, Cryn Fredericksz., was retained by the West India Company for the purpose of staking out a fort in New Netherland. The Commissioners issued a set of special instructions to him, signed by van Rensselaer and Godyn, which reflect well the commercial nature of the company establishment, or colony, projected for New Netherland.[68] He was also provided with sketches of five plans, lettered A through E, for laying out this establishment in conformity with the wishes of the Commissioners. The sketches have not survived. The detailed instructions, however, suggest that the Commissioners had an ideal "model" in mind for a company establishment, probably derived from experience gathered in the Far East or elsewhere. It was to be a military garrison and commercial complex. The engineer's job was clearly one of execution rather than of innovation, for the Commissioners quite pointedly added in the last paragraph:

> *All of which we desire to have observed without any alteration*
> *unless some evident mistakes have been committed herein, which*
> *may be duly corrected by the Commissary, the surveyor, and the*
> *Council, provided they advise us of the reasons for such change.*[69]

The military and commercial complex outlined in these plans was to consist of a fort, within which were to be the dwellings of the principal officials of the company, the storehouses, and various public buildings such as a church, schoolhouse, and hospital. Described in Plan C, the fort was to have a circumference of 3,150 feet. Plan D divided the area within the fort into streets and building lots and provided for a market place in the center.[70] The fort was also to have its own moat, or inner ditch, 54 feet wide and at least 8 feet deep.[71] Between the outer limits of the fort and the surrounding moat was to be an area 200 feet in depth, within which were to be placed the "dwellings of the farmers and their gardens." These were reserved for

Seal of the Province of New Netherland 1623. Courtesy of the Museum of the City of New York.

The First Known View of New Amsterdam about 1626–1628. This view,
engraved in reverse, is the earliest known representation of Manhattan.
The book, "Beschrijving Van Virginia, Niew Nederlandt (etc.)" was
published in Amsterdam in 1651 by Joost Hartgers. Courtesy of
the J. Clarence Davies Collection, Museum of the City of New York.

the company's head farmers and for lesser company officials; their size was carefully detailed in Plans A and D.[72] At the backs of these houses, according to Plan A, the outer ditch or moat was to be constructed, 24 feet wide and 4 feet deep. There was to be only one bridge over this with a single, guarded gate. The encircling moat was designed to have only three sides — the fourth being open to the water. One side was to be 2,000 feet long and the remaining two sides each 1,600 feet in length.[73] Outside the moat, the land was to be divided into farms as provided for in Plan B.[74] Additional farm houses were to be constructed in these lands in accordance with Plan E.[75]

The main block of houses within the fort were to be of the same size, each 25 feet square and so constructed that they were all joined together. The reason for this was dictated by commercial needs.

> *The second story of all the adjoining houses, 9 feet high and 25 feet square, shall throughout be reserved for the use of the Company, to store therein at first all the provisions belonging to the Company, as well as all the trading-goods and furs and whatever else belongs to the Company, and after other suitable places therefor shall have been found, they shall be used as grain-lofts, which applies to all the houses in the entire fort, but the garrets above the second story shall be for the use of the respective houses.[76]*

The instructions also specified that the Commissary's house should be located in the center of these because, "From his own house the Commissary must be able to go into all the lofts on the right-hand side, as well as in all the lofts on the left-side, along the entire street, doors to be made from one to the other." [77]

As projected by the Commissioners, the company establishment in New Netherland was, thus, to be primarily a tightly organized working community. The emphasis throughout was on uniformity. Housing facilities had to be provided but great care was taken that they should be of the simplest variety and no individual adornment was to be permitted. The "Further Instructions for Verhulst," also issued in April of 1625, specifically warned against:

> *. . . permitting any one to construct anything special that another has not, not even excluding from this rule the Commissary,*

whose house in front on the street must be in line with the oth-
ers, in order not to break up the general arrangement, but who
may build out somewhat further in the rear.[78]

The selection of a site for this company establishment was left
pretty much to the discretion of the Director and his Council and to
engineer Fredericksz., although the Commissioners did establish some
criteria. That the commercial center and the farmers or colonists were
conceived of as forming one unit is evident from a reference in Verhulst's instructions of January, 1625, urging him to find a suitable
place for a "fortification and the dwelling places of the colonists and
farmers." Another reference in the same document mentions settling
in one place "all the families together with the hired farmers and the
cattle." [79]

A "suitable place," the Commissioners defined as 800 or 1,000
morgens (1,600–2,000 acres) in extent, "abandoned by the Indians or
unoccupied," and located on either the Delaware or Hudson Rivers,
the principal points of the fur trade.[80] In the earliest instructions the
Commissioners seemed inclined to favor the Delaware as the best location. The instructions of 1625 spoke of Verhulst's "usual place of
residence" as being there.[81] "High Island" on the Delaware was mentioned as a possibility, as was Noten Island (Governor's Island). "But
if in the North River [Hudson] a still more suitable place" was
found, the Commissioners were willing to have the headquarters of
the company in New Netherland located there.[82]

The site selected was Manhattan Island.[83] It not only met the requirements laid down by the Commissioners but it was also central,
lying between the Delaware and the Hudson Rivers. It was larger
than Noten Island — some 22,000 acres — and, having been inhabited
by the Indians, it possessed a good portion of cleared land or "flats."
It certainly made greater sense to locate the company establishment
at Manhattan than at Fort Orange (Albany) on the upper Hudson.
Van Rensselaer later referred to Manhattan as "the place of rendez-
vous," and this was precisely what it was.[84]

It seems clear, then, from the foregoing, that the early settlement of
the West India Company in New Netherland was designed as a self-
sufficient commercial center. The expectation was that this colony
would permit the company to extend greatly the operations of the fur
trade as well as to examine the area more minutely and systematically
for other potential sources of profit. And, in terms of these objectives,

the colony attained a real measure of success. Between resupply from home and the cultivation of provisions in New Netherland, the colony was able to survive and even grow. The resident population in 1628 was estimated by Wassenaer at around three hundred.[85] Unlike Virginia or Plymouth in its early years, no "starving time" is recorded for New Netherland during the years 1623–1629.

The presence of three hundred people in New Netherland necessitated the establishment of some form of government. This had not been overlooked by the Commissioners for New Netherland in drawing up their various instructions. But, in the passages dealing with law, administration, and justice, the procedures established reflect more the outlines of a quasi-military than a political community. They tend also to reinforce the interpretation advanced in this chapter that the company establishment was not seen as an attempt to form a new or permanent society in New Netherland.

Although the Director was authorized to administer corporal punishment for wrongdoing, the severest and most effective punitive device placed at his disposal was that of removing offenders from the colony. In the Instructions of January 1625, Verhulst was ordered:

> . . . to expel from the colony and to send hither all adulterers
> and adulteresses, thieves, false witnesses, and useless persons
> among the Christians, likewise also the lazy persons who draw pay
> from the Company, in order that they may be punished here ac-
> cording to their deserts.[86]

Within the community, arbitration and conciliation were seen as the most useful means of preserving harmony:

> He shall see that all misunderstandings and disputes among the
> Christians be settled by proper means, and if anyone show an un-
> ruly, wanton, or disobedient spirit, without being willing to lis-
> ten to admonition, he shall have such person again brought
> hither, with the evidence of his delinquencies, to be punished
> here according to the circumstances.[87]

The application of sanctions or of punishment was regarded more as a matter of maintaining the efficiency of this commercial community than of catering to the civil and political needs of the community. It was suggested, for example, that idlers should be left, "to suffer want if they are unwilling to do their duty, so that they may thereby be compelled to devote themselves more to work." [88] The Director was charged to review periodically the classification of workers in the colony so that "if he has too many or too few people of any kind, he must advise us, but not let any one go idle." [89]

Thus, while punishment was provided for, it was felt that the best way to maintain order would be by carefully controlling the composition of the colony, "to the end that each one may be in his proper place and the work may be done and the needs be supplied by the common labor and diligence of all." [90] Punishment within the colony was, therefore, a temporary expedient. The solution was to remove the chronic offender from New Netherland:

> . . . *upon committing such an offense for the second time, the delinquent shall, in addition to forfeiting the whole of his earned wages, inclusive of tithes, etc., be punished by the Council as a common thief and be kept in prison until by the first ship returning to the fatherland he can be sent back as a rogue, together with a pertinent account of his delinquencies and the sentence passed upon him.*[91]

The notion of each colonist's "proper place" permeated the Commissioners' instructions for setting up a company establishment in New Netherland. By "proper place" they meant the performance of assigned tasks, of an economic role, within an essentially commercial structure. In the eyes of the Commissioners, employees and colonists alike were overseas laborers who would dwell in New Netherland for a specified period. Despite the differentiation in status, the residents in New Netherland were seen as employees of the company. They assumed, therefore, that an identity of interest existed between these overseas laborers and themselves at home. And far from believing that they were establishing a separate society in New Netherland, they looked upon their outpost there as forming an integral part of society at home.

This then was the plan for New Netherland as fashioned by the Commissioners. And this view of the role or function of New Netherland was to remain a dominant part of the thinking of Netherlanders regarding their possession in North America down to 1664. Even in the early years it met resistance on the part of those who chose to emigrate to New Netherland. In its encounter with reality in the years 1623–1629, this plan for New Netherland came off badly.

CHAPTER FOUR

"A WILD COUNTRY"—
NEW NETHERLAND
1623–1629

The early efforts of the Commissioners in Amsterdam were devoted to realizing their plan for New Netherland. In attempting to do this, however, they encountered obstacles at home and, quite unexpectedly, in New Netherland. At home, the "contrary minded" only grudgingly permitted the Commissioners to go ahead with their scheme. But they were never fully convinced of the wisdom of spending money on what they considered a vain attempt to increase the profitability of New Netherland. Disparaging the labors of the Commissioners in this trifling business, their opposition took the form of repeated attempts to block those measures that were designed to implement more fully the plan for New Netherland. When forty soldiers for the defense of New Netherland were requested, for example, they informed the States-General that they "would rather see it secured by friendly alliance." [1]

In New Netherland, the Commissioners ran up against obstacles of a quite different nature. Experience slowly demonstrated that their assumptions about the wealth to be discovered in New Netherland were ill founded. So too, it was learned, were their assumptions about the ease with which desirable export commodities could be cultivated. And ultimately far more important, they painfully became aware that an identity of interest did not in fact exist between themselves and their overseas employees. The emigrant laborer they sent out acquired a distinct interest of his own when he landed 3,000 miles away as a New Netherland immigrant. Although a separate society in New Netherland had not been envisioned by the Commissioners, it nevertheless grew up over the years. The peculiar nature of that society in the period 1623–1629 is the subject of this chapter.

Only a few descriptions of New Netherland during these years have survived. Two were written by men who had never ventured from the Netherlands — Johannes de Laet and Nicolaes van Wassenaer.[2] Both of these accounts were essentially promotional tracts, designed to encourage emigration to the West India Company's possessions in the New World. De Laet was one of the first directors of the company and, after 1629, a participant with van Rensselaer and others in the plan to establish patroonships in New Netherland. Wassenaer wrote his *Historical Verhael* (Historical Account) in twenty-one semi-annual parts, the second of which he dedicated to the West India Company.[3] Of the two, his account is the more romantic, though both works pictured New Netherland in idyllic terms and made frequent and pointed reference to its "great prospects." In one passage, after comparing the efforts of the West India Company in New Netherland to the colonizing activities of the Old Testament patriarchs, the Assyrians, and the Greeks, Wassenaer concluded with an exceedingly flattering reference to the Romans:

> *The Romans domineering over the western world, spread colonies all over it, as it proved by the carved stones found everywhere; but what order they observed herein is well known to us. Those sent thither, must acknowledge the senders as their lords, pay them homage, and remain under their sovereignty; they were also protected by these by suitable weapons furnished also to them. And whereas, God be praised, it hath come about that the Honorable Messrs. Directors of the West India Company, have, with the consent of the Noble High and Mighty Lords States General, undertaken to plant some colonies, I shall give the particulars of them . . . .[4]*

What order the Romans maintained in their colonies was certainly unknown to Wassenaer. Still, it must have been stirring to an overseas laborer to have his efforts compared to the Greeks and the Romans. Undoubtedly, the works of de Laet and Wassenaer greatly aided the Commissioners for New Netherland in their recruiting program.

Of greater historical value are the descriptions of New Netherland recorded in the letters of the Reverend Jonas Michaëlius,[5] the first minister in New Netherland, and in the letters of Isaack de Rasière,[6] who resided briefly in New Netherland as secretary of the company established there. Both men were employees of the company who wrote their descriptions from firsthand experience. Although their accounts are permeated by romantic notions of what life in New Netherland ought to be like, they do provide glimpses into the actual conditions of the company settlement in New Netherland during the early years.

From these four sources and from other scattered references, it seems clear that the Commissioners began immediately to launch their plan for New Netherland. The obvious first step was taken — the sending of some company representatives to New Netherland, "in order to continue the possession of those quarters and to maintain the trade in peltries."[7] As de Laet noted, the yacht "Mackreel" was accordingly dispatched in the summer of 1623. It traded along the Hudson through the winter of 1623–1624 and arrived back in Holland sometime during the summer of 1624.[8] Whether any colonists were aboard or whether any personnel were left behind in New Netherland by the "Mackreel" cannot be determined. The purpose of this voyage was, however, primarily to assert the West India Company's claim to the region and to prevent any interruption of the fur trade in New Netherland. It officially signaled the end of private trading there.

In November, 1623, the company turned down the request of one of the private traders, Pieter Boudaen Courten, for permission to send one more ship to New Netherland "to trade their merchandise and bring home their people." The company proposed instead that the Amsterdam chamber fit out a ship which might "take with them 5 or 6 families of the colonists, in order to make a beginning of settlement there and on that occasion bring back here the goods secured in return for the aforesaid merchandise, and the people."[9]

Once continuity in the conduct of the trade had been provided for, the Commissioners could then proceed with their more ambitious plan for developing the fur trade in New Netherland through the creation of a company establishment. The Commissioners were fortunate in having some volunteers at hand — a group of Walloons or French-speaking Protestants from the area of what is now northeastern France and Southwestern Belgium.

The leader of this group was Jesse de Forest, a native of Avesnes, who in 1615 established himself in Leyden. As a spokesman for some fifty or sixty Walloon and French Protestant families in 1621, he had petitioned James I, through the English Ambassador to the Netherlands, Sir Dudley Carleton, for permission "to go and settle in Virginia, a country under his rule, and whether it would please him to undertake their protection and defense from and against all and to maintain their religion." [10] The petition was referred to the directors of the Virginia Company, who in August, 1621, informed the king that "the exhausted stock of the Company prevents them from affording any help." [11]

In the following months, de Forest attempted to solicit support for his project within the Netherlands, turning first to the States of Holland and West Friesland and then to the States-General. Since the West India Company was in the process of formation, his petitions were ultimately passed on to its directors. In all, de Forest probably gathered together upwards of three hundred people who had expressed a willingness to emigrate within the bounds of the West India Company's charter. If the company had had any scheme in mind at the time for a great settlement effort in New Netherland, such a group would have provided the basis for an excellent beginning. That no such plan was entertained is evident from the action taken by the company on these petitions:

> *The Directors of the West India Company report that they have*
> *examined the paper relative to the* Families to be conveyed to
> the West Indies, *and are of opinion, that it is very advantageous*
> *for the Company, and therefore that an effort ought to be made*
> *to permit it, with a promise that they should be employed.* . . .[12]

Thus, their attitude was similar to that of the Van Tweenhuysen Company's directors toward the Pilgrims. They felt that the group might be useful to the company but saw the members of it as so many potential employees.

The first members of this group to be "employed in the service" of the company were sent not to New Netherland but to Guiana. Like the Virginia Company, the West India Company was somewhat appalled by the size of the group and the expense that the transportation of so many people would entail. The sending of such a colony to Guiana was, after all, an experiment — but a costly one since, as employees, they would be on the company's payroll. The directors, therefore,

> . . . thought it better before carrying over the above-mentioned families, to send a certain number of the heads of families with the said Jesse deforest to inspect the region and themselves select their place of abode. . . .[13]

This small group of Walloons, 10 heads of families led by Jesse de Forest, left for Guiana in July 1623. In January, 1624, most of the heads of families began the journey back to the Netherlands. De Forest, along with two Walloons and six crew members, remained behind in Guiana. Soon after, de Forest died and the projected colony in Guiana came to nought.[14]

Who were these Walloons and what were their aims in venturing to the New World? Many writers have attempted to see in this group a Dutch counterpart of the English Pilgrims of Plymouth. The evidence to support such a contention, however, is not very convincing.

Since de Forest was in Leyden in 1620, the departure of some of the English Pilgrims there to America undoubtedly attracted his attention. What was the nature of this attraction? Unlike the Pilgrims, the Walloon émigrés formed in no sense a tight cultural and religious enclave within Dutch society. Most were multilingual and therefore faced no great difficulty in assimilation. Many were in need of jobs, though, and this did present a problem in view of the great number of émigrés from Catholic countries that poured into the Netherlands at this time because of the religious wars. But the Walloons came individually or in families and the informal communities they formed in the Netherlands did not resemble that of the English Pilgrims. No restrictions were placed on the public exercise of their religion in the Netherlands. Nor could the determination to preserve their own language have presented itself as forcefully to them as it did to the English Pilgrims. It is, therefore, difficult to imagine that Jesse de Forest, "brooded, till the idea of leading a colony of Protestant Walloons to the New World became a veritable obsession." [15]

In proposing to emigrate to English Virginia, the Walloons had, understandably, sought assurances of protection for their Protestant religion and for their French language. In exchange for this, they pledged themselves to submit to "such fealty and obedience as loyal and obedient subjects owe to their King and Sovereign Lord." [16] No such conditions were attached to their request for employment to the West India Company. Rather than a flight for religious purposes, de Forest's group seems to have been more of a business venture. What had probably interested de Forest in the Pilgrims' venture was their ability to obtain financial assistance from English merchants. This was what he sought in the Netherlands.

De Forest was not a very successful woolen cloth merchant and dyer. He had a large family, and his personal finances generally hovered on the edge of debt. His role in the Walloon venture was thus as an entrepreneur rather than as a religious leader such as the Reverend John Robinson, pastor of the English Pilgrims in Leyden. Although himself a Walloon, he cast his net wider for potential emigrants to the New World, asking the States-General in 1622 for:

> . . . *authorization to inscribe and enroll, for the colonies, families of the Christian reformed Religion willing to make the voyage to the West Indies for the advancement and service of the West India Company.*[17]

His drive for recruits was thus not directed exclusively at the Walloon community in the Netherlands, nor even at one area of the Netherlands, but extended to "the various cities where he might enroll his colonists."

There is no indication that the group de Forest gathered together intended to settle overseas as one community or that the members of it intended to remain permanently abroad. The evidence does suggest that they were interested in seeking their fortunes in the New World, and that Guiana or New Netherland would do just as well. Mrs. de Forest, the family's most recent biographer and editor of the "Journal of a Voyage to Guiana," has made this point clear:

> *Holland was now swarming with refugees whose only plea was for employment, and Jesse also was ready to be satisfied if the company would convey his families across the seas and promise to employ them after arrival.*[18]

Some members of this group — and the reference of Wassenaer to "mostly Walloons" now becomes clearer — made up the first colonists which the Commissioners sent out to New Netherland aboard the "Nieu Nederlandt" in 1624.[19] In all probability they went over to New Netherland with the status of employees of the West India Company rather than as free colonists. In 1628 Michaëlius noted that: "A number of the Walloons are going back to the Fatherland, either because their years here have expired or else because some are not very serviceable to the Company." [20]

The initial task of these first company residents in New Netherland was twofold. They were to begin the cultivation of provisions in New Netherland and to staff temporarily the known outposts of the fur trade until such time as additional personnel could be sent over. In order to accomplish these aims, therefore, the colonists were divided when they arrived in New Netherland. According to a deposition of Catelina Trico in 1688, recalling her arrival some forty-odd years earlier, this was done in the following manner:

> As soon as they came to Mannatans now called N: York they sent
> Two families and six men to harford River Two families & 8
> men to Dalaware River and 8 men they left att N: Yorke to take
> Possession and ye Rest of ye Passengers went with ye Ship up as
> farr as Albany which they then Called fort Orangie. When as ye
> Ship came as farr as Sopus which is ½ way to Albanie, they light-
> ened ye Ship with some boats yt were left there by ye Dutch that
> had been there ye year before a tradeing with ye Indians upont
> there oune accompts & gone back again to Holland & so brought
> ye vessel up; there were about 18 families aboard who settled
> themselves att Albany & made a small fort. . . .[21]

With company relations established at the principal places of trade, and with additional farmers, company employees, and livestock arriving from the Netherlands, it became possible to adhere more closely to the Commissioners' plan for New Netherland.[22] Sometime after the arrival of engineer Fredericksz., and probably early in 1626, Manhattan was selected as the site for the company establishment in New Netherland. The farmers who were scattered about doing double duty by raising provisions and also serving as agents in the fur trade, were then ordered to withdraw with their families to Manhattan. There was now a sufficient number of regular traders and commercial

agents in New Netherland to permit the colonists to devote them-
sclvcs to thcir main task of agriculturc. Rcferring to Fort Orangc in
1626, Wassenaer wrote:

> *There were eight families there, and ten or twelve seamen in the*
> *Company's service. The families were to leave there this year—*
> *the fort to remain garrisoned by sixteen men, without women*
> *— in order to strengthen with people the colony near the Man-*
> *hates, who are becoming more and more accustomed to the*
> *strangers.*[23]

The same course of action was taken in the Delaware region. At
one point in his account, Wassenaer stated, "Those of the South
River will abandon their fort, and come hither [to Manhattan]." [24]
At another point, he stated, "The fort at the South River is already
vacated, in order to strengthen the colony." [25] Both of these references probably mean that the families or colonists, originally sent to
the Delaware, had moved, like those at Fort Orange, to Manhattan.
Certainly the area was not abandoned by the traders, for, as Wassenaer pointed out, "Trading there is carried on only in yachts, in
order to avoid expense." [26] This would be entirely in keeping with
the Commissioners' plan for developing the fur trade in New Netherland. It seems likely that the traders would continue to use the small
fort whenever they were in the area. In 1626, de Rasière urged the
building of a "small fort on the South River." Since there was already
a fort there, de Rasière may have had in mind a different location on
the Delaware for it or the erection of a stronger fort. Both considerations were probably involved, for de Rasière seems to have regarded
the area as a potential source of great profit for the company. And
thus, in his view, a fort was necessary:

> *First, to keep possession of the river, in order that others may not*
> *precede us there and erect a fort themselves. Secondly, because,*
> *having a fort there, one could control all the trade in the river.*
> *Thirdly because the natives say that they are afraid to hunt in*
> *winter, being constantly harassed by war with the Minquaes,*
> *whereas, if a fort were there, an effort could be made to reconcile*
> *them.*[27]

The concentration together of colonists and the main headquarters
of the company in one place was in accordance with the desires of the
Commissioners. Manhattan was thenceforth to be the "permanent res-

idence" of both the colonists and the company in New Netherland.[28] The various instructions of the Commissioners make it clear that the term "permanent" simply meant a suitable place to build the fort and commercial compound. This distinction of "permanent" was opposed to the "temporary" out-forts at the various points of trade in New Netherland. These out-forts were to be less solidly constructed since their location might well change as the fur trade expanded further inland.[29] It would be the function of the permanent fort, or company establishment, to supply the out-forts with provisions and articles of trade.

Wassenaer has recorded a description of the company establishment at Manhattan in 1626, which should not, however, be taken too literally:

> The colony is now established on the Manhates, where a fort has been staked out by Master Kryn Frederycks, an engineer. It is planned to be of large dimensions . . . The counting-house there is kept in a stone building, thatched with reed; the other houses are of the bark of trees. Each has his own house. The Director and Koopman live together; there are thirty ordinary houses on the east side of the river, which runs nearly north and south. The Honorable Pieter Minuit is Director there at present; Jan Lempou schout; Sebastiaen Jansz. Crol and Jan Huych, comforters of the sick, who, whilst awaiting a clergyman, read to the commonalty there, on Sundays, texts of Scripture and the commentaries. François Molemaecker is busy building a horse-mill, over which shall be constructed a spacious room sufficient to accommodate a large congregation, and then a tower is to be erected where the bells brought from Porto Rico will be hung.
>
> The council there administers justice in criminal matters as far as imposing fines, but not as far as corporal punishment. Should it happen that any one deserves that, he must be sent to Holland with his sentence . . . Every one there who fills no public office is busy about his own affairs. Men work there as in Holland; one trades, upwards, southwards and northwards; another builds houses, the third farms. Each farmer has his farmstead on the land purchased by the Company, which also owns the cows; but the milk remains to the profit of the farmer; he sells it to those of the people who receive their wages for work every week. The houses of the Hollanders now stand outside the fort, but when that is completed, they will all repair within, so as to garrison it and be secure from sudden attack.[30]

Thus by 1626, the plan for New Netherland, drawn up by the Commissioners in Amsterdam, was seemingly well on the way to becoming a reality. From this relatively early high point of organization in 1626, Commissioner van Rensselaer later stated that the condition of the colony began "continuously deteriorating." He laid the blame for this at the door of the "contrary minded," the directors and Commissioners who opposed the plan for New Netherland:

> *Now when the aforesaid farmers and animals had been sent thither and when, as is generally the case with new undertakings, everything did not succeed at first as might be wished, certainly not nearly so well but that the contrary minded could find occasion for fault-finding. . . .*[31]

Van Rensselaer bitterly denounced the "contrary minded" for their shortsightedness. Preferring to reap a quick profit from New Netherland, they had initially only been lukewarm toward the Commissioners' plan. But once the scheme had been launched, they expected, in van Rensselaer's view, too much to be accomplished in New Netherland in too short a period of time:

> *. . . since there were now farmers and animals, they decided that little or no provisions ought to be sent, not considering that it takes time to clear the land before it can be plowed or cultivated and that in the beginning several horses and cows perished which they would not replace, whereby the people were forced to take the merchandise and trade it for provisions, thus damaging the Company to an incredible number of thousands. . . .*[32]

Thus, van Rensselaer charged that the niggardly policy of the opposition had not only impeded the Commissioners in putting their plan into full operation, but, indeed, had added greatly to the already high costs of colonization.

But particularly grating to van Rensselaer, who had been appointed a director by the "chief participants" or trading interest within the company, was the whole approach of the "contrary minded" or political interest toward the development of the New World. He castigated their methods as being hopelessly bureaucratic and inefficient, pointing out that in most circumstances one or two persons could easily "do all the business for which the Company

needs at least 25." [33] Their handling of the shipping to New Netherland he cited as a case in point:

> . . . *instead of an ordinary freighter of large hold which would
> need to sail only once a year, they have sent usually two, three and
> more small vessels, so overloaded with skippers, officers, provisions
> and ammunition that the three together could not take in half as
> much for the country as the larger alone while the latter would
> not have cost much more than each of the small vessels in view of
> the fact that usually many people sail back and forth who could
> man the large ship but would overload the small ones, which
> error has cost the company . . . .*[34]

The "contrary minded" agreed that the condition of New Netherland was continuously deteriorating but preferred to place the blame
for this on van Rensselaer and the Commissioners who were privately
profiting from New Netherland at the expense of the company. And,
indeed, there was some truth to this charge.

The transportation of livestock to New Netherland was an integral
part of the Commissioners' plan. Yet the livestock was sent over from
Amsterdam not in ships of the company but in private ships. The
profits from the first shipment of animals to New Netherland, according to Wassenaer went to:

> . . . *the worthy Pieter Evertsen Hulft, who undertook to ship
> thither, at his risk, whatever was asked of him, to wit; one hun-
> dred and three head of live stock — stallions, mares, bulls and cows —
> for breeding and multiplying, besides all the hogs and sheep that
> they thought expedient to send thither.*[35]

But Hulft was not the only merchant involved, for he and another
Amsterdam merchant, Pieter Rans(t), signed a charter agreement on
May 27, 1625, with a skipper from Hoorn to ship animals to New
Netherland. Both Hulft and Rans(t) were directors of the Amsterdam
chamber of the company. Commissioners van Rensselaer and Godyn,
and two other directors of the Amsterdam chamber signed a charter
agreement for the same purpose on May 28, 1625. The skipper of this
latter venture also agreed to carry over eight or ten persons "for account of the charterers." The ship was later captured by the Turks
and never arrived in New Netherland.[36]

How many other ships were sent to New Netherland in which the Commissioners held a private interest cannot be determined. But that some of the Commissioners were profiting by virtue of their office seems obvious from the loud protests continually made by the "contrary minded." Nor was this an unusual occurrence. Scandals such as this were frequently brought to light which involved the directors of the East India Company. The general knowledge of such practices explains the insertion of article XXXI in the West India Company's charter which specifically prohibited the directors of the company from delivering or selling to the company "any ships, merchandise, or goods belonging to themselves in whole or in part" during their term of office.[37] Special permission was, therefore, required for these private livestock ventures to New Netherland on the part of some of the directors. It would have been needed anyway because private trading of any sort within the limits of the company's grant was expressly forbidden by the charter. But, by virtue of their office, the Commissioners had much to say about when and to whom such special permissions should be granted.

The profits in these private ventures came not only from freight charges and the merchandise shipped, but from the opportunity they provided for privately engaging in the fur trade in New Netherland. The "contrary minded" were particularly outraged by the profit making of the Commissioners in 1629 when one of their members, Samuel Godyn, imported furs amounting to 5,600 florins from New Netherland. Godyn had sent over two men in December, 1628, in advance of the public announcement of the initiation of the patroon system, in order to buy lands from the Indians — another example of the Commissioners benefiting from their positions. The agents of Godyn were provided with merchandise for this purpose and were also authorized to exchange the "remaining merchandise for furs." It would appear that a considerable amount of merchandise must have been left over, for Godyn's agents purchased furs to such an extent that their value represented roughly one-twelfth of the company's annual fur imports. It hardly seems surprising, then, that the "contrary minded" confiscated the furs; Godyn's only recourse was to institute suit for recovery.[38]

The private interest of the Commissioners was furthered in other ways in New Netherland. Many of the officials in New Netherland maintained close personal ties with the Commissioners who had en-

gaged them for the company's service. De Rasière, for example, began
his letter to Samuel Blomaert, one of the Commissioners, by stating:

> As I feel myself much bound to your service, and in return know
> not how otherwise to recompense you than by this slight memoir
> . . . I will beg you to be pleased to receive this, on account of my
> bounden service. . . .[39]

When a new slate of directors began to recall some of the early company officials in New Netherland, van Rensselaer, observing that
"new lords make new laws," feared that "no one of the old servants
would remain there." He acknowledged to another old servant, Director Krol, that "I helped to promote you to the directorship, which I
did with pleasure." [40]

The feud in the Netherlands between the van Rensselaer faction
and the "contrary minded" reflected a basic disagreement in approach to operations in New Netherland. The van Rensselaer faction
saw New Netherland pretty much in commercial terms and was willing to invest some capital in order to obtain greater profits in the
long run. The members of this faction were not adverse to profiting
privately from their official capacity. But they did at least have a
comprehensive plan for New Netherland. They attempted to place
this plan into full operation through both the company's activity and
their own private efforts. Well aware that New Netherland was not
another Mexico, they still doggedly persisted in the hope that some
profit could be wrested from there. Furs and timber were the only
known products of value in New Netherland and their plan, therefore, revolved around an organized and vigorous exploitation of the
area for these two products.

The "contrary minded" for their part had no plan for New Netherland. Composed mainly of the more politically oriented directors and
Commissioners, this faction of the West India Company was after
much bigger game than New Netherland. Because of this they never
really came to terms with the question of what ought to be done in
New Netherland. Van Rensselaer complained sharply that they:

> . . . had no other aim than to send their ships from here to trade
> in the aforesaid places, notwithstanding that it was clearly pointed
> out to them that such trading could bring no profit to the Com-
> pany but rather decided damage and continual loss, since the

amount of furs coming thence — seeing that the trading places are
so distant from each other — could bear no heavy outlays; besides,
that other nations of adjoining regions, when our ships should
be away from there, would immediately seize and occupy these
and keep us out, as they now do in Virginia, Canada, New En-
gland and elsewhere.[41]

The attitude of the political faction of the company toward New
Netherland was, therefore, ambivalent. On the one hand, they were
not interested in New Netherland and were willing to allow the trading interest a certain amount of latitude in exploring the possibilities
of making New Netherland pay. On the other hand, they were unwilling to give the trading interest too free a rein. In the absence of
any plan of their own, the "contrary minded" were forced to go along
with and support the Commissioners' ideas. But they did so only with
reluctance. Annoyed with the Commissioners for privately profiting
from New Netherland, they would not, however, support a more vigorous expansion of company activity there.

Throughout the history of New Netherland this split within the
company greatly influenced the relations between company and colony. In view of the frequent changes in directors, the working out of
a consistent policy for developing New Netherland became difficult at
best. The Commissioners at any one time were attacked as much for
their general position vis-à-vis New Netherland as they were for the
specific happenings there during their administration. More often
than not an event of small consequence in New Netherland could be
blown up enormously if the ear of the right director in the Netherlands could be gained. Company politics thus became one of the
major disruptive factors affecting the creation of a stable situation in
New Netherland.

Much as company politics may have contributed to the "continuously deteriorating" condition of New Netherland, there were other
factors of greater significance. Implicit in van Rensselaer's comment
was the recognition that the Commissioners' plan for New Netherland simply was not working out. In casting about for reasons to ex-
plain this, he seized upon the dilatory tactics of his opponents at
home as the key to the difficulties in New Netherland. But it was not
that simple. Even if the "contrary minded" had cooperated fully with
the Commissioners, it would have little altered what was taking place

in New Netherland. For it was within the colony itself that the root of the difficulties lay.

The Commissioners' plan for New Netherland assumed that the residents would be so many laborers in the employ of the company who would serve out their time and perhaps even extend or renew their contracts before ultimately returning home. A number of people were needed quickly in order to place the plan into operation. To get them, the Commissioners launched a promotional campaign designed to appeal to the imagination and self-interest of prospective employees. Fantastic claims were made about what life would be like in New Netherland. Promises were glibly given and then promptly forgotten once a contract had been signed. The minister, for example, was promised land to support himself in lieu of the free board to which he was entitled. But after arriving, Michaëlius soon discovered that such a promise was "worth nothing. For their Honours themselves knew perfectly well, that neither horses nor cows nor labourers are to be had here for money." [42]

The recruiting policy of the Commissioners produced side effects which worked to their disadvantage. In the first place, since little care was or could have been exercised in the selection of persons for service, the appeal to self-interest attracted mainly those who, in Michaëlius's words, came "to get rich, in idleness rather than by hard work." The company, it seems, had actually encouraged the "rather rough and unrestrained." [43] Qualifications could not be too carefully inquired into with the result that many of those engaged were unable to perform their expected duties once they arrived. In some cases it was difficult to find any job they could adequately perform:

> With regard to the making of tan and oak bark peelings I have no doubt that Minuyt will have informed your Honors of Gerrit van Gelder's incapacity, so that upon those things not much dependence can be placed, as he is a person who pays little attention to his duties and oath and who is very unfit for farming, he having no knowledge of it himself and being unable to keep any men under him. He had a quarrel with Heindrick Conduit, in which they called each other rogues and thieves.[44]

In the second place, the surprised reaction of the eagerest of immigrants, when he compared the reality at hand to the picture presented to him before sailing, was bound to affect adversely the smooth functioning of the company establishment there. Many immigrants, as a result, spent much of their time murmuring against the company and doing as little as possible in the way of service. De Rasière, too, spoke of some of them as a "rough lot who have to be kept at work by force." [45] Surveying the situation for the directors at home in 1626, his view was that:

> As the people here have become quite lawless, owing to the bad government hitherto prevailing, it is necessary to administer some punishment with kindness, in order to keep them in check, to break them of their bad habits, and to make them learn to understand their bounded duty and the respect they owe your Honours both in writing and speaking. . . .[46]

Although the Commissioners had hoped to establish a stable, well ordered, commercial community in which each would work at his assigned task, the type of person who could be found to take up a temporary residence overseas made the realization of their plans virtually impossible. Lured to New Netherland by reports of the fabulous fortunes which could be quickly made there, the new immigrant thought more of his obligation to himself than of his obligation to the company. Some quite openly stated that:

> . . . they had not come to work, that as far as working is concerned, they might as well have staid at home, and that it was all the same what one did or how much one did, if only in the service of the company.[47]

The new immigrant's hope of making a fortune in New Netherland was quickly dimmed soon after he arrived. No mines of gold or silver were found, nor were any other extractive minerals of value discovered. The making of salt, bricks, tar, pitch, and the like was constantly referred to as "possible beyond doubt." [48] And yet repeated failure in such enterprises was always the result. The reason, too, was always the same — the lack of experienced people. Plea after plea went home from the officials in New Netherland to send over more industrious people "who understand the work and [will] occupy themselves with it." [49] De Rasière warned:

> *Greater diligence will have to be applied than has hitherto been done, under the superintendence and management of sober, industrious persons, of whom, may God better it, there is a great lack here. At times I cannot sufficiently wonder at the lazy unconcern of many persons, both farmers and others, who are willing enough to draw their rations and pay in return for doing almost nothing, without examining their conscience or considering their bounden duty and what they promised to do upon their engagement.*[50]

Increasingly the new immigrant's interest was drawn to the one source of sure profit in New Netherland, the fur trade. Employees and free colonists alike competed with the company for the furs of the Indian trappers. This inevitably drove up the price which the company had to pay for furs, as de Rasière noted:

> *It happened one day that the wife of Wolfert Gerritsz came to me with two otters, for which I offered her three guilders, ten stivers. She refused this and asked five guilders, whereupon I let her go, this being too much. The wife of Jacob Lourissz, the smith, knowing this, went to her and offered her five guilders, which Wolfert's wife again told me. Thereupon, to prevent the otters from being purchased I was obliged to give her the five guilders.*[51]

The company officials in New Netherland were in a quandary about this. If they did not meet the price demanded, then the residents would find other ways of disposing of their furs for a profit. They would either sell them to foreign traders who happened into the area or else they would attempt to ship them home to the personal account of one of the West India Company directors, with whom a prior arrangement had probably been made.[52] De Rasière was appalled at the latter because it so flagrantly violated the rule that residents were required to sell their furs only to representatives of the company in New Netherland. He remarked that the residents were very much:

> *. . . stirred up, and said that they wished to send the skins to the honorable Directors, who would give them three guilders for each skin, good or bad. One is at a loss to know who put that into their head: I presume that it must have been Fongersz, for I have heard no one say this in the Council but him.*[53]

To prevent price inflation and the attendant damage to the fur trade, the Commissioners placed a ban on individual participation in the trade.[54] Only the company was to be permitted to trade in furs. While this measure may have restored some order to the trade, it did nothing to mollify the sullen spirits of the New Netherland immigrant who was now to be shut off from the only source of profit there. Little wonder that van Rensselaer complained of the "continuously deteriorating" condition of New Netherland.

The leading officials of the company in New Netherland were cut from the same cloth as the workers. They were as interested in furthering their own personal fortunes as the farmers or artisans. In a letter of 1630, Michaëlius condemned strongly the conduct of Director Minuit and his Council:

> For besides cheating our Company, whose servants they are, in unworthy ways to their own profit, and having an eye only to their own interest, they also oppress the innocent, and they live so outrageously that they seem not only to be wicked, but even to propagate wickedness. And although they sometimes do not agree, whether through ambition or by reason of some thievish profit, still when they come together (that they may better defraud the Lords of the Company and not give each other away mutually, to the common loss of all) they amalgamate again, according to agreement, and slyly play into each other's hands.[55]

This same Minuit and his Council, de Rasière would have us believe, removed the former Director, Willem Verhulst, for his corruption:

> . . . banishing him now and forever from the limits of your Honors' charter. This was done because he gave out here that if he were not serving the honorable gentlemen here he knew other masters who would help him and would know how to avenge himself.[56]

Ironically, Minuit later entered the service of a Swedish commercial company and returned to the area to establish a colony on the Delaware in 1638 for his new masters. Van Rensselaer, well aware of the high degree of self-interest which motivated the company's leading officials in New Netherland, urged against too frequently:

> *. . . calling home all the officials, who having no other occupa-*
> *tion will spy out the land, this one on behalf of France and that*
> *one on behalf of England as has already happened and as will*
> *happen again.*[57]

Thus the picture of New Netherland which emerges from these accounts of de Rasière and Michaëlius is quite different from the idyllic one drawn by the propagandists who remained at home. The minister summed up his impression of New Netherland in 1628 this way:

> *Thus we lead a hard and sober existence like poor people. This*
> *should be otherwise forsooth, though suffering is salutary, as the*
> *saying is among the nuns, for they themselves know quite well,*
> *that empty cupboards make dull Beguines.*[58]

"We live here very plainly," was de Rasière's comment.[59] The great strides forward suggested in Wassenaer's tidy view of New Netherland in 1626, are belied by Michaëlius's notation in 1628 that the residents in New Netherland were only then "beginning to build new houses in place of the hovels and cots in which heretofore they nestled rather than dwelt." [60]

New Netherland in the years 1623–1629 was, as Michaëlius wrote home, "a wild country." [61] Its first immigrants did not see themselves in the role of laying the foundation of a permanent community in the wilderness. Rather, they were seeking to improve their lot in the world by a temporary fling at what had seemed at home like a good get-rich-quick scheme. Their tie of loyalty to the Netherlands was an extremely tenuous one since many of them were not even Dutch but French, or Walloon, or English. Their sense of loyalty to the West India Company was weakened considerably once promises were painfully matched with reality. Ultimately, their only loyalty was to themselves. An unidentified "Journal of New Netherland" noted that in the early years "no one calculated to remain there longer than the expiration of his bounden time, and therefore did not apply himself to agriculture." [62]

The immigrants to New Netherland in these years were, for the most part, men in motion — footloose, ambitious, and adventurous. Once set in motion it became difficult for them to sink down roots anywhere. Many of the names that appear in New Netherland during these years drop completely from sight. A number of them returned to the Netherlands, disenchanted with what they had found overseas or regarded as unsuitable by the company. Other early residents in New Netherland led quite peripatetic lives after their service there had expired. De Rasière was in Brazil from 1635 to 1651 where he owned several sugar plantations, in Holland in 1654, and in Barbados in 1669. Joost van den Boogaert was in New Netherland in 1625, in Brazil in 1637, and in the settlement of New Sweeden in 1640. Minuit died at St. Christopher in 1638. The first schout, or sheriff, in New Netherland was an Englishman, who returned with Minuit to Holland in 1632. Director Krol was in New Netherland four times between 1623 and 1645 and probably died in the Netherlands. Even Domine Michaëlius was influenced by wanderlust and the hope of brighter prospects outside the Netherlands. Before coming to New Netherland he had been in the West Indies and in Guinea. As for staying permanently in New Netherland with his family, Michaëlius wrote to a friend in 1628:

> *I cannot say, whether or not, I shall remain here any longer after the three years have expired. I expect to be guided in this matter by the fruits of my ministration and the convenience I find in living here with my family.*[63]

He extended his contract for a while, returning to the Netherlands in 1632. He thought once more of coming back to New Netherland in 1637 but was denied an appointment by the West India Company.[64]

The character of the community in New Netherland during the years 1623–1629 is surprising only if seen from within an interpretation posited on an assumption of intended permanency. Compared to the early years of West Indian settlements or even Virginia and the pre-Puritan period of Massachusetts, the experience in New Netherland was quite similar. Richard Pares, surveying British and French colonies in the seventeenth century, concluded that, "The first colonists can only be described as tough guys. They quarreled and drank and disobeyed." [65] The letters of de Rasière and Michaëlius amply document the presence of such traits in New Netherland during these years.[66]

The first residents in New Netherland were, moreover, a mixed group of many nationalities. The principal strains represented were Dutch, French, Walloon, German, Scandinavian, and English. Wassenaer mentioned in his account of 1626 that there were also two Portuguese.[67] De Rasière suggested to the directors that "10 or 12 Norwegians" be sent over in order to make a better beginning in the production of tar and pitch.[68] The Commissioners needed as many laborers as they could possibly get to carry out their design for New Netherland. Their only major requirement, therefore, was a willingness to venture overseas. But the cosmopolitan cast to New Netherland in the beginning was far from unique. Hansen notes:

> The Virginia Company had made use of aliens skilled in trades — Dutch, French, Italians, Germans, Poles — even a "John Martin, the Persian," appears in the early records.[69]

And this picture is extended by Diamond, who notes that Virginia in 1613 also "contained eighteen prisoners — fifteen Frenchmen, including two Jesuits and several members of the nobility; a Spanish spy . . . a renegade Englishman in the pay of Spain; and an Indian princess, Pocahontas." [70]

With such a diverse group in New Netherland, devoted largely to pursuing their own interests, the Commissioners' dream of an efficient, well ordered, commercial community suffered many setbacks. Reports on the behavior of officials and other employees in New Netherland filtered back to the Commissioners and provided them with a number of indicators that their plan was not working out in fact. In addition to the turmoil and dissension in New Netherland, they learned that the accounts of business transactions were so poorly kept that in some cases no record existed of the monthly wages due to employees there. Indeed, de Rasière complained that company affairs were so jumbled that he,

> . . . had to go from one person to the other, asking after one thing and another in order to get information about their names and monthly wages, when they came and how much was still due to them.[71]

The response of the Commissioners to this unexpected turn of events in New Netherland was to explore ways of remedying the defects in what they still regarded as essentially a good plan. An obvious step was to seek better employees — ones who would be more docile and who actually possessed the artisan and farming skills so desperately needed. They also attempted to prune out the malcontents and incompetents already sent to New Netherland. Both of these measures were frequently urged upon the directors by the officials in New Netherland.

Still, it was difficult in practice to do this. Michaëlius applauded the actions of the directors in excising some of the troublemakers from the community, as he informed a friend, "This sort of people are, in course of time, re-shipped home as useless ballast." [72] While it was relatively easy to follow this course of action with respect to lesser employees, it was quite another matter when the chief troublemaker was, as the minister charged, Director Minuit himself. Michaëlius could then only despair and hope for an alteration of conditions:

> And although it was sufficiently clear to the Directors of the Company, so from my letters as well as from the complaints of those who returned to the fatherland, that we did not complain without cause, I do not know how it happens, that we are not freed from the unbearable yoke of this cruel man, or that we ourselves are not called back to the fatherland.[73]

Disappointed and frustrated, Michaëlius longed for happier days when "it might be granted to each honest man to live in peace, after this ballast had been thrown over, and to busy himself with his own affairs." [74]

Given the type of person most likely to be attracted to service in a company's overseas establishment, the prospects were not very good that the Commissioners would be able to upgrade the quality of their employees in New Netherland. At best such an approach could only hope to be effective in the long run. More and more the Commissioners' interest was drawn to ways in which the situation could be stabilized in New Netherland itself. With very little conscious awareness of what they were undertaking, they increasingly moved in the direction of attempting to regulate better the commercial establishment there. These efforts, begun in the interest of improving the efficiency of the operation in New Netherland, ultimately involved the company in the much greater task of ordering a political society. The necessity of this, as all European commercial companies engaged in settlement in the seventeenth century discovered, was inescapable.

To be sure, the Commissioners had made some provision for the conduct of essential public business in New Netherland. The question of punishment has already been mentioned. In addition, they directed that "All wills, marriage settlements, contracts, and other instruments upon which any one might base a claim to title or mortgage of real estate should be duly entered by the secretary in a public register." [75] It was expressly stated that all such matters should be handled in accordance with accepted practices at home. But the expectation was that any such public business would require very little time and that all complicated matters would be referred to the Netherlands for final disposition. The instructions further specified that the residents:

> . . . shall not be permitted to pass any new laws or ordinances or to sanction any new custom, unless such have previously been sent over to us, together with the reasons why under their condition they consider their adoption advisable, whereupon, the same having been examined by the Assembly of the XIX, they shall follow our orders and instructions as regards their confirmation or rejection.[76]

Thus, while it was recognized that a modicum of public business would have to be carried on, the Commissioners made it abundantly clear that the primary responsibility of everyone was to the company:

> . . . one and all, in addition to obeying these instructions, articles, ordinances, and directions already issued by us or that may hereafter be sent over, shall promise the Council upon their solemn oath that they shall, each in the matters entrusted to his care, look after the Company's interests, manage their farm, exercise their trade and perform their labor with the greatest profit and least expense . . . and conduct themselves in all things as faithful servants and obedient subjects are bound to do. . . .[77]

It was found through experience, however, that the administration of public matters in New Netherland could not be handled in such a tidy fashion. Nor did the officials and residents there consider public matters quite so marginal to their existence, for as de Rasière informed the Commissioners, there was "more to be done here than your Honors themselves realized." [78] Moreover, the company officials, who were also required to serve as the public officials, had little skill in such things. They were, as Michaëlius noted, "good people, who are, however, for the most part simple and have little experience in public affairs." [79] De Rasière spoke frankly of his "incapacity," pointing out to the Commissioners, that "I have never before had such matters to deal with." [80] He urged the sending over of "depositions according to the style and usage in such matters in the city of Amsterdam, in order that we may regulate ourselves accordingly when the occasion presents itself." [81]

Although the Commissioners in Amsterdam had conceived of New Netherland as a place of work and of its temporary inhabitants as so many workers in the service of the company, life could not be ordered so simply even in a wilderness three thousand miles away. Leading officials and lowly employees alike did acknowledge, no matter how grudgingly, their relationship to the company. But they also conceived a larger role for themselves, apart from the company, as members of society. It mattered little how primitive that society might be or how temporary their residence in it. Accustomed to the various institutional ways of a settled society, they could not, when uprooted, merely become integers in a company's "table of organization." [82] They looked out on their small but bewildering world and not only saw a commercial company but remembered institutional ways. Michaëlius put his finger on this when he observed that "many things are mixti generis . . . nevertheless the matters and offices, proceeding together, must not be mixed but kept separate, in order to prevent all confusion and disorder." [83] But it was by no means easy to separate out the two roles of company servant and private citizen in a community with so little form.

The minister, for example, a servant of the company under contract for only three years' required service and uncertain of whether he would stay, saw his role in New Netherland not as a chaplain ministering to the needs of an overseas commercial establishment but rather as the founder of a church. His appearance was apparently unexpected for he mentioned that many of his potential flock "had forgotten to bring their certificates with them, not thinking that a church would be formed and established here." [84] Elaborately, Michaëlius went about setting up a church in New Netherland in much the

same way as he would have in the well settled society of the Netherlands. With three months, or perhaps even less, he chose two elders
for the church, Minuit and his brother-in-law, Jan Huygens. These
two, along with Krol who was stationed far away at Fort Orange, he
formally styled, in this community of only some two hundred-odd
souls, his "consistory." Because of the commercial offices they held
within the community, he assumed they would also be the natural
leaders of society in such areas as church organization. While this
might have been expected by a minister in the Netherlands where an
established social order existed, it was not the case in New Netherland. The authority which adhered in commercial offices simply could
not be transmitted to other areas of life by the conference of a title.
For Michaëlius this was profoundly disturbing. He could only ex-
plain it by attacking the officials for their lack of piety. Unrecognized
was a far more basic factor — the inability of officials to play expected
institutional roles in a society so essentially lacking the semblance of
a social order. He immediately launched a large scale program to
convert the Indians by separating children from their parents, insisting that "we must procede in this direction, although it would be attended with some expense." [85]

As the only clergyman in New Netherland, Michaëlius expected
that his position in the community would be the same as a leading
minister at home. Anticipating that his advice, therefore, would be
much sought out by the good but simple officials in matters of public
importance, he wrote home that "I should have little objection to
serve them in any difficult or dubious affair with good advice, provided I considered myself capable and my advice should be asked." [86]
His advice apparently was not sought after and instead he became
embroiled in a number of controversies with the Director and his
Council in New Netherland. The substance and details of his quar-
rels with Minuit are not known. But that an aspect of them involved
his sense of being slighted can be inferred from one of his comments:

> Not willing to conive at all these things, I thought I should be
> silent, until their affairs, being more than transparent enough,
> they could be absolutely convinced by me and they could not con-
> ceal themselves in any hiding-places. When this took place gradu-
> ally, it is inexpressible with what kind of friendship the governor
> tried to silence me and to make me hated in the meantime,

through secret complaints by the Lords of the Company, and at
last has tried to eject me out of this place, branded with a mark
of shame.[87]

De Rasière, too, approached his duties in a similar manner. Appointed by the company to the dual posts of Merchant and Secretary to the Council in New Netherland, he felt it was impossible to perform both jobs once he had arrived. He proposed to expand one or the other into full time tasks. This was in part because he objected to the low salary which the position of Secretary paid compared to other offices there. But of greater weight was the manifest disappointment of de Rasière with the status accorded to him in New Netherland. It seems obvious that his expectations in coming to New Netherland were not at all met. Denied a vote in Council meetings because of the Secretary's position, he protested vehemently to the Commissioners:

> . . . *in matters of legislation and administration my vote and*
> *seat would come next to those of Minuyt, If it be your Honors'*
> *intention that I am to have no vote in any matters so long as I*
> *act as secretary, it were better for me, instead of the honorable*
> *gentlemen giving or allowing me one hundred guilders a year for*
> *this position that I should pay 50 guilders extra to get rid of it.*[88]

To attain the standing in the community that he felt he was entitled to, de Rasière began to transform his commercial offices into political ones. The reactions he encountered from officials and residents were sharp and immediate. Complaining that the previous Director had ruled "without any legal formality, but merely on his own authority," he began holding court sessions and cracking down on the inhabitants' lack of respect for company regulations and officials.[89] He recommended the introduction of a system of fines and penalties in order to deal with the unruly inhabitants before or instead of sending them back to the Netherlands. De Rasière reported that the residents, for their part, found it:

> . . . *very strange that we now begin to inquire into their affairs*
> *and that they are summoned before the court to defend their*
> *cause. They consider that great injustice is done to them if they*
> *are ordered to speak of your Honors with reverence and without*
> *using such profane words as they have heretofore been accus-*

tomed to use and as have been listened to with deaf ears and
been allowed to pass without their being punished therefore.[90]

In dealing with his fellow members of the Council, the reaction was more vitriolic. Eager to maintain or enhance their own standing, members of the Council minced no words with de Rasière when he threatened to tighten his control over the conduct of commercial transactions. One member, assistant commissary Fongersz., pointedly told him "I do not consider you a big enough man for that." [91] Outraged by the conduct and comments of Fongersz., de Rasière fumed that this man, whom he considered his inferior, had actually been "put above" him by the Commissioners:

> *He maintains he owes me no respect, as having no voice in the*
> *Council, and I cannot put up with much from such a drunkard*
> *and idiot, so that I fear that we shall get into further disputes. I*
> *therefore beg the honorable gentlemen to take such measures*
> *as shall separate us, or else to give me more authority in order to*
> *clip the wings and check the insolence of such a half-senseless*
> *person.*[92]

In the eyes of de Rasière, then, the situation could only be improved if his position in New Netherland were improved and a greater formality introduced into the conduct of public affairs. Accordingly, he suggested that the Commissioners "send me and the schout other instructions and . . . order the Council to assist us better." [93] Minuit and the Council won out, however, and de Rasière was back in the Netherlands at least by 1628. De Rasière later married a niece of one of the directors of the company. An attempt was made in 1634 to appoint him to the office of Director in New Netherland but it ultimately failed.[94]

Thus, company politics and the type of immigrant who could be induced to undertake service overseas were only two factors in what van Rensselaer saw as the "continuously deteriorating" condition of New Netherland. They were certainly important factors since they constituted elements of instability on the New Netherland scene. But far more basic — though not clearly recognized by the Commissioners — was the situational problem posed by New Netherland itself. To the Commissioners, New Netherland was simply a business venture, a place to send laborers for the profit of the company. But to the workers themselves, it was more than that. They did not consider themselves merely employees of the company — as, for example, members of the armed services or corporation employees in the twentieth century do when sent overseas. They had ambitions of their own in New Netherland, outside of their role as company employees. It was unfortunate for the Commissioners' well laid plans that the source of profit for both the company and private ambitions was the same — the fur trade. The method of operation was as easy for one as it was for the other. The result was that the expected identity of interest between company and colony never materialized. The temporary employee acquired a separate interest, distinct from the company's. And it was engendered by the situation of New Netherland.

In an attempt to stifle this separate interest and thus to realize their plan for New Netherland, the Commissioners were increasingly led into matters of a noncommercial nature. To deal with the problem of discipline, they became involved in the administration of justice and other institutional considerations in New Netherland. For the most part their steps in this direction did little to increase the efficiency of commercial operations. More often, in fact, they led to demands for an expansion of noncommercial functions. The cost of this was high and ultimately had to come out of the profits of the trade. And yet no considerable gains were recorded as a result of greater organization in New Netherland. The greater involvement of the company in attempts to order society there had other effects. It added to the already existing separate interest within New Netherland as the officials sent over to manage these noncommercial matters became caught up in disputes over social and political precedence in the community.

In the years 1623–1629 New Netherland was a small scale operation. Compared to the early years of Virginia or the Puritan beginnings in Massachusetts, three hundred people in six years did not represent an energetic or auspicious start. And in terms of the coming and going of company servants in these years, this figure may even be unreliable. But an analysis of these years does show that questions of a political and social nature did emerge even though the number of inhabitants was small and even though no Mayflower compact was formally drawn up. These problems were inherent in the situation rather than a result of numbers — they only became more apparent and disturbing as population increased in New Netherland.

The situation of New Netherland, the type of immigrant drawn there, and company politics at home were all factors contributing to the difficulty of establishing a stable order — either commercial or political — in New Netherland. As a result, the Commissioners' view of New Netherland as a self-contained commercial unit never became a reality. Such a view persisted, however, in both the Netherlands and New Netherland, even though it became increasingly overlaid with considerations more societal than commercial in nature. Beginning in 1629 still another factor of instability was introduced into New Netherland when the company legally permitted private merchants to operate within the limits of its monopoly grant.

CHAPTER FIVE

THE RESURGENCE
OF PRIVATE INTEREST
IN NEW NETHERLAND

From a population of three hundred in 1629 New Netherland grew over the succeeding thirty-five years to an estimated population of ten thousand in 1664 when West India Company and Dutch rule came to an end. How had this population been attracted? What were the aims and aspirations of those who came to make up the resident population of New Netherland? And what kind of society was formed during these years? The remaining chapters will attempt to frame answers for these questions.

Earlier historians of Dutch New York have assumed that a distinctive, well formed Dutch society was created during these years. Brodhead, for example, concluded that "Against all the withering influences under which they laid the broad foundations of a mighty state, the colonists of New Netherland steadily achieved their own purposes, and by degrees, won for themselves the franchises of their brethren who remained at home." [1] But had they, in thirty-five years, laid such broad foundations and were the foundations designed to support the building of a uniquely Dutch society in America?

That the Dutch did not accomplish more in these thirty-five years and that they ultimately lost New Netherland to the English, Brodhead attributed to the inhibiting, indeed the pernicious, influence of the West India Company. "The province," he observed in the same passage cited above, "had been unwisely intrusted to the government of a close commercial corporation, than which no government can be less favorable to popular liberty." Yet this is an oversimplification which distorts the relationship of New Netherland to the Netherlands. The choice which Brodhead implied simply never existed. The States-General could not itself have administered the colony of New Netherland. The only alternative to company rule, therefore, was to leave New Netherland to its own devices. But if it did so, the States-General feared that New Netherland would be swallowed up by its English or French neighbors. And however worthless New Netherland might have appeared, no one could advocate abandoning territory to the English or French. Such an alternative was, therefore, never seriously pursued. The experience of the private merchants in the years before 1623, moreover, hardly suggests that New Netherland would have fared any better in private hands even if the English had not moved in.

It has been necessary to dwell at length in the previous chapters on the first twenty years of New Netherland, the years 1609–1629. For during this period basic attitudes were formed toward New Netherland which shaped its later development. The attractiveness of New Netherland, as we have seen, to private merchants before 1623 and to the incorporated merchants of the West India Company after 1623, lay in the opportunities it seemed to present for commercial exploitation and profit. The steps taken by either group of merchants were consequently directed toward commercial goals. To neither group did it seem to be an area suitable for transplanting a distinctively Dutch society in the New World; nor did it even seem desirable. The idealism which surrounded the utterances of Usselinx, the promotional literature of de Laet or Wassenaer, or even the statements of Commissioners for New Netherland such as van Rensselaer should not obscure the fact that no one cared to establish societal institutions except as they might contribute to the success of commercial operations in New Netherland. Much less was anyone aware of the difficulties of dealing with an overseas population that constituted a *de facto* society by virtue of its situation.

There were no large, discontented groups in the Netherlands who saw mass emigration to New Netherland as a solution to present difficulties. Nor were there in the Netherlands any harassed religious groups such as England possessed in the Pilgrims or the Puritans. There was even no great number of younger sons of the burgher aristocrats for whom New Netherland might represent a not-to-be-missed opportunity. Rather the perennial problem down to 1664 was one of finding any person willing to emigrate. Van Rensselaer discussed this in 1633:

> *Nothing can be accomplished there by poor people, who are like a dying plant or leaking roof, also that the rich and well-to-do will not go there themselves, but that a good work can be accomplished by the two . . . the rich may stay at home and send their money thither and the poor may go and perform their work with the money of the rich. To this end freedoms and exemptions were needed in order to raise up patroons who should send out many laborers. . . .*[2]

While it is true that various judicial and political institutions were introduced in the years 1623–1629, it would be a mistake to see in them a seed from which an ultimate flowering of institutional forms developed. They were rather a means of better ordering the commercial community there and thus of enhancing the possibility of making a commercial success of New Netherland. The experience of 1623–1629 revealed, however, that societal considerations could and did overshadow the commercial interests of the company to such an extent that they came, in effect, into competition with those interests. The Commissioners for New Netherland were by no means pleased with this development. They were after all in the business of trying to make a commercial success of New Netherland rather than of trying to create a political society there. To cater to the societal needs of New Netherland only added to the expense of operations without necessarily adding to their profitability. And yet it seemed to those best informed that in the better ordering of the community in New Netherland lay the only real hope of future profit.

If, then, an institutional seed was not implanted during these years, how did society ultimately take shape in New Netherland? The history of the later years suggests that the primary problem was not how to introduce an institutional seed but rather how to make it take root and come to fruition. And one must conclude from the years 1629–1664 that the roots of a distinctively Dutch society were never firmly established in New Netherland. Institutions require time and a measure of stability in order to take hold. And both of these factors were denied to the Dutch venture in New Netherland. Thirty-five years proved to be too short a period of time, and conditions both in the colony and at home conspired to keep New Netherland in a constant state of disruption rather than to induce the requisite degree of stability. Widely separated areas of New Netherland were indeed brought under cultivation during the Dutch period. But it proved impossible to root deeply enough the institutions that were introduced and which in time might have indelibly stamped a Dutch cast on society in that area.

Down to 1664 groups of Netherlanders were continually making a beginning in New Netherland but rarely going much beyond that stage. The initial efforts of the West India Company in New Netherland in the years 1623–1629, examined in detail above, were repeated over and over again in the following years — in Rensselaerswyck, by the Swedes on the Delaware, by the city of Amsterdam in its colony of New Amstel, and by others in such places as New Haarlem, Brooklyn, or Bergen. The pattern of these beginnings were everywhere the same. Complex commercial arrangements were elaborately detailed or formal provisions were made for institutional needs. But all such schemes faltered in the hands of persons in New Netherland who had little experience in such matters and who, moreover, had interests of their own to which they assigned a higher priority by virtue of the hazards they faced in undertaking to live in the wilderness of America.

It has been traditional to structure the history of New Netherland after 1629 in terms of the gradual development of institutions from forms already planted. Yet the facts of the period are quite intractable to such an approach. Institutional forms planted in New Netherland were ephemeral things which never acquired any real definition throughout the Dutch period. The forms were there but people moved restively beneath the forms, struggling to create some kind of a recognizable social order on which a viable institutional life might then have been erected. In all the repeated beginnings that were made the result was the same — a struggle over who would occupy the preferred places within a particular community of New Netherland.

Only by the end of the period does an outline of a social order begin
to emerge in New Netherland and by that time the days of Dutch
rule were numbered. In retrospect it is easy to see that real roots
could only be established if purposeful action had been taken in New
Netherland or at home to further the consolidation of institutional
forms. But it was the fate of New Netherland that action in either
place tended instead to fragment even more the nature of society
emerging in the colony and to impede or arrest institutional development.

Thus the history of New Netherland in the years 1629–1664 is not
the story of the gradual development of a distinctively Dutch society
in the New World but rather the story of why such a society did not
take shape. This latter story can best be exhibited through an analysis
of the actions and interactions of the three principal groups involved
in New Netherland during these years — the West India Company, the
private merchants trading to New Netherland, and the inhabitants of
New Netherland.

These three groups were responsible for the shaping of events in
New Netherland in the years 1629–1664. As for the States-General of
the Netherlands, it exercised virtually no positive direction over the
course of the colony's development. A delegate from the States-
General sat in on meetings of the West India Company but it seems
clear that policy decisions of the company were reached with little or
no regard for the wishes of his masters. In most cases the company
paid scant attention to any requests from the States-General. For
nearly eight years, for example, the States-General pleaded with the
company to take action on the complaints of Lubburtus van Dincklagen, schout under Director van Twiller who was dismissed in 1636
soon after he arrived in New Netherland. In the end van Dincklagen
obtained redress not through the efforts of the States-General but
rather because favorably inclined directors of the company came into
power and exercised their influence on his behalf.[3]

Although the States-General frequently complained that it was un-
informed or that it received "unreliable information on the affairs of
New Netherland," it rarely attempted to do more than mediate
among the three major conflicting interests there.[4] Increasingly over
the years it heard grievances from all parties involved in New Netherland but could only urge them to "settle their differences by agreement and mutual accord." [5] Indeed, the ineffectualness of the States-

General in dealing with New Netherland was openly derided there according to one inhabitant who claimed that "the opposite party jeer . . . saying, when they do anything — 'Go and complain to the States.' " [6]

Thus the States-General did not and could not provide the disinterested leadership to build a political society in New Netherland such as Brodhead and other historians have assumed. Not only did the States-General lack power in the Netherlands to champion such a program but it is not at all clear that in the beginning at least it even saw any reason for doing so. Only very gradually did the usefulness of an overseas colony, not dependent on the exploitation of an indigenous population but based instead on a society nearly as highly organized and differentiated as that in the Netherlands, become apparent. And even when it did the likelihood that a sufficient number of native Netherlanders could be induced to emigrate permanently with their families to New Netherland was remote. The States-General, therefore, was cast throughout these years in the role of mediating between the groups that for one reason or another found it to their advantage to become involved in New Netherland.

If the States-General lacked both the vision and the means for implementing the development of New Netherland in more than a commercial way, where then was the impetus for building a Dutch society in New Netherland to come from? It can hardly be discerned in the actions of the three groups that were most intimately connected with New Netherland in the years 1629–1664. All three groups — the West India Company, the private merchants, and the inhabitants — were far more interested in pursuing their own interests, in advancing their own personal and economic well-being. Each group tended to clothe, indeed to identify, its interest with notions of a separate, public interest in New Netherland. Yet this was for the most part so much trimming: When the chips were down, it was private interest rather than public interest which mattered most. Since the ways of producing a profit in New Netherland were the same for each group, a running clash between them was inevitable. As outlined in the previous chapter, a struggle between the company and the inhabitants flared up immediately in the years 1623–1629. The struggle between these two groups continued in the later years but became more complicated as private merchants began gradually entering New Netherland in the following decade. The general sense of disappointment with New Netherland which prevailed in the Netherlands as a result of the company's experience in the first six years created a mood which made it possible for private merchants to look once again to New Netherland as a possible place of operation.

By 1629 both the company and the inhabitants had found New Netherland disappointing. The carefully laid plans of the Commissioners were never accomplished. And the high hopes of the emigrants to New Netherland were never fulfilled in their encounter with the wilderness. As van Rensselaer and the Commissioners for New Netherland summed up their analysis of the first six years, "The conduct of the people was not regulated; the expenses were high, and the want of success beyond expectation." [7] Many within the company favored a policy of retrenchment. Others were inclined to abandon New Netherland altogether. But still others continued to hope that a commercial success could somehow be made of New Netherland.

The fate of New Netherland was very much in the balance in 1629. By the terms of the company's charter the first slate of directors was scheduled to retire that year. Some changes were bound to be introduced by the new directors, especially since they were predominantly drawn from among the more politically oriented members of the company.[8] But what could the company do with New Netherland in 1629? It certainly could not abandon the colony which was, after all, Dutch territory. And the directors were reluctant to turn it over to anyone else, the States-General included, unless as they later wrote, "they derived profit by it." [9] The prospect of this was not at all likely. The States-General might have reimbursed the company for its losses in New Netherland but it could hardly have taken upon itself the administration of the colony. And there were no other groups in the Netherlands clamoring to take over this failure from the West India Company. The company was, therefore, stuck with New Netherland; it neither could nor would give it up.

Thus the problem for these more politically oriented directors was really one of devising a new policy for New Netherland. Yet here, too, the directors were restricted in their choice. They were not at all disposed to embark on an extensive program to develop New Netherland. This would only put the company to greater expense and the experience of the first six years had amply indicated how uncertain the returns were from such a course. The only choice, therefore, was to retain New Netherland, continue the policy already launched, and hope for the best. In the absence of a more acceptable solution, the new directors slipped into this course of action by default. Since the new directors were men who were far more interested in other operations of the company, this meant that the policy established by the first Commissioners for New Netherland would be maintained but would not be very vigorously pursued. No attempt was made to broaden the policy of the first Commissioners during the next decade and no new approaches were taken. As far as company operations in New Netherland were concerned, they were destined to an official policy of drift for ten years.

An alternative which the new directors had quickly rejected was the opening up of New Netherland to unrestricted free trade for private merchants in the Netherlands. The directors were not in favor of this because they had already invested so much in the colony and because such a step might provide a precedent for attempts by private merchants to extinguish the company's grant of monopoly elsewhere within its patent. Besides there was always the outside chance that New Netherland might somehow prove to be a source of profit in time. Such a course was tempting, however, since it held out the possibility of reducing company expenses in New Netherland. But not until 1638 did the company open up the fur trade in New Netherland to everyone on the payment of prescribed duties.[10]

The new directors were not the only ones who resisted lifting the monopoly ban on private trading to New Netherland. Far more vigorous in their opposition to such a step were the old Commissioners for New Netherland — the van Rensselaer faction. The basis of their opposition was not that such a policy would be against the public interest but rather that it would interfere with their own private interest. Before their retirement they had won support within the company to push through a measure for their own benefit — a West India Company charter entitled "Freedoms and Exemptions for the patroons, masters or private persons who will plant any colonies in, and send cattle to New Netherland, drawn up for the benefit of the General West India Company in New Netherland and for the profit of the patroons, masters and private persons." [11]

This charter of "Freedoms and Exemptions," the basis of the so-called patroonship system in New Netherland, was, in effect, the first break in the company's monopoly over New Netherland. Participation in the "Freedoms and Exemptions" was restricted to large stockholders of the company on record as of 1623. Yet it is clear from the first patents taken out under the charter that it was designed principally for van Rensselaer and his faction of the old Commissioners for New Netherland. The charter of "Freedoms and Exemptions" was obtained because of the great influence of this faction within the West India Company and because of the prevailing feeling in the Netherlands that little profit could be expected from ventures in New Netherland. To be sure many Netherlanders objected to this preferential treatment of the old Commissioners. It was construed as a grab at the time and, indeed, there were certainly elements of this involved. Writing in 1641 de Vries stated, "When the work began to progress, these persons were directors of the Company and commissioners of New Netherland, and helped themselves by the cunning tricks of merchants. . . ." [12] In fairness to the Commissioners it should be pointed out that de Vries was no less cunning but he had been unable to apply for a patroonship under the "Freedoms and Exemptions" of 1629 because he was not a major stockholder of the company. Throughout 1633 especially, van Rensselaer was under severe attack by critics of the charter.[13]

But the fact of the matter is that there was no great rush of applications besides those of van Rensselaer and his faction to take advantage of the charter of "Freedoms and Exemptions." [14] The reason for this seems obvious. Despite the lure of participation in the fur trade, New Netherland remained an area, especially after the company's experience in the first six years, which involved a high degree of risk for prospective merchant speculators. Other ventures could be found which held out equally good chances for large profits but which also offered greater security.

From their experience as Commissioners, van Rensselaer and his colleagues had gained considerable knowledge about and interest in New Netherland. Few other Netherlanders could have been as intimately aware of the prospects for private gain there as these first Commissioners. And few were as well circumstanced to take advantage of the "Freedoms and Exemptions." Unlike many another merchant who might have been attracted to the patroonship scheme, they had many personal contacts with company employees and others already residing in New Netherland who could further their interests on the spot. The Commissioners had engaged every person sent out to New Netherland during the years 1623–1629. Some were their relatives or friends and with all of them the Commissioners maintained close touch. By holding out the hope of greater preferment in their service than in the company's, it was an easy matter for these former Commissioners to make use of the residents already there for their own projects. And this in fact was what the members of the van Rensselaer faction did in getting their patroonships started in New Netherland.

Despite all that has been written on the feudal aspects or implications of the patroonship system, the motive which inspired it in the beginning was exclusively commercial. It arose out of the disenchantment with the way things had been handled in New Netherland by the company during the first six years and also out of the desire of the old Commissioners, particularly van Rensselaer, to continue their connection with New Netherland. Over the years, the problem of how to derive a profit form New Netherland became virtually an obsession with van Rensselaer. Although he ultimately failed, his imprint on the history of New Netherland was nonetheless considerable. For well over half the years that New Netherland was under the rule of the West India Company, van Rensselaer — as Commissioner for New Netherland, as patroon of Rensselaerswyck, and as a man of great influence within the West India Company — played a leading role in shaping its development.

As a document, the "Freedoms and Exemptions" of 1629 was an exceedingly curious one. Phrased in heavy feudal terminology, it was quite anachronistic in the far from feudal condition of the Netherlands in the seventeenth century. "The term 'patroon,'" as Nissenson notes, "was not known to Dutch political nomenclature of the period, nor had it any association with the economic or administrative aspect of any bygone feudalism. It was merely the equivalent of the English word 'patron.' . . ." [15] Indeed, in terms of the time at which it was introduced into New Netherland and the conditions prevailing there, it bears a greater resemblance to the "particular plantations" of Virginia than to an earlier feudalism.

Van Rensselaer or others had no working knowledge of the system of feudalism. "Here in Holland," van Rensselaer wrote in 1641, "fiefs are rare and unusual, but in Gelderland they are common and they are fiefs of all kinds and of all forms of succession. . . ." [16] Yet it is perfectly clear from his correspondence and instructions that he knew nothing of the legal, economic, or administrative functionings of feudalism. The patroonship system was rather an improvised amalgam of the peculiar conditions of New Netherland and the commercial aspirations of van Rensselaer. That a complicated feudal order in New Netherland could have been erected on the basis of the imprecise understanding of van Rensselaer seems incomprehensible. And if van Rensselaer himself knew little of the workings of feudalism, his employees in New Netherland knew even less. He described Arent van Curler, his grandnephew and an official for many years in Rensselaerswyck, as "too weak to take charge of . . . matters." "The persons who hold office," van Rensselaer wrote of his officials, "are not of much capacity." [17] Also, he frequently complained that the colonists sent out were very simple people, noting with resignation that "one can not always get the best to go thither." [18]

The patroonship of Rensselaerswyck, the only successful one in New Netherland or elsewhere, was a commercial venture, not an attempt to impose an anachronistic social order. Van Rensselaer's arguments on feudalism presented in the Netherlands were rationalizations for maintaining control of the colony in his own hands. He presented them so often, he may have begun to believe in later years that he actually was a feudal lord. But the commercial nature of the venture was always clear to his copartners. De Laet, for example, saw no difference between the patroonship venture in New Netherland and other commercial ventures. He described the "Company of Ten," which he, van Rensselaer, and the other Commissioners formed to develop their patroonships as similar to "companies for the diking of land." [19] Van Rensselaer's arguments on the feudalistic aspects of the Company of Ten did not appear until years later and seem to be based for the most part on a superficial knowledge of the subject gained by "a certain person who studied up to the time of taking his degree"—in all probability Adriaen van der Donck, a young man of twenty-one whose first job was as an employee of van Rensselaer in New Netherland.[20]

In the eyes of the copartners and, indeed, in terms of van Rensselaer's own operations in New Netherland, the patroonship system was a commercial venture. Opinion among the various patroon's, however, was strongly divided just how New Netherland should be approached commercially. Commissioners Godyn, Burgh, Bloemaert, and van Rensselaer banded together to form the "Company of Ten" to develop collectively the areas they individually staked out in New Netherland.[21] They all undoubtedly hoped to profit greatly from the furs of New Netherland. Yet they were initially disappointed in this expectation because they were unable to obtain from the company the kind of charter they wanted. Largely responsible for this were the activities of Bloemaert in trading for furs even before the "Freedoms and Exemptions" of 1629 were officially approved by the directors of the West India Company.[22] This touched off a furor in the Netherlands which, together with the prevalent suspicion that the charter was solely a preferential license for the Commissioners to profit at the company's expense, pressured the company into withholding the right of participating in the fur trade from the patroons, continuing it thus as a monopoly of the company. This probably made the patroonship scheme seem far less attractive to speculators in the Netherlands.

Nonetheless the old Commissioners went ahead with their plan for establishing patroonships. Opinion among the various patroons, how-approached commercially. The lure of quick profits from New Netherland continued to exert a strong pull, even on the Commissioners who should have known better from their experience in the years 1623–1629. But this attraction seemed to remain constant throughout the history of New Netherland. People apparently felt that although others had failed they would somehow find success by applying the same techniques. While van Rensselaer approached New Netherland with a view toward long range profits, it seems clear that his copartners were attracted by the hope of quick profit.

Van Rensselaer insisted time and again in memorials and letters that the risks inherent in the trade could only be reduced by stationing personnel in New Netherland the year round to conduct trading operations and to fend off the constant threat from foreign interlopers or conquerors. This would involve a great deal of expense which could only be turned to profit over a long period of time. Van Rensselaer was well aware that ship captains or small traders might occasionally strike a windfall in trading there, but he also knew that they might more often obtain nothing for their efforts in New Netherland if they happened there at the wrong time or were driven away by Indians or foreigners. He feared, moreover, that such hit-and-run trading operations might, as they in fact did later, proliferate to such an extent as to nearly ruin the trade. Van Rensselaer was after long-term profits. He was willing, and as he frequently pointed out he was financially able, to bear the heavy expense of initial investment to attain his desired ends.[23]

Burgh, Bloemaert, Pauw, and Godyn were not willing. The history

of their patroonships tends to confirm this. The ones staked out by
Burgh and Bloemaert in New Netherland were never even started. In
1636, after seven years and with no profit to show for their efforts,
Godyn and Pauw sold their patroonships of Swanendael and Pavonia
back to the West India Company. The patroonships projected for the
Caribbean came to nothing. Indeed, all the patroonships carved out
in New Netherland between the years 1629–1655, with the sole exception of Rensselaerswyck, ultimately failed in every sense.[24] Rensselaerswyck, it is true, never produced the long awaited great profit
envisioned by its first patroon. But it was at least a functioning enterprise throughout the Dutch period and became a source of profit in
time to the American van Rensselaers.

The fur trade was to New Netherland what tobacco was to Virginia. In the beginning everyone hoped to make a fabulous fortune if
only he could participate in — or better still control — the trade. There
is no evidence to indicate that anyone ever made the fortune in the
fur trade in New Netherland of which he so fondly dreamed. Certainly the company throughout the years of its connection to New
Netherland never did. Neither van Rensselaer nor any other single
merchant in the Netherlands made any large scale profits in the
trade. The profits that were made seem rather to have been spread
out more extensively. And increasingly over the years the opportunity
for profiting from the trade tipped in favor of those actually resident
in New Netherland.

Disappointed in their patroonship ventures, prominent speculative
merchants such as Burgh, de Laet, Godyn, and Bloemaert turned
their energies and their capital to more promising investment opportunities. Godyn was involved in the Northern Company and as early
as 1620 had the reputation of being "one of the greatest current account
customers of the Amsterdam Bank of Exchange." [25] Bloemaert was later
Accountant General of the West India Company and actively engaged
in a number of speculative ventures throughout Europe, especially in
Sweden. He was a large investor in the Swedish company which established a colony on the Delaware in 1636.[26] Burgh later became a
burgomaster of Amsterdam and an ambassador to Russia and to Den-
mark. Pauw was later a minister to France for the Dutch Republic
and involved as a merchant in Venice.[27] Some of them continued
to participate in small trading ventures to the colony of Rensselaerswyck as members of the Company of Ten. But for the most part,

even though these merchants together owned at one time 60 per cent and later 40 per cent of Rensselaerswyck, through their invest- ment in the Company of Ten, they were quite content to leave the management of it entirely in the hands of Kiliaen van Rensselaer. Not until 1641, when van Rensselaer began to suggest that the future looked much brighter and after he had wrestled alone for twelve years with the difficulties of his colony, did his partners once again begin to show any interest in Rensselaerswyck.[28] And then they were more interested in trading to Rensselaerswyck than in contributing to its development.

The approach of van Rensselaer was quite different from that of his fast-profit seeking copartners. No less interested in profiting from New Netherland, van Rensselaer, whether as a Commissioner or as a patroon, was in all respects a merchant, not a conscious builder of society. He was quick to recognize that the peculiar circumstances of New Netherland made it necessary to establish certain forms of polit- ical and social institutions. The efficiency and profitability of opera- tions depended upon the maintenance of order in New Netherland. But in making provisions for this, van Rensselaer's eye was never de- flected from his main task of pursuing commercial success there. He was no more anxious than the company to assume great expenses in connection with the necessities of government. To the company or to van Rensselaer this type of activity could only be regarded as so much overhead which cut into the margin of expected profit. Worn down by the incessant litigiousness of his colonists in Rensselaerswyck, van Rensselaer made his position on this quite clear:

> *I should not like to have them waste their money and time
> checkmating one another with pleadings, for which I should have
> to pay the bills on both sides. These contracts are also not
> permanent but made for a certain number of years. When the
> people are their own masters and have their own money and
> property, let them plead and appeal all they please, but I will
> not allow my servants to do so.*[29]

The anticipation of eventual profit was the mainspring of all of van Rensselaer's labors in New Netherland.

Other motives besides profit undoubtedly influenced his actions. Never tempted to emigrate to New Netherland himself, he hoped that opportunities might be created there for his sons when they came of age. Religious zeal may also have been a factor influencing him to press the development of New Netherland. He frequently contrasted his motives with those of the company:

> *. . . the Lord will bless our undertaking, as we have a much better object than the Company in this matter, since we seek to populate the country and in course of time by many people to propagate the teaching of the Holy Gospel. . . .*[30]

It should be noted, however, that it was thirteen years before van Rensselaer engaged a minister for his own colony in New Netherland.[31] As a man of wealth and position in the Netherlands, he spoke often of the obligations which men of his class had toward the poor. In terms of his social philosophy, New Netherland presented an opportunity to discharge that obligation and in a way which he felt would also be profitable. He urged, therefore, a partnership between rich and poor as the best means of developing New Netherland — the rich to provide the money and the poor to venture in person. Yet it seems quite clear from other statements of van Rensselaer that he by no means intended the laborer to rise too high on the economic or social scale through service in New Netherland. He attempted to keep a tight rein on the acquisitiveness and ambition of his own colonists, pointing out that "one man must not have too much." [32] Nor did he want his colonists ever to forget that his interest was their reason for being in New Netherland, for as he frequently reminded his officials, "If everyone seeks his own interest, it cannot go well with the patroon." [33] The colony, he continually stressed, was established for his profit, not for the profit of his colonists. "I should not like to have my people get too wise and figure out their master's profit, especially in matters in which they themselves are somewhat interested." [34]

Important as these influences and the desire for profit may have been, there was in van Rensselaer's case an additional motive. He developed an abiding conviction in the correctness of his view on how New Netherland should be developed. New Netherland represented a challenge to him. Increasingly he devoted more of his time to devising schemes that would enable him to reap the long awaited profit. Van Rensselaer blamed the failure of the plan he had devised as a Commissioner on the bungling ineptness of company officials in executing it in New Netherland. In his own hands, he reasoned, the plan would work. Much of the remainder of his life was devoted to attempts to prove this.

The approach which van Rensselaer took toward the development of his patroonship in New Netherland was essentially the same as the one he had espoused, and in all probability drafted, for the West India Company during its first years of operations. He was convinced that a program of colonization and agriculture was necessary to provide a base for any other possible modes of developing New Netherland. As a Commissioner he had argued that this was necessary if the fur trade were to be expanded. As a patroon he hoped that he would ultimately be legally permitted to enter the fur trade, in which case an agricultural base would be essential. But he saw agriculture as both a supporting activity and as a potential source of profit in its own right. Wheat and tobacco presented themselves as possible agricultural staples.

In this he was influenced by the example of Virginia, where he noted that "about 4,000 people . . . live mostly by tobacco." While working for a change in the company's policy that would permit him to participate in the fur trade, van Rensselaer began working on the development of agriculture in Rensselaerswyck. He informed his nephew, Wouter van Twiller:

> . . . my eye is mainly fixed on tobacco planting by which I can support many people, and as every morgen of land needs not less than five or six men to do well and will produce some 6000 lb, I would get the start of all the English in Virginia and the French on Cristoffel, by reasons of the extreme duties and returns paid to the king and the officers.[35]

Knowing that the new Commissioners for New Netherland were not at all favorably disposed to extending the company's participation in colonizing and agricultural pursuits, van Rensselaer hoped that his colony might profit from the traders and soldiers which the company would have to maintain there. His patroonship in effect would take over the support activities of the company establishment in New Netherland and derive a profit by so doing. "We have various strings to our bow," van Rensselaer wrote to his copartner de Laet:

> The company will have to keep at Fort Orange yearly some 25 men, from which by providing them with everything we may draw

some 2500 guilders a year and therewith pay the laborers' wages.
As soon as there is a supply of grain on hand I intend to erect a
brewery to provide all New Netherland with beer . . . and when
there is more grain, I intend also to erect a brandy distillery. . . .
I also intend to grind meal with a view of selling the same to the
Brownists toward the north or to the English toward the South.[36]

Van Rensselaer plunged vigorously into the task of developing his
agricultural base. He was greatly assisted in engrossing the livestock
necessary for agricultural operations by relatives and friends residing
in New Netherland, particularly his nephew, van Twiller, who was
the company's Director-General there. He knew exactly how to proceed on this:

If we had cattle we should have money and if we had
horses we should have wheat. I take good care to avail myself
of all opportunities to acquire cattle, which makes many jealous
of me, but they have to stand it, as everyone is free to do what
is best for himself.[37]

In a number of ways van Rensselaer chipped away at the company
establishment in Manhattan, hiring away company servants and obtaining company livestock. His efforts met with such success that he
was nearly able:

. . . to nulify completely the company's effort at agricultural
development around New Amsterdam, for, of the six farms in-
augurated there, all but one, hired for himself by van Twiller,
were in this way made destitute of animals, and even of the
animals on van Twiller's farm, some were sought, after his de-
parture, to be sent up to Rensselaerswyck.[38]

By raiding the company and by sending over some himself, van
Rensselaer was successful in obtaining the livestock necessary for
farming in New Netherland. But he was no more successful in dealing with the question of organizing the people in his colony into an
efficient community than the company had been with the assorted
population which made up its commercial establishment in the years
1623–1629. The experience of the early years of Rensselaerswyck was
in many ways exactly the same as the early years of the company's es-

tablishment at Manhattan. And the problems which both the company and van Rensselaer faced were the same.

One problem was recruiting colonists to go to Rensselaerswyck. In 1632 van Rensselaer feared that he would be unable to obtain the fifty persons which he was required to send to New Netherland during the first four years as a condition of holding a patroonship under the 1629 charter of "Freedoms and Exemptions." If he could not obtain the requisite number, he expected that "then certain partial people would soon call for action" in the Netherlands against him.[39] Van Rensselaer at times blamed this on such things as "the great mortality which there has been in this country." [40] But it seems clear that few people in the Netherlands were willing to emigrate to New Netherland. Apparently van Rensselaer went so far as to engage recruiting agents, for he complained of "the expense of travelling, board and agent's commissions which I have before I can get any servants." [41] Like the company he was, therefore, forced to accept those emigrants who offered themselves as volunteers. This meant, as it had for the company, a mixed group of nationalities. Of the eighty-two emigrants to Rensselaerswyck in the years 1630–1639, some thirty-two colonists, or nearly 40 per cent, were from such places as England, Norway, and various German principalities.[42]

Because of this difficulty, van Rensselaer, too, was forced to make a variety of contracts with his colonists, some of whom were "free colonists" and some of whom even entered into partnership arrangements with him for the performance of specialized functions, such as the cultivation of tobacco or the operation of saw mills. The types of emigrants who could be persuaded to venture to Rensselaerswyck were also similar to the ones who presented themselves as servants of the West India Company. Many of them were young — eager for adventure and eager to make their fortunes. And most of them were probably as van Tienhoven, Secretary of the company under Kieft, describe them, "country or seafaring men," with little experience but with great ambition.[43] Van Rensselaer preferred to describe them as "poor beggars" who became puffed up with personal ambition when they arrived in New Netherland. This was largely because they tended, in his view, to place their interest above his. Van Rensselaer sought to console his minister in the colony, the Reverend Johannes Megapolensis, who showed signs of despair after his initial encounter with the people of Rensselaerswyck:

> *That you do not find the people in the colony what we should*
> *both like them to be is apparently and without doubt due to the*
> *luxuriousness of the country, the small number of people (for*
> *people usually fear more the opinions of others than the pene-*
> *trating eye of the Lord), lack of a good pastor, the natural*
> *tendency towards evil and the fact that the best people seldom*
> *go far across the sea.*[44]

Van Rensselaer touched on the root of the problem in this passage but he continued to expect that people would conduct themselves in New Netherland either as economic robots or as members of an established social order. The fact, however, was that there was no stable social order and that it could not be imposed merely by titles or offices. Throughout his life, van Rensselaer proceeded on the assumption that a social order could be imposed in such a fashion.

The officials in the colony of Rensselaerswyck were also simple men of little experience. Arent van Curler, the patroon's grandnephew, was sent over as an officer at the age of eighteen and van Rensselaer repeatedly attributed reverses in the colony to Curler's youth and inexperience. In 1639 he observed that "I have as yet no one among my people who has any business training." He distrusted his officials so much that he refused to appoint a resident director of the colony during his lifetime. The first Director, Brant van Slichtenhorst, did not arrive in Rensselaerswyck until 1648, eighteen years after the colony was first begun.[45]

Much of the incompetence which van Rensselaer complained of can be traced to his own unwillingness to establish any clear lines of authority in the colony during his lifetime. The administration in Rensselaerswyck was so hydra-headed that van der Donck described it as a system where one official was sent out solely for the purpose of spying on an earlier appointed one. Van Rensselaer bristled in reaction to van der Donck's accusation that he was sending "informers into the country" and charged him in return with mainly aspiring to the office of Director:

> *If your desire inclines to high office, your efforts will be directed*
> *more toward your own advancement than toward my ad-*
> *vantage . . . If you have imagined that you can extort the*
> *directorship from me, you will be much deceived, for that is not*
> *the way to get it.*[46]

Van Rensselaer, more successful at the task of developing agriculture in New Netherland than the company had been, nonetheless ran aground on the same insoluble problem that the company had — the organization of society. Benefiting from the experience of the company's first six years in New Netherland, van Rensselaer carefully took steps to solve this problem. He felt that by keeping control tightly in his own hands he would avoid the factious difficulties which had plagued the administration of New Netherland by a group of Commissioners. His belief that company operations in New Netherland had been impaired by too many hands at the tiller was reinforced by the experience he and the other patroons had had with the patroonship of Swanendael. "When we got so many participants in Swanendael," van Rensselaer wrote, "then came our confusion." [47] Yet by attempting to keep the reins of control entirely in his own hands he erred on the other side. The colony in New Netherland could not be effectively run from 3,000 miles away.[48] By pressing everyone in the colony to write to him directly, he tended only to subvert the authority of his officials there. His unwillingness to consolidate authority in any one person in Rensselaerswyck only added to the difficulties there. The examples of both Virginia and Massachusetts Bay in the early years suggest that order and stability could only be maintained if a somewhat authoritarian structure of control were present in the colony itself.

Aware of the necessity of introducing institutions of a political and administrative nature into his business enterprise of Rensselaerswyck, the patroon overdid it. Nearly everyone in the colony in the beginning was invested with some office:

> When there were still less than a score of inhabitants, the
> patroon appointed Rutger Hendricksen van Soest, one of his
> farmers, as "officier and schout," and Gerit Theusen de Reux,
> Brant Peelen and Roel of Jansen, the farmers in charge of the
> three remaining farms, Marinus Adriaensen van der Veere, who
> was in charge of an attempted tobacco plantation, and Laurens
> Laurensen, in charge of the sawmill, as "schepens" of the patroonship, collectively designated as its court or council.[49]

And, as Nissenson has pointed out, the instructions which he provided for these officers had more to do with commercial functions than with matters of government. The patroon continued to increase

the number of officers in his colony and to assign duties to offices
which bore no relations to matters that would have come under the
authority of comparable offices in the Netherlands. Only confusion
could be expected from such an arrangement. Van Rensselaer knew
well that the persons he named had no experience whatsoever with
the execution of these offices. He attempted to buttress their inexperience by providing them with the traditional symbols of office — black
hats with silver bands for the schepens and councilors and a silver-
plated rapier with baldric and a black hat with plume for the officer
and schout.[50] The effect must have been truly comic in this tiny
wilderness community of only a few souls.

And yet to the people of the community it was not at all comic.
The ones who had been appointed to office attempted to use their
new authority while their fellow colonists, who could see little social
difference or any grounds on which to distinguish the officers from
themselves, contested bitterly the officers' right to do so. The fact that
the community was 40 per cent non-Dutch did not help the situation.
The result was that Rensselaerswyck was continually racked by suits
and countersuits over petty matters. None of these legal actions had
anything to do with the main business at hand of clearing the land
and creating the material conditions which would enable the community to survive and prosper. But in a community so uniformly recruited from the same stratum of society in the Old World and composed of ambitious, self-seeking "Country or sea-faring men," a struggle for creating some semblance of a remembered social and political
order was virtually inevitable. Men who were perhaps a notch above
most of the colonists, men such as van Rensselaer's relatives or Adriaen van der Donck, soon learned that their position in the old country counted for very little in the new.

The patroon never quite understood the nature or the dimensions
of this problem. Nor did he realize that the very reason which
prompted his colonists to emigrate to Rensselaerswyck would make
them more prone to place their interests above his. Van Rensselaer
always construed the disturbances in the colony as deliberate attempts
to cheat him out of his long awaited profits. Although he frequently
spoke of his willingness to wait patiently for long term profits, it
seems clear that he pressed hard for more immediate returns. He
seemed to suspect, therefore, that his colonists were making huge
profits at his expense — and indeed some of them may have. But he
went a little too far when he suggested that "My people complain

because they have it too well." And the contrast he sketched between
life in the New World and the Old was hardly a valid one:

> *The people there live in too much luxury, those who are located*
> *here on the frontiers where war is would thank God to have such*
> *conditions.*[51]

The explanation he most frequently seized upon was that his
officers were not exercising sufficient care in supervising his business
interests in Rensselaerswyck. He constantly complained of his officials'
laxness and ordered them to be more strict with his recalcitrant colonists. But for the most part the difficulty was a situational one:

> *The accounts remained unsettled because there was not the*
> *wherewithal to pay. . . . In these circumstances, resort to force*
> *or to legal proceedings was of little avail, and, in this small*
> *community, resulted only in an apparently inescapable personal*
> *animosity.*[52]

Van Rensselaer saw it in much simpler terms:

> *My people have thus far not observed proper order in the*
> *administration but have thrown my insructions in a corner and*
> *they have mainly studied their own benefit and advancement.*[53]

The dream of van Rensselaer was to establish a stable social order
in New Netherland by attracting more "suitable" emigrants. In this
way it would be possible, he felt, to rule his colony "through representatives from different orders of society according to the custom in
this country." [54] Both van Rensselaer and the company failed to find
such suitable people for New Netherland. But even if they had, such
persons would have had to compete with the ambitious adventurers
who did find New Netherland attractive. As it was, much social unrest was to precede the emergence of a natural social order in New
Netherland.

The struggle for social and political position in Rensselaerswyck by
1639–1640 so upset van Rensselaer that he wrote van Curler:

> *I am surprised that they dare call themselves an independent*
> *community, as they are altogether my servants and subjects . . .*
> *If they rise up against me, they will ride an [un]easy horse.*[55]

Although he had elevated simple and inexperienced people to official positions in his colony, he now spoke of teaching "the peasant councilors to mutiny against their lord." Far from solving the problem of forging an economic rather than a political organization out of his community in New Netherland, van Rensselaer's efforts were as much a failure as the company's had been in Manhattan during the years 1623–1629. The similar beginnings of these two communities in New Netherland — Rensselaerswyck and the company establishment at Manhattan — suggest how situational the kernel of their difficulties was. There simply was no correlation between administrative machinery and increased efficiency as van Rensselaer painfully recorded:

> *Whereas I have been inclined to have a large number of people*
> *in my colony, I become disgusted with it, seeing that the greater*
> *the amount the worse the bargain and the better I regulate every-*
> *thing the more everyone looks out for himself, from which dis-*
> *order proceeds.*[56]

The examples of Rensselaerswyck and the company establishment at Manhattan demonstrate that it was one thing to introduce institutions into New Netherland but quite another thing to have them take root. Both had been planned as primarily commercial ventures and yet it had proved impossible to organize them along these lines. Seemingly, no one knew his place, much less kept his place, once he arrived in New Netherland. However small the community, it was disrupted by disputes between council members over matters of precedence and by clashes between officials and others on the proper management of things public and things private.

The elaborate titles given to the officials of the company or the patroon were descriptive only of the duties they were expected to perform rather than any duties that were necessarily performed. Little continuity in the functioning or execution of offices can be discerned in these years. However much the scope of an individual's activities might have been defined at home, they were actually determined by the figure he cut in New Netherland.[57]

Not only were these individual communities beset by internal chaos but forces from without continually impinged upon them in such a way as to impede even more the development of institutional forms. The "Freedoms and Exemptions" of 1629 ushered in a period of private merchant activity in New Netherland which in short order virtually destroyed the agricultural underpinnings of the company's establishment begun at Manhattan in 1626. The competition of the patroons, especially of van Rensselaer, for colonists and for livestock was chiefly responsible for this. Indeed, the creation of the Rensselaerswyck community was at the expense of the Manhattan community. In terms of societal considerations it upset whatever start had been made at Manhattan. The Vingboom map of 1639 indicates that none of the company farms were in operation then, and that little if any of Manhattan had been under cultivation just before this time.[58]

An examination of the beginnings of these two areas provides useful points of comparison. Considerably more information is available on the beginnings of Rensselaerswyck which tends, by analogy, to throw light on the early years of Manhattan. In both instances a struggle soon developed between the inhabitants, on the one hand, and either the company or the patroon, on the other. The nature of the struggle was essentially social. An earlier generation of historians, assuming that societal institutions could be easily transferred from the settled society of the Netherlands to the frontier wilderness of North America, chose to regard these clashes as evidence of the oppressive character of commercial company or feudal landlord rule. Others have chosen to see the period in terms of simple anarchy, a kind of Hobbesian state of nature. Neither is correct. The language used by the participants in these clashes indicates that the nature of constituted authority was not called into question. All of the participants had much the same conception of how society ought to be organized. Instead, the clashes revolved around the exercise of authority by individuals who, in terms of a more settled society, did not possess the expected background for holding office. While these clashes certainly impeded the development of institutional forms, they were essentially the means by which a recognizable social order ultimately emerged, upon which, institutions capable of exhibiting continuity might be erected.

Although piqued by the crafty maneuverings of van Rensselaer, the new Commissioners for New Netherland were not altogether unhappy about the company's elimination from agricultural activities in New Netherland. The company's involvement in this had created more problems than it seemed to be worth. And it was also quite expensive. If patroons or others could be induced to take up the plow, the company was quite willing to abandon it to them, thereby reducing their own overhead expenses in New Netherland. In the decade after 1629 the company began casting about for ways to economize on its establishment in New Netherland. Increasingly this led to a shift away from the company's direct participation in agriculture and ultimately even in the fur trade. Van Rensselaer reduced the West India Company's difficult position in New Netherland to its simplest terms:

> *If they wish to keep it [the fur trade] to themselves with few*
> *people, which is most profitable to them, they can not defend the*
> *country, and with many people they suffer loss; and others will*
> *not care to populate the country unless they have the free trade.*[59]

Since they had no real choice but to defend the country, they were drawn by economic necessity into encouraging immigration to New Netherland. "It is the Company's intention," one of its directors reported in 1638, "to cause those countries to be peopled and brought into cultivation more and more." [60] The peculiar circumstances of the colony made it impossible for the company, as they well knew from ample experience, to make a commercial success of it on its own. Thus, as a consequence of this, and not from a heightened awareness that an attempt to create, literally, a New Netherland ought to be undertaken as a state policy, the company threw open the fur trade in New Netherland to all inhabitants of the Netherlands or its allies on the payment of fixed duties to the company. This change in policy necessarily meant that the company would be more concerned in the future with administrative and governmental functions in New Netherland than with direct trading. Although it continued to maintain traders on its own account until 1644, it began after 1639 to consolidate its supervisory personnel at Manhattan and Fort Orange.[61]

The decade 1629–1639 bore witness to no progress in the emergence of a differentiated society in New Netherland. The roots that had been set down in Manhattan at such great cost to the company were in effect wrenched up and carefully transplanted in the soil of Rensselaerswyck. The quick-profit seeking partners of van Rensselaer retired from the field after a brief but intense moment of sowing unrest by a vain attempt to develop their abortive patroonships. They were, in effect, the harbingers of the new era of small, private traders that followed. The stand-pat attitude of the company's directors during these years while they worked out a new policy contributed little to the development of New Netherland. Van Twiller, the company's Director-General there, in fact presided over the liquidation of the start that had been made, and in so doing contributed to the success of his uncle's venture along the banks of the upper Hudson. At home the "contrary minded," now the Commissioners for New Netherland, thwarted van Rensselaer at every turn to make sure that the remote chance of his profiting hugely from New Netherland would never become a reality. They went out of their way, for example, to issue a placard against anyone participating in the inland fur trade — knowing full well that the only one so circumstanced was van Rensselaer.[62]

The emigrants who went out to New Netherland with their families in the service of van Rensselaer or the company by no means necessarily intended to settle permanently there. Their hope was for a spectacular windfall, and failing in this many of them returned home on the expiration of their contracts. Others moved about considerably, taking service now under the patroon, and now under the company, or even frequently going off on their own to try their luck. Of the eighty-two known immigrants to Rensselaerswyck during the years 1630–1639, nearly half of them returned home or wandered elsewhere in New Netherland.[63] Illegal private trading abounded in New Netherland and neither the officials of the company nor of the patroon could do very much about it. Indeed, many of the officials were themselves involved privately in the fur trade. De Vries characterized the inhabitants of the colony of Rensselaerswyck this way: "Every boer was a merchant." [64]

Aggressive entrepreneurs such as David de Vries or Adriaen van der Donck, intent upon making fortunes for themselves in New Netherland, avariciously sought out any conceivable position or post that held out the promise of profit or power. With reckless abandon they covered with slanderous tales any potential rival. De Vries, a skipper-merchant who had sailed to the Mediterranean and the East Indies before venturing to New Netherland, was approached by the partners in the Swanendael patroonship scheme to serve as their chief official there. He agreed to their proposition but insisted that he would "have to have a status equal to that of a patroon." [65] He obtained it in name but the colony still failed.

De Vries repeatedly attacked Director van Twiller, complaining home of his incompetence and lack of quality for the office. In a pointed reference to van Twiller he expressed surprise,

> . . . that the West India Company would send such fools into
> this country, who know nothing, except to drink; that they could
> not come to be assistant in the East Indies; and that the
> Company, by such arrangement, must come to nought.[66]

Yet if any of these charges were true, they must be weighed against the fact that de Vries was simultaneously conducting a campaign to obtain the job of Director-General in New Netherland for himself. He was ultimately disappointed in this for the directors at home ruled on de Vries' request that "a more capable person is needed for Director." [67]

And as if all these factors were not sufficient in themselves to keep New Netherland constantly stirred up and to make virtually impossible the growth of institutions, two events involving foreigners completed the picture of near total disruption during the decade. Jacob Eelkens, one of the pre-West India Company traders to New Netherland, returned to the area in April of 1633 in the service of an English commercial company and attempted to trade for furs near Fort Orange. Described in the heavily formalistic terms that so characterized the language used by officials in nearly all seventeenth-century European colonies, this simple, illegal trading venture was cast in terms of an international tilt between two great powers in America. In retrospect it appears only as *opéra bouffe* and yet it touched off a violent debate over Dutch and English claims to the area which rocked the colony and its officials and even reached back to England and the Netherlands.[68]

A final source of instability for New Netherland in this decade was the establishment of a Swedish commercial colony on the Delaware by New Netherland's former Director-General, Pieter Minuit. The venture was the result of a combination of Dutch and Swedish capital. Its aims were the same as those of the West India Company — the commercial exploitation of the area, with particular reference to the fur trade. To the officials of New Netherland it represented a constant irritant which would one day have to be removed. In the overall picture of the decade it meant simply another community beginning which had little capacity for developing any real roots.

But it did serve to extend further the already wide geographical dispersion of the population in New Netherland.[69]

Thus in 1639, thirty years after the discovery of the area by Hudson, New Netherland showed few signs of any settled society or even of permanency. To individuals at the time, the year 1639 was seen as still another beginning for New Netherland. The directors of the West India Company, for example, armed with a new approach toward the question of emigration, began to project ahead the arrangements that would be necessary for "the first commencement and settlement of this population." [70] The nature of this "new" beginning merits the same close examination as the decade 1629–1639 in order to determine whether society in New Netherland in the following years would be drawn together or fragmented even further.

CHAPTER SIX

A MAELSTROM OF INTEREST:
NEW NETHERLAND
1639–1650

The condition of New Netherland in 1639 was analogous to that of Virginia in 1624. Both the West India Company and the Virginia Company had initially gone into their respective areas with the expectation of reaping great profits only to discover that North America did not lend itself to such an approach. After the first wave of disappointment, each company experimented with subsidiary organizations in an attempt to come to terms with the sources of failure in the early years — the Virginia Company tried "particular plantations;" the West India Company, patroonships. Neither of these stopgap measures made very much headway against problems that were essentially situational in nature. Both companies learned that "colonization required . . . more than the transportation of their people to this new land of plenty." [1]

Up to the point at which Virginia and New Netherland were each recognized as commercial failures, their patterns of development had been quite comparable. After that they diverged sharply. In 1624 Vir-

ginia was simply written off the books as a failure by its sponsoring
company in England. The company's dissolution, as Craven has detailed it, was brought about by intercompany struggle over control
and by political maneuverings in England, heightened and brought
to a climax in the milieu of commercial disappointment which surrounded the experiment in Virginia. Although Virginia nominally
acquired the status of a royal colony in 1624, it was many years before
a well defined British colonial policy emerged. As a result, Virginia
was left to develop largely on its own during the next forty years
until a "new interest became manifest in the plantations old and
new, not as colonies or areas of land but as adjuncts of trade." [2]

New Netherland, on the other hand, was not written off the books
by the West India Company in 1639 when its failure as a commercial
venture became fully apparent. The central government of the
Netherlands could not have taken over the colony. Indeed, the States-
General was quite content to see New Netherland remain under the
charge of the company. Since the West India Company was not narrowly based in one area of the New World nor near the brink of
bankruptcy as the Virginia Company was, it could, therefore, afford
to carry or subsidize the unprofitable area of New Netherland. Noting that New Netherland had occasioned the company a net loss of
550,000 guilders between the years 1626–1644, the weight of a lengthy
report by the company's Board of Accounts in 1644 was nonetheless
against discontinuing operations there:

> Inasmuch as the Company has, by its conceded Freedome,
> promised to take all Colonists, as well freemen as servants, under
> its protection, and to aid in defending them against all foreign
> and domestic wars; and as the improvement of affairs by good
> orders from here, and better government there, is not altogether
> hopeless, so that this place may be preserved, in the first instance,
> with small profits, or at least without loss; we are, therefore,
> of opinion, under correction, that the Company cannot decently
> or consistently abandon it. [3]

In fact the West India Company repeatedly maintained that it encouraged the promotion of New Netherland and took offense easily
when accusations of neglect were leveled against it. The directors of
the Amsterdam chamber of the company, for example, sharply up-
braided Stuyvesant in 1664 for his remarks in this vein against the
company:

But we also insist that you will not, whilst complaining accuse
us . . . of having so little understood the state of New Nether-
land as that you and our people should call themselves
abandoned.[4]

But while the West India Company did not abandon its colony in
North America after 1639, it saw no reason why it should not profit
or at least break even on operations. In opening up the fur trade to
private traders the company was not now consciously taking upon itself the disinterested task of building a political society in New Netherland. Rather it was merely trying a new commercial approach with
its white elephant in North America which seemed to fit no known
pattern of successful commercial development. This shift in policy resulted from the company's experience in the previous years which had
clearly indicated that an efficient commercial outpost could not be
maintained with profit in New Netherland. Two main reasons were
seen as being at the root of the company's failure — the peculiar conditions of New Netherland and the inability of company officials in
New Netherland to make the inhabitants pursue the company's interest rather than their own. The directors pointed out that

. . . all the population cannot be settled on one place, but must
be disposed according to the inclination of those going thither,
and the circumstances of affairs there. . . .[5]

But since it was obliged to continue its connection with New Netherland, the company now sought ways of doing this which would involve the least possible expense.

The company seemed somewhat resigned to the fact that New
Netherland would not produce any great profit and so began to ad-
dress itself to its new role as caretaker of New Netherland. The principal problem in 1639, as the company and the States-General saw it,
was simply one of retaining control of the territory of New Netherland. To do this, more people were required to offset the threat posed
by the growing population of New England. "The inhabitants of foreign princes and potentates," the States-General reported, "are en-
deavouring to incorporate New Netherland, and if not seasonably
attended to, will at once entirely overrun it." [6] Thus as a result of
the commercial failure of the early years and the threat of losing territory, the West India Company in 1639 was drawn into throwing

open the fur trade to inhabitants of the Netherlands and friendly ⟵ allied nations.

In exchange for granting this privilege, the West India Company established a schedule of duties on goods sent out to and received from New Netherland.[7] The receipts from this, it was hoped, would pay for the costs of the limited company establishment which would have to be maintained and would perhaps even provide a small measure of profit. Besides the new duties, the company would derive some income from its charges for warehousing and transportation of goods in company ships. Until 1644 it maintained some of its own traders in New Netherland and continued to participate in the fur trade directly. It also sold goods directly to the inhabitants of New Netherland until around 1650.[8]

The main advantage which the company sought to derive from the new policy was a reduction in its overhead expenses in New Netherland. If a sufficient population could be established there, the company could eliminate its farmers, artisans, and later even its traders from the payroll. In so doing its functions could be reduced to three — collection of duties, defense of the colony, and the maintenance of the bare minimum of government consistent with good order. In the minds of the company directors these functions could be performed by a rather small establishment in New Netherland. This can be seen in the plan which the West India Company's Board of Accounts outlined in 1644, proposing that New Netherland could be effectively managed for the company by a director, an assistant who might also serve as a factor and receiver of company goods, a fiscal or officer of justice, two commissaries, a secretary, a clergyman, a school teacher, a surgeon, and sixty soldiers. The Board estimated that the total cost of this establishment of sixty-nine persons would be 20,000 guilders annually. It felt that "These officers and servants would be sufficient for the business; and carpenters, masons, smiths and such like ought all to be discharged, and left to work for whomever will pay them." [9]

There was, then, no significant change in the company's attitude toward New Netherland as a result of its policy shift in 1639. It still continued to regard itself as engaged primarily in a commercial operation. The means by which it hoped to profit from New Netherland changed, but the pursuit of profit itself did not. Nor was there anything in the company's experience during its first sixteen years to suggest that it ought to have altered fundamentally its pursuit of profit in favor of an all-out policy of building a Dutch society within the geographical limits of New Netherland. Earlier historians of the period have attacked the company at this point for continuing its commercial policy and for failing to recognize what its task should have been. O'Callaghan wrote:

> Had they filled the land as the English were doing, with thousands of moral, hardy pioneers; had they transported cattle, and encouraged the planting of towns and villages in the wilderness, instead of building solitary forts to serve as a rendezvous for lazy Indians and a few isolated traders, rendered the more defenceless by their isolation, the tide of encroachment from New England would not, at this date, have threatened to wash the walls of Fort Amsterdam. . . .[10]

But such a view emerges from a combination of hindsight and wishful thinking rather than from a proper regard for the insights available at this time to the participants in the history of New Netherland. In the first place, the intimation that the English government was consciously pursuing a policy of filling up New England is misleading. The English emigrated to New England for a wide variety of reasons rather than in response to an articulated plan which clearly saw the possibilities which North America offered for the building of a new English society. In the second place, there were no thousands of inhabitants of the Netherlands clamoring to fill the land in New Netherland. Both the company and the patroons had found it very difficult to attract people from home or elsewhere to venture to their overseas possession. Finally it was not at all clear to the company, or for that matter even to the English, what the future of New England would be. The margin between success and failure in New World ventures in the seventeenth century was exceedingly slim. It is too much to expect that the Massachusetts Bay Colony after only eight or nine years overwhelmingly presented itself as a model for the Dutch to follow in North America.

Brodhead's view, too, was predicated on what the Dutch ought to have known and, consequently, on what they ought to have done. For him, the company after 1639 perversely "adhered to a system of onerous imposts, for its own benefit." [11] But while the change of policy was, of course, for the company's benefit, the company hardly looked upon its schedule of duties as in any way onerous. The company expected to obtain something in return for granting privileges and undertaking to defend New Netherland. It did not regard its desire to profit from or break even on its operations in New Netherland as incompatible with advancing the development of New Netherland.

With very little knowledge of the magnitude of the task involved, the company was placed in the difficult position of having to assume a dual role in New Netherland. To its stockholders, the company's role was seen predominantly in commercial terms. To inhabitants of New Netherland and to many critics of the company's operations, the company's role was seen preeminently in terms of its responsibility for organizing society there. It was an impossible position for a seventeenth-century company to occupy. The situation of New Netherland, thus, made it unlikely that the new commercial policy of the company would be any more successful than the old one had been. As an historian of economic organization during these years has pointed out:

> Conceivably (though even this is not certain) a vast monopolistic corporation might have been able to organize purely commercial interests in the West; but to combine those interests with the organization of settlement . . . was beyond the capacity of any seventeenth century company.[12]

And in shifting from a policy of direct commercial participation to one of commercial regulation, the West India Company unwittingly only became more involved in the organization of settlement in New Netherland. However much the company preferred to see its role in New Netherland as a commercial one, the company's servants and the inhabitants in New Netherland pushed it increasingly into a governmental one.

The company was certainly not opposed to the peopling of New Netherland. In fact it now hoped to profit by the presence of people there. But it could not justify to its stockholders the expenditures of vast sums of money without some expectation of profit. The company, along with the inhabitants, the States-General, and private traders, dreamed at times of a great flourishing center of trade rising in New Netherland. But dreams require money to be actualized and the company was unwilling to shoulder the sole burden of responsibility for developing New Netherland. It would and did help; but it expected that others would contribute as well.

Despite eighteen years of experience in New Netherland, the company continued to believe that business and politics could be neatly separated in its administration of the colony. The small size of the establishment proposed by the Board of Accounts suggests that the company still felt that the functions of government in such a small wilderness community would be quite minimal and could easily be handled by a few company officers on a part-time basis. A large measure of voluntary cooperation was also sought from the inhabitants themselves in matters of government. In 1638, for example, the company proposed that,

> *Each inhabitant should be bound willingly to accept, and*
> *honestly and faithfully to discharge at his place of residence . . .*
> *all public burthens and duties, such as the office of magistrate*
> *and those of honor or authority; also those in any way relating*
> *to works of piety, such as churches, without claiming any rec-*
> *ompense or reward for so doing.*[13]

The company's sanguine expectation as to the degree of cooperation it might obtain from the inhabitants was never realized. In opening the fur trade to private individuals it also opened the door to an influx of people whose struggles for an economic, social, and political place in New Netherland kept the colony in a constant state of disruption down to 1664. In place of the orderly development which the West India Company envisioned, the years 1639–1650 witnessed instead a maelstrom of competing interest in New Netherland.

Incredible disorder resulted initially from the opening up of the fur trade in 1639. People already residing in New Netherland abandoned their farms and trekked far inland in the hope of establishing better trading relations with the Indians for furs. According to one source, "every one thought that now was the acceptable time to make his fortune." So assiduously were trade relations with the Indians cultivated that the same account spoke of the inhabitants not only inviting the Indians to their homes, but of,

> *. . . admitting them to Table, laying napkins before them, pre-*
> *senting Wine to them and more of that kind of thing, which*
> *they did not receive like Esop's man, but as their due and desert,*
> *insomuch that they were not content, but began to hate, when*
> *such civilities were not shown them.*[14]

The announcement of the opening of the fur trade produced a similar effect in the Netherlands, attracting not the farmer and artisan as the company had hoped but rather the fortune seeking private merchant who came on his own account or as an agent for an Amsterdam company. New Netherland began to abound with rootless, private traders whose only interest was in the profits which the fur trade offered. Not only did they compete with the old inhabitants of New Netherland but they tended to drive the price of both furs and goods up. Secretary van Tienhoven charged that these private traders added a 100–200 per cent markup to goods which they brought with them from the Netherlands.[15] By 1643 the West India Company began to complain that:

> *The plan of opening the trade to said place, produces no true effect according to the intent, inasmuch as many will go thither to trade without acquiring a domicile there; and therefore, population scarcely increases there, whilst trade is seriously ruined.*[16]

Both the company and those who considered themselves old inhabitants of New Netherland, were greatly disturbed by this influx of private traders. The inhabitants proposed taxing the private traders, since those "who had drawn excessive profits from the country, by their injurious usury, should contribute something to the public service."[17] For its part the West India Company considered from time to time restricting the trade to inhabitants or to those who would at least maintain a domicile in New Netherland.[18]

The furor touched off by the activities of the private traders was not an easy matter for the West India Company to deal with. It involved one of the most difficult, recurring problems of these years — how to determine who was a temporary and who a permanent resident of New Netherland? There was so much coming and going in the years before 1639, when the company had mainly looked upon its servants and others as so many transient laborers, that few could have laid claim to having been in the colony since its beginning in 1623. Men such as O. S. van Cortlandt, Thomas Hall, Hendrick Hendricksen Kip, who had been in New Netherland no more than eight to twelve years, referred to themselves in 1649 as "We . . . who have resided there a considerable time."[19] And many signers of the "Remonstrance of 1649," leaders of New Netherland in the fight against the West India Company, could remember little before the beginning of Kieft's administration in 1638 since "most of us were not here at that time." [20]

Thus in the years following 1639 it was not easy to distinguish between petty private traders and men who, while engaged in trading, claimed to be devoting their chief energies solely to the better development of New Netherland. For the men who became spokesmen for the inhabitants — or "commonalty" as they came to be called — in the struggles with the West India Company during the years 1642–1650 were themselves comparative newcomers to New Netherland. A number of highly ambitious men, many of them young, began arriving in New Netherland in the last years of the 1630's. Many of them were undoubtedly attracted by the opportunity to participate in the fur trade. But all were interested in seeking their fortunes one way or another in New Netherland.

Adriaen van der Donck arrived in Rensselaerswyck in 1641 as a young man of twenty-one. Frustrated in his desire to become director of the patroon's colony, he severed his official connection in 1643. He continued to operate a farm there and to engage in a variety of ventures throughout New Netherland before taking up residence in Manhattan in 1646. He married the daughter of the Rev. Francis Doughty, the controversial English minister who was one of the original patentees in 1642 of the English town of Mespath (Newton) on Long Island.[21]

Olaf Stevenson van Cortlandt came to New Netherland as a soldier in the service of the West India Company in 1637. His brother-in-law, Govert Loockermans, had preceded him to New Netherland four years earlier. Loockermans was a factor for the Amsterdam firm of Gillis Verbruggen and Company. Favored by Director Kieft, van Cortlandt held a number of company posts in New Netherland from which he prospered. Michael Jansen Vreeland was a servant of van Rensselaer when he first arrived and apparently did so well that he was reported to have "made his fortune in a few years in the Colonie." By 1646 he, too, had taken up residence in Manhattan.[22] Jan Evertsen Bout had been in New Netherland several times before he became an official at the patroonship of Pavonia in 1634. He later moved to Brooklyn where he farmed, traded, and speculated in real estate.[23] Jacob van Couwenhoven was an official under van Twiller and a tobacco planter at Manhattan. While in Amsterdam in 1650,

Bout, van der Donck, and van Couwenhoven served as contractors for supplying and transporting two hundred emigrants to New Netherland.[24]

David de Vries, merchant in the East Indies, merchant-skipper to Newfoundland and Italy, and an ambitious place-seeker who had tried to unseat van Twiller as Director, took up residence in New Netherland in 1638 and devoted his energies to developing a colony on Staten Island.[25] An acquaintance and fellow East Indian merchant of de Vries' who had been in Danish service, Jochem Pietersz. Kuyter, came to New Netherland in 1639 and also began a colony.[26] Cornelis Melyn, a friend of both these men, arrived in 1639 and began his own colony. Melyn had previously shipped many times as supercargo for Kiliaen van Rensselaer to such places as Canada, France, and New Netherland.[27] Augustine Herrman, son of a Prague merchant, was a latecomer to New Netherland, not arriving on the scene until 1643. He came as a commercial agent or factor for one of Amsterdam's leading mercantile companies, Gabry and Company.[28]

These men became the leaders of the so-called "commonalty" of New Netherland. Beginning in 1642 these men, variously referred to as the "Twelve," the "Eight," or the "Nine," contested with the officials of the West India Company in New Netherland and at home for control over the future development of New Netherland. Appealing over the heads of the directors of the company to the States-General at a time when the company was seeking subsidies and a renewal of its charter, they came close to having their own way in New Netherland. Their tilts with the company in the years 1642–1650 served to keep New Netherland in a continual state of turmoil. But their efforts ultimately contributed in some measure to the development of a recognizable social order in New Netherland.

The struggle between the leaders of the "commonalty" and the West India Company grew out of the condition of New Netherland which resulted from the rapid pace of development in the years 1638–1642. Inhabitants and new immigrants had ranged widely throughout New Netherland in quest of furs and flat, cultivable land. Emigration from the Netherlands had been prodded by the company's offer of free passage. And people from Virginia and New England crossed over the boundaries into New Netherland to plant tobacco or to escape the regimen of a tightly ruled Puritan colony. A description in 1643 noted that among the population of Manhattan "there were men of eighteen different languages." And while the established religion was Calvinism, "this is not observed; for besides the Calvinists there are in the colony Catholics, English Puritans, Lutherans, Anabaptists . . . etc." [29] Besides the start of English colonies in New Netherland, people such as Cornelis Melyn, David de Vries, and Myndert Meyndertsz. had also begun colonies which showed great signs of promise. Indeed, the future of New Netherland as a whole seemed bright, and "there was an appearance of producing supplies in a year for fourteen thousand souls, without straightening the country." But even in flourishing times the plea was for more population, for "had there not been a want of laborers or farm servants, twice as much could be raised." [30]

The accelerated rate of development, however, had been accompanied by severe growing pains. The increase in population and the movement of people throughout New Netherland in these years gave the Indians cause for alarm. For the first time they began to feel pressed by the advance of the New Netherlanders into the interior. Some of the inhabitants tried to make servants of the Indians, while others plied them with liquor and sold them guns and powder in return for great quantities of furs. The outcome of this intense period of activity in New Netherland might well have been predicted — an Indian uprising and an Indian war. It came, and it was called "Kieft's War," after New Netherland's Director-General during these years.

The Indian scare demanded the formulation of an Indian policy. And yet in a community so diverse and so highly individualistic, unanimity could hardly have been expected. In 1641 Director Kieft consulted with the inhabitants, who chose representatives to advise him of their views on the matter — the "Twelve" as they were called. In 1643 the "Twelve" became the "Eight" which, however, did little to reduce the division of opinion which prevailed. Nearly everyone was in favor of attacking the Indians but few could agree on when or where such an assault should take place. The divided opinion of the "commonalty" produced only anxiety and procrastination. When Kieft eventually took action he was attacked by members of the "commonalty" for being a warmonger. Because he drowned on his return to the Netherlands in 1648, his side of the story could only be asserted by subordinates or friends. And yet it seems clear that the "commonalty" was no less inclined to war against the Indians, provided the time and place was "subject to God and opportunity." The

"Journal of New Netherland" stated the problem well: "occupied as each one was, in taking care of his own, nothing beneficial was adopted at that time." [31]

The main activity of the Indian wars in the years 1641–1643 occurred on the frontiers of New Netherland — on Staten Island, Long Island, in Westchester County, and in Pavonia (Jersey City). These areas coincided with the centers of recent Dutch settlement efforts. The Indians not only resented the intrusions of the whites into what had been hitherto unspoiled territory, but were forced into daily contact with the settlers from which incidents were bound to result. It was a potentially explosive situation which required little to touch off war at any time. Tempers flared, fears emboldened men to hasty action, and when peace returned the results were much the same as in any other Indian/white encounter — many more Indians than white men were killed and the land remained in possession of the white settlers.[32]

The conduct of the war became a cause célèbre. Director Kieft and his supporters were castigated as the prime instigators of the war who had inflicted great suffering and damage on New Netherland because of their bitter and unreasonable hatred of the Indians. Kieft and his supporters, on the other hand, placed the blame on the inhabitants' aggressive grasping after furs and land which had spread the population so thin as to invite Indian attack. Charges and counter-charges filled the air on both sides of the Atlantic. Historians have taken sides on the question, blaming one individual or another as chiefly responsible. The evidence, however, is not such as to indict or exonerate fully any single individual. Both the charges and counter-charges were probably in large measure true.

To the men of the times, the issue of the war was cast in extremely personal terms. But it was also intimately bound up with the problem of how a community in the wilderness of New Netherland should be organized. Disappointments arising out of the precarious nature of life in New Netherland found their focus in the issue of the war. The running battle between the "commonalty" of New Netherland and the West India Company, which began as a result of the Indian uprising and which was argued in terms of Indian policy, was actually a struggle over the organization of society and settlement in New Netherland. It was fed by the hardships and disappointments encountered there and involved the personal interests of a number of highly ambitious and intensely opinionated men. The struggle, moreover, was framed by the slowly emerging awareness that the development of a differentiated society — based on an agricultural economy operated by European immigrants — might well provide a comfortable living to those who would make their permanent home in New Netherland. This was a new awareness for immigrants coming to New Netherland and it was derived in large measure from the example of the English in North America. Unplanned and with little conscious awareness on their part, the English in North America were developing a model of colonial success far different from either the East Indian or Spanish model. New Netherlanders, in close touch with developments throughout North America, slowly began to see both the virtues and the possibilities of such an approach.

The leaders of the commonalty were after more than the figurative scalp of Kieft, for even when he was replaced by Stuyvesant in 1647 their struggle with the West India Company continued. What they sought was a greater influence in the management of affairs in New Netherland. From the first petition of the "Twelve" in January 1642 it becomes clear that the demands revolved around a greater participation in the offices of government. At that time it was requested that four members of the commonalty be permitted to appear in the Council to represent the interests of the inhabitants. They also suggested that the Council, essentially composed of the officers of the company, ought to increase its members to five so that it might better resemble "the Council of a small village in Fatherland." Kieft was obviously annoyed at this bid for power and thought it odd "that the commonalty should comment considerably on the smallness of the Council." He pointed out that the question, after all, was "whether any one has cause to complain of unjust decisions." [33]

But the question of government touched on here was precisely the point in the struggles between the commonalty and the West India Company in the years after 1641. It seems clear that both held the same view of government and that it was a static conception brought with them from home. But their remembered view of government was predicated on a traditional, well ordered society in which most people knew their place by custom. Whatever social mobility there was at home was easily accommodated within a long established framework of society. In New Netherland, however, there was no long established framework and it was notorious that people there neither knew their place nor kept it. Thus while the company officials and the leaders of the commonalty shared the same view of what government ideally ought to be, neither felt that it was even being approximated in New Netherland. The leaders of the commonalty accused Kieft of hankering after "princely power and authority." [34] They complained bitterly:

> . . . that one man who has been sent out, sworn and instructed by his Lords and masters, to whom he is responsible, should dispose here of our lives and properties at his will and pleasure, in a manner so arbitrary that a King dare not legally do the like.[35]

The company officials for their part looked upon the efforts of the leaders of the commonalty as so many attempts "to rid themselves of all government," and the leaders themselves as ones who wished "to live without government or order." [36]

As the struggle progressed, it became clear that what the leaders of the commonalty wanted was to eliminate the company from the direction of affairs and to install themselves in positions of government.[37] They repeatedly insisted that the government of New Netherland should only be entrusted to those who were most interested in the country — by which, of course, they meant themselves. "It is impossible ever to settle this country," the leaders of the commonalty wrote in 1644, "until a different system be introduced here. . . ." [38] The company, on the other hand, upheld the system and denounced the leaders of the commonalty, who "by their complaints would fain filch the country from the Company, and pay nothing." [39]

At issue between the leaders of the commonalty and the West India Company was a proper definition of public interest in New Netherland. The company looked with suspicion on private traders such as Melyn and de Vries who were so vociferous in championing the public interest of New Netherland so soon after they had arrived there. The history of their entrepreneurial activities before coming to New Netherland was not such as to inspire confidence in the extent of their commitment or devotion to this new country. Were they interested merely in quick profits or did they have some long range plan for the development of New Netherland? The officials of the company really had no sure grounds for answering these questions. Did these men who had only been in the country a few years but who claimed to be the leaders of the commonalty intend to reside permanently in New Netherland? There was really no way of knowing at the time. De Vries later returned to the Netherlands after a series of disappointments. Melyn and Herrman stayed on. But after the struggle of the forties had spent itself, they found better futures elsewhere — the one in New Haven and the other in Maryland.[40] Nor was the company reassured by the leaders' protestations of devotion to New Netherland when nearly each petition was accompanied by veiled threats of their removing to the English settlements in North America if their demands were not acceded to.

The company had had a great deal of experience in the years before 1639 with men who had used their official position in New Netherland to further their own private interest. If they viewed private interest in New Netherland with a somewhat jaundiced eye, their experience with the patroons over the years was enough to confirm and sustain their innate suspicion. As late as 1660 the directors were even skeptical of the intent of one of their former colleagues, Baron Hendrick van de Capellen, when he began to seek patroon's privileges for the development of Staten Island.[41] Patroon van Rensselaer was no less skeptical than the company of the intentions of highly ambitious individuals who used their connection with Rensselaerswyck to advance their own fortunes. "No man should have too much" was the advice which van Rensselaer tried to impart to his officials in the colony as he attempted to deal with the problem of private interest in opposition to his own interest.[42]

If there was a question of the capacity of private individuals pursuing their own interest to adopt a larger public view, there was also the question of whether the company itself could adopt such a course. In the eyes of the leaders of the commonalty, the West India Company could hardly pass as the repository of any purely detached public interest. And it was indeed difficult for the company to draw the line between commercial interest and public interest in its dealings with New Netherland. The company's servants were frequently known to "bite sharp and carry away" while performing their functions of commercial regulation and collecting duties owed to the company on goods shipped to or from New Netherland.[43] The mixture of private and public interest extended even to the Directors in New Netherland, who,

. . . being at a distance from their masters, looked close to their own advantage. They have always known how to manage their own affairs handsomely, with little loss to themselves, yet under plausible pretexts, such as public interest & c.[44]

In their denunciations of the company, the leaders of the commonalty did not spare the directors at home, whom they regarded as having "adopted wrong plans and in our opinion looked more to their own profit than to the country's welfare, and turned more to interested than to sound advice." [45]

In sifting such charges and counter-charges it is difficult to see just where any "sound advice" on public interest might have been found. Both the company and the leaders of the commonalty identified their own interest with notions of a detached public interest. It was easy for both to condemn the actions of the petty traders to New Netherland as destructive of the public interest. But the question might well be raised whether their attack on the petty traders proceeded from a concern for any public interest or from the threat which the petty traders posed to their own interests in New Netherland. Both the company's officials and the leaders of the commonalty held up an image of a well ordered, prosperous, and populous New Netherland as the object of their strivings, but when it came to implementing plans for the development of this, both insisted that their way was the only correct way.

The ringing, highly formalistic rhetoric which attended the clashes between these two groups on the surface has managed to obscure the large measure of general agreement existing between their views on the condition of New Netherland and the course which its future development ought to take. There was, for example, no disagreement between the officials of the company and the leaders of the commonalty on the necessity of populating New Netherland if it were ever to amount to anything. Both groups made efforts to enlist people to cross the Atlantic. Many more merchants than farmers were attracted to New Netherland which did little to alleviate the crying need for the latter. But the fact was that it seemed impossible to obtain many farmers in the Netherlands who were willing to emigrate. Frequently the company sent over a number of people whom they supposed were farmers only to discover that it had unwittingly added to the number of petty traders there. "We regret to learn," the company's directors wrote to Stuyvesant:

*. . . that so little advantage is to be expected from the free
people who, from time to time, have been conveyed thither at
the Company's expense; in regard that the third part are not
what they represented themselves here, namely agriculturists and
such like.*[46]

Amsterdam merchants were so familiar with this problem that
when the City of Amsterdam started its colony of New Amstel on the
Delaware they urged:

*No Hollanders but other foreign nations must be employed and
attracted for this purpose, the Swedes and Fins (who are already
there in reasonable numbers) being, among others, hereunto
particularly fitting. . . .*

But it was a difficult task to recruit foreigners and it was a slow process to rely on their being "notified by their Countrymen in the aforesaid Colonie of the good opportunity there." [47]

The leaders of the commonalty tended to regard the efforts of the
company on recruiting population for New Netherland as weak and
ineffective. And they attributed the failure of the company to obtain
emigrants not to the difficulties of recruiting but rather to the "company's harsh proceedings and want of means." The argument was
somewhat circuitous but it provided them with an explanation for
the poor condition of New Netherland and a point on which to attack the company in their own quest for a freer hand in New Netherland. The company quite reasonably took offense when many of the
"farm laborers" they sent out turned traders once they arrived and
then lashed back at the company for failing to populate the country.
The problem of population could readily be solved, according to the
commonalty leaders, if all ships were merely obliged to transport
some emigrants to New Netherland on each voyage. In the face of experience to the contrary and with no recognition of the difficulties of
the problem, they weakly insisted that then "many friends would, no
doubt, emigrate within a short time to New Netherland." [48]

There was also a great degree of underlying agreement between the
leaders of the commonalty and the company on the necessity of consolidating settlement in New Netherland. Indeed, the company had
long championed such an orderly approach to the development of

New Netherland. Kieft himself had attempted to put such a policy into effect during the years when the rapid increase in population took place. The company found it strange, then, when the future organization of settlement in towns or villages became a demand of the leaders of the commonalty and also one of their grievances against the company. The company was accused of paying more attention to the fur trade than to providing for the closer grouping of people in New Netherland.[49]

Thus the inhabitants blamed all the ills of New Netherland on the company and the ruinous policy they alleged it had followed. A petition of the leaders of the commonalty to the States-General, dated July 26, 1649, summed up its indictment of company policy by listing the causes of the "very poor and most low condition" of New Netherland. The causes, the petition stated:

> *We presume to be First, Unsuitable government; 2 Scanty*
> *privileges and exemptions; 3 Onerous imposts and duties, ex-*
> *actions and such like; 4 Long Continued War; 5 The loss of the*
> *Princess; 6 A superabundance of Petty Traders and pedlars and*
> *a want of Farmers and Farm servants; 7 great dearth in general;*
> *8 and lastly, the insufferable arrogance of the Natives or Indians*
> *arising from our small number, etc.*

They then proceeded to show how the company was responsible in each instance for what had happened.[50]

The surviving literature on the struggle between the leaders of the commonalty and the company contains point-by-point indictments of the one, together with point-by-point refutations by the other. The language of the literature consists largely of half-truths, innuendoes, insinuations, outrageous overstatements, and incredibly petty personal character attacks. The verification of most of the statements would be an impossible task to undertake and in all probability an unrewarding one. A few examples will convey the flavor of the literature. Under a section entitled "Of Justice," the leaders of the commonalty charged:

> *The Directors have written to Kieft that he, instituting an action*
> *against the Colonists should, where there was no cause of action*
> *count one default, and reckon half a fault as a whole one. . . .*

In a section pompously labeled "Of the Church, Ecclesiastical Property and Benevolent Institutions," it was charged that "The Directors have made no effort to convert to Christianity either the Indians or the Blacks or Slaves, owned by the Company there." Replying to the first charge, the Company demanded proof that the statement had ever been made, adding "They cannot believe that such orders emanated from the Assembly (of the XIX)." As for the second charge, the company retorted:

> *Every one conversant with Indians in, and around New Nether-*
> *land, will be able to say, that it is morally impossible to convert*
> *the adults to the Christian faith. Besides, 'tis a Minister's business*
> *to apply himself to that, and the Director's duty to assist him*
> *therein.*

And so the charges and counter-charges ran on, numbering into the sixties. Charges were parried rather than answered; hearsay advanced seriously as truth.[51]

To cast the struggle between the West India Company and the leaders of the commonalty in terms of a contest between the forces of tyranny and the forces of democracy, or between a grasping commercial company and a struggling group of freemen, fails to do justice to the dimensions of the historical problem involved. In their respective visions of what New Netherland ought to be like if it were properly developed, there was fundamentally very little difference between the two groups. Even in their approach to the steps that needed to be taken in order to develop New Netherland there was general agreement. The wide gulf which separated them was caused by their inability to see the magnitude of the task before them — the task of building a society in the wilderness of New Netherland composed of transplanted Europeans. And there was good reason for this.

The Dutch had neither knowingly nor consciously entered upon this task. No European nation had fully done so. From its discovery in 1609, New Netherland's lure had been the possibilities it offered for commercial exploitation. Private merchants and the incorporated merchants of the West India Company had approached New Netherland in this fashion and not with any view of establishing a permanent society on its shores. In the early years of West India Company activity in New Netherland, the people sent to reside there were not

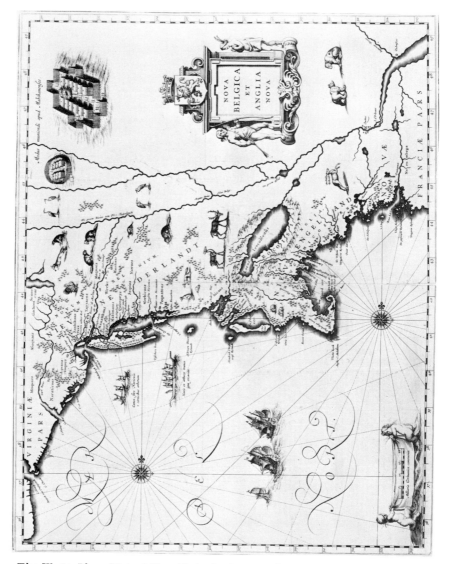

The W. Jz. Blaeu Map of New Netherland, 1635. This map, copied by Blaeu from Adriaen Block's Figurative Map and entitled "Nova Belgica et Anglia Nova," contained the first use of the name "Nieu Amsterdam." Courtesy of the J. Clarence Davies Collection, Museum of the City of New York.

NOVA AMSTELDA

The Ffort and Cittie of New Amsterdam. The de Wit view about 1652. Copper engraving. Courtesy of the Museum of the City of New York.

NIEUW AMSTERDAM OFTE NUE NIEUW IORX OFT TEYLANT MAN

New Amsterdam Now New York on the Island of Man(hattan) 1650–1653. View taken from the East River. The prototype view. Reproduction of a water-color drawing (probably by Vinckeboons). Courtesy of the Museum of the City of New York.

regarded as forming a separate society, distinct or cut off from the
Netherlands. Rather, they were seen as overseas employees, integral
members of society in the Netherlands who would in all probability
return home on the expiration of their contracts or, in the case of free
men, when they struck it rich. Emigration was looked upon not in
terms of severance but of circulation. In 1634, for example, a new
charter of "Freedoms and Exemptions" made explicit reference to this
circulating view of emigration:

> *Their High Mightinesses shall exert themselves to provide the*
> *Patroons with persons bound to service, who shall be obliged to*
> *serve out their bounded time, in all obedience, for their board*
> *and clothing only, which being done, on bringing to this country*
> *a certificate thereof from the Patroons or their Commissaries,*
> *such persons shall be here restored to their former state and*
> *freedom.*[52]

Before 1639 many Netherlanders and other nationalities circulated
between New Netherland and wherever home happened to be. Some,
of course, stayed on, finding life in New Netherland bearable even
though they had been disappointed in their expectations of wealth.

Even within these small colonies of Europeans in New Netherland,
at Manhattan or Rensselaerswyck, the need for institutions and the
need to recreate remembered ways was present. Present, too, was the
need for a recognizable social hierarchy in which to place others as
well as oneself. In a group so mixed as to nationality and yet so similar in social origins and personal ambitions, the establishment of any
social order proved to be a difficult task. The same factors made it
difficult to maintain the identity of interest which the directors at
home had presumed would exist between them and their overseas
laborers. Cut loose physically from society at home, they seemed to
show allegiance primarily to their own private interest. They strug-
gled for existence, working out their contracts or drifting off on their
own. Never large in numbers, and widely dispersed, there were few
elements present in New Netherland to contribute to the stability of
the colony, much less to the development of an institutional life with
any continuity. Indeed, there was little if any awareness of the need
for the creation of a separate institutional life. Their sojourn in New
Netherland was, after all, seen in temporary terms. Before 1639 New
Netherland may well be compared to pre-Puritan Massachusetts.

With the influx of people after 1639 a new understanding of the possibilities of New Netherland began to emerge. Experience slowly acquired began to alter men's views of New Netherland. But altered, too, was the situation of North America when compared, for example, to 1623. There were now many Europeans dwelling throughout the continent. To the south in 1642 there were ten thousand Englishmen; to the north, perhaps another ten thousand.[53] The activities of these large numbers not only provided a model of what might be done through the development of agriculture but their mere presence meant a market for goods as well.

It is difficult to draw the line between when New Netherland was regarded primarily as an area of temporary residence to be exploited and when it began to be considered as an area where something more might be accomplished.

In the case of the company, the directors inherited a largely commercial approach to New Netherland and elements of this persisted even as the possibilities of permanently populating it took on a new urgency. In a detailed and lengthy report of the company in 1648 this new awareness began to appear. The report noted that the,

> . . . places within the Charter where the Company maintains government, forts, or quarters, ought to be considered under two divisions, some being of a nature not to demand any cultivation or population, affording simply trade; others again, where the lands must necessarily be first improved by population if they are to render any return of moment.[54]

New Netherland was, of course, in the second division. In the company's new view, New Netherland might become a bread basket colony, supplying provisions to Brazil and other areas in the West Indies. But even the new approach was mixed with elements of an earlier mode of operations and no clear view of how New Netherland might be developed was yet articulated. For the company also recommended that slave labor in New Netherland:

> . . . be more extensively cultivated than it has hitherto been, because the agricultural laborers who are conveyed thither at great expense to the colonies, sooner or later apply themselves to trade, and neglect agriculture altogether.[55]

And the new policy was also seen more in terms of what it might do for unemployment in the Netherlands than in terms of engaging the nation in building a society in New Netherland.[56]

Nor in the case of the inhabitants themselves can any clear line be drawn between their seeing it as the place of a temporary job or opportunity for quick profit and as a place of permanency, where an agriculturally based society might be erected. In the beginning they, too, were mainly interested in the profits of the fur trade and whatever else offered itself for quick exploitation. Gradually, for the inhabitants, a close scrutiny of developments in New England and Virginia was decisive in crystallizing a new view. Throughout the controversy of the 40's, the leaders of the commonalty cited the experience of the English in North America, particularly in New England. Their knowledge of what was taking place there was quite detailed, indicating a degree of intercolonial cooperation in the seventeenth century which deserves closer analysis by historians. In reiterating their demands for immigrants and greater privileges, the leaders of the commonalty were quite explicit: "New England and Virginia especially, afford a clear example that this policy causes prosperity." [57]

Prices of cattle, livestock, and goods in New England circulated readily to New Netherland. Secretary Tienhoven even had in his possession a list of "Public Charges in New England." [58] And the details of government in New England were carefully used by the leaders of the commonalty to suggest that the inhabitants of New Netherland should likewise play a greater role in the direction and management of their own affairs. In requesting the introduction of municipal government in New Netherland, the example of New England was again emphasized as well as reference made to local government in the Netherlands. They wanted a form that was "suitable," "adapted to this Province, and somewhat resembling the laudable government of our Fatherland." They clarified this by adding "in form of a State, like the government of this country [the Netherlands], especially as in this case there is no difference, but fundamentally a similarity between it and our neighbors of New England." [59]

But while an awareness that New Netherland had possibilities beyond quick exploitation began to emerge on both sides of the Atlantic, an understanding of precisely how New Netherland might get in step with New England was necessarily vague. The definition of the steps to be taken constituted the point of division between the company and the leaders of the commonalty. And, in balance, this cleavage resulted not because of personalities or malice on either side, but rather from a gross misunderstanding by both groups of the difficulties and expense involved in creating a society in New Netherland.

The costs of establishing a society overseas were enormously high and yet they were universally underestimated by all European nations involved in settlement in the seventeenth century. As Pares has pointed out, the most essential thing was the "mere removal of the colonist from one side of the ocean to another." And "at the very least, it was a costly business to charter shipping and to feed the emigrants, perhaps even before they got on board." [60] Certainly the West India Company was aware of the costs and while it paid for the passage of many an immigrant to New Netherland, the directors found it annoying when some of them turned traders. The inhabitants, on the other hand, took a rather cavalier attitude toward the costs of emigration and expected the company or the States-General to provide willingly ample funds for this purpose. When attacked for their attitude on this, they tended to respond merely with platitudes such as "People are bound to pray for their benefactors, and if they do not, virtue is always its own reward and God recompenses it." [61] To the private individuals, to the company, and to the States-General, who were all constantly harangued for their failure to support emigration vigorously enough, such an approach was not likely to make purses any more responsive.

The expectation of the inhabitants that the company or others should lay out vast sums of money altruistically or with only a long-term hope of profit was not confined merely to the matter of immigration. It extended throughout the range of public requirements. Time and again the leaders of the commonalty and the company crossed swords in a way which indicated that there could be no meeting of minds on two such conflicting attitudes toward public expenses. The leaders of the commonalty charged that "The Company hath never yet undertaken anything special for the advantage of New Netherland whereby it has improved." The reply of the company was invariably the same, "We think the Company has done enough." The directors of the company replied hotly to such insinuations in one case by a personal reference, "to wit, in carrying over at the Company's expense, numbers of people, among whom were Jacob Couwenhoven's father and brothers, together with cattle and other necessaries." [62] Couwenhoven was one of the leaders of the commonalty, loud in his denunciations of the niggardly policy of the company. The hard attitude of each group toward the behavior of the other ruled out any rational discussion of the issues involved. The company always felt it was doing more than it financially should, considering the fact that the colony had always been a loss. The inhabitants, on the other hand, always felt that the company never did enough. But how much was enough? And who could determine this? No answers could reasonably be given to such questions.[63] They became instead the focus of polemical disputation.

The leaders of the commonalty complained bitterly of the company's failure to provide such things as churches, schoolhouses, and even orphan asylums to minister to the institutional needs of the people. In a fit of pique at one point an official of the company in New Netherland inquired,

> *Are the company or the Directors obliged to have constructed*
> *any buildings for the people out of the duties paid by the trader*
> *in New Netherland on exported goods, particularly as their High*
> *Mightinesses granted those duties to the Company to facilitate*
> *garrisons and the payment of the expenses attendant thereupon,*
> *and not for building Hospitals and Orphan Asylums, Churches*
> *and School-houses for the people.*[64]

Secretary van Tienhoven attempted to demonstrate, besides, that the company had spent a great deal on public buildings in New Netherland with little gratitude shown by the inhabitants. Credit subscriptions, for example, were made by the inhabitants for the erection of a church but the company disbursed the funds and was still owed the money in most cases. In Kieft's War the inhabitants went so far as to offer to mortgage New Netherland to the English in return for their assistance against the Indians. As it was, the support of the English troops was paid for by drafts drawn on the credit of the company.[65]

"If the people require institutions," van Tienhoven stated, "they must contribute toward them as is the custom in this country." [66] Such a plea fell on deaf ears as far as the inhabitants were concerned. There were few wealthy inhabitants who had emigrated to New Netherland, unlike New England as it was pointed out, and so the inhabitants felt that the company should absorb all such charges.[67]

The company officials in New Netherland attempted to turn the arguments of the leaders of the commonalty around when they continually cited the example of New England. Although there was greater participation of the inhabitants of New England in the management of their affairs there, the officials pointed out that New Englanders also took upon their own shoulders the support of public requirements. Van Tienhoven noted that "all expenses, allowances and wages are also proportioned there among the people." [68] The leaders of the commonalty offered no direct reply.

The "Remonstrance of New Netherland," published in the Netherlands in 1650 by the agents of the commonalty, contained the clearest statement of the recognition that a new view toward New Netherland had in fact emerged.[69] It was also in many ways the most unjust attack on the company. Armed with a new insight into the future course of New Netherland's development, the writers of the "Remonstrance" went after the company with infallible hindsight. In effect they blamed the company for not having recognized that New Netherland should have been developed as a permanent, agriculturally based society from the beginning. They had "adopted wrong plans" which only meant that "unnecessary expenses [were] incurred from time to time." Admitting that the company had brought some livestock and people to New Netherland, the "Remonstrance" however, accused the company of failing because "it did not persevere, so that little advantage followed; it had, also, no proper commencement, for 'twas done as if without any plan." In fact, of course, it was not a question of perseverence but of experience having engendered a new conception of the potentialities of New Netherland. That the "Remonstrance" was based on this new perception, drawn largely from an intimate knowledge of New England on the part of the commonalty's leaders, is apparent from the frequent references to the model which New England now presented for the development of North America. Had the West India Company only acted purposefully along the same lines, the writers suggested, "New England would not have outstripped us so much." After twenty-seven years of experimentation and heavy financial loss on the part of the company, this was perhaps the cruelest attack that could be made.[70]

The basic attitude of the two groups toward each other, and their combined misapprehension and underestimation of the dimensions of the problem, made an impasse inevitable. But the ire of the company's directors was aroused even more when the leaders of the commonalty appealed over their heads to the States-General to air their grievances. Ineffective as that body was, it could stir up a hornet's nest by requests for information and by endless discussions of the difficulties that were complained of. At a time when the West India Company was itself seeking a new charter and subsidies to support its far-flung commitments, the leaders of the commonalty sought to have the States-General take New Netherland under its immediate administrative control and remove entirely the influence of the company in New Netherland.

The leaders of the commonalty hoped by such a step to receive greater financial support for emigration and greater financial assistance for the establishment of public institutions. Their aim was clear:

> *Your High Mightinesses must at first meet the outlays. For the country cannot sink in the beginning into helplessness, and New Netherland will come into condition if some gentlemen privately, or what in our opinion would be better, if your High Mightinesses were to make some disbursements.*[71]

The company was outraged by this approach of the leaders of the commonalty, insisting that "they would have performed their duty much better, had they first submitted to their Lords and Patroons [the company] whatever observations they might intend to offer." [72] They were more than annoyed by the uproar which the delegates from New Netherland were creating in the Netherlands and which was upsetting the company's plans for getting subsidies for itself. The company countered by stringing out the discussions to great length and by attempting to inconvenience the delegates of the commonalty as much as possible.

The hope of the leaders of the commonalty was an unrealistic one. After urging their advice on the company, the States-General in the end perforce had to go along with the policy of the West India Company. It could not directly administer New Netherland itself, much less undertake the heavy subsidization which the leaders of the commonalty anticipated. The company made it quite clear that the "country belongs exclusively to them" and not to the States-General. It was reported in New Netherland that "The Directors have written not to pay any attention to their High Mightinesses' safeguards or letters, but to theirs." Van der Donck, one of the commonalty's agents, reported that he had been informed that "their High Mightinesses had not the least authority over New Netherland." [73] And this was true in an effective administrative sense. The result was that the leaders of the commonalty lost their battle in the Netherlands to have New Netherland become a direct charge of the States-General. When the States-General brought up complaints of the same nature about New Netherland again in 1652, the company replied in a manner which clearly conveys the relationship of the company to the States-General:

> We cannot omit observing that we have already communicated our opinion in writing on the aforesaid draft . . . and have conferred, at divers times since, with the Lords, and your High Mightinesses' deputies, so that we concluded that your High Mightinesses had designated laying aside the unfounded complaints of the Delegates and ill-affected Committee of some malcontents in New Netherland, and we are surprised at a draft being now brought up, which for so long a time has been considered as disposed of.[74]

In the final analysis the problem was much too large for the leaders of the commonalty or the company to win or lose in such an encounter. It gradually became clear to everyone that the Netherlands simply could not effectively populate New Netherland, and the apprehension, perhaps even resignation, rose that it would only be a matter of time before English encroachments would overpower the West India Company's colony in North America. It gradually became clear also that the dimensions of the task of forming a society in New Netherland far exceeded the expectations of all groups concerned. Such a task required great experimentation and much building on earlier failures. There were no simple answers to the difficulties involved in this task and the experience of New Netherland on this point amply attested to the fact that there were also no guidelines:

> "Tis not with us as in our Fatherland, or as in Kingdoms and Republics which are established and settled by long and well experienced laws and fundamentals, best agreeing with the condition of the people. But in our little body, made up of divers members, namely folks of different nations, many things occur

in the laying of a foundation for which there are no rules nor examples. . . .[75]

The importance of the struggle between the leaders of the commonalty and the company in the decade of the 40's was that it helped to lay the foundation of a social order in New Netherland. And it was the undercurrents of the social struggle taking place in New Netherland that so charged the atmosphere of the controversy. The "Eight," the "Twelve," and the "Nine" were no more than *ad hoc* groups, composed of individuals who considered that their voice should carry some weight in the management of affairs in New Netherland. To trace the roots of such groups back to ancient Dutch practices tends to obscure the social struggle of which they were a manifestation. Rootless, these groups also did not perpetuate themselves over the final years of the history of New Netherland. Once municipal government was formed in New Amsterdam, such titles and such groups dropped quickly from view.

That any "commonalty" arose as a group and elected these men as their representatives, cannot be imagined in a community so diverse and drawn from such similar social backgrounds. Rather, the reverse was true, that the leading figures elected the population to "commonalty" status. There was too much emphasis on formality and procedure to suggest any sense of easy familiarity with positions of government and authority. The highly legalistic and formalistic petitions and grievances, which portrayed the struggle in classical terms, were the work of two individuals with legal trainings — van der Donck and van Dincklagen — neither of whom had probably ever practiced law or held positions of authority in the Netherlands. Van Tienhoven was caught at one time by the leaders of the commonalty inserting in the record the words "the whole of the commonalty" to suggest that the people in New Netherland were supporting the company's position.[76]

In a society so nearly equal in terms of social background, individuals expected that the titles they bore would grant them what their experience or birth could not. The leaders of the commonalty saw no difference between themselves and the officials who were placed in positions of authority over them. In the decade of the 40's the leaders of the commonalty challenged the officials on these grounds; the officials fought back on the same grounds. The officials of the company in New Netherland complained of the need for "persons of rank" in the country to occupy seats in the Council rather than appointing them from the leaders of the commonalty, who were described as those men who "separated themselves from the well-disposed and secretly induced a few low inhabitants to sign their names." [77] Both sides went out of their way to refer to the presumed social qualifications of their own men. The fact that van der Donck and van Dincklagen were "Doctors of Law" was frequently mentioned. The "Remonstrance" touched on the essentially social nature of the struggle in New Netherland when it noted that the leaders of the commonalty were made out to be "about the biggest villains in the country, where they had shortly before been recognized the best of persons and most deserving of children." [78]

The leaders of the commonalty were successful in obtaining the right to organize the municipal government of New Amsterdam in 1653. And with this began the first local institution of government in New Netherland with any real roots and with any continuity of development. The eleven years between the establishment of local government in New Amsterdam and the coming of the English in 1664 hardly provided sufficient time for Dutch institutions of government to impress any distinctive cast on the society of New Netherland. The social struggle of the 40's, however, had created the outlines of a social structure in New Netherland which made it possible for the men at the top to shift easily to new forms once the English took over. The struggle of the 40's had created a base on which institutional life could be built and from which a distinctive society in New Netherland might have emerged had there been time.

EPILOGUE

An era came dramatically to a close on September 8, 1664 when Director-General Peter Stuyvesant and the garrison of Fort Amsterdam marched out with "drums beating and colors flying" to surrender up the province of New Netherland to the English Colonel Richard Nicolls. The grave formality of the scene, actually comic when contrasted with the conditions of life in America in 1664, was by no means an unusual practice in the New World during the seventeenth century and, indeed, had been insisted upon by Stuyvesant a few days earlier. Amid such fanfare New Netherland became New York and, with the exception of a brief six-month interlude of no lasting consequence in 1673–1674, remained an English province until the Revolution.

To the English Colonel the surrender meant that the wedge separating New England from Virginia had been driven out. To the citizens of the renamed province it scarcely seemed to make any difference. One nameless "Dutchman of quality" was even reported to have "rejoice[d] that the Dutch had done so well." The Town Council of New Amsterdam struck a note of philosophical resignation when it reported the surrender to the directors of the West India Company: "Meanwhile since we have no longer to depend on your Honors' promises of protection, we, with all the poor, sorrowing and abandoned commonalty here, must fly for refuge to Almighty God, not doubting but He will stand by us in this sorely afflicting conjuncture and no more depart from us. . . ." [1]

By any standard, the transition from Dutch to English rule was an incredibly smooth one: schepens became sheriffs, Fort Amsterdam became Fort James, and even Stuyvesant, that irascible warhorse who had thundered before the surrender that he would rather be carried out dead than submit to the English, retired peaceably and quietly to his New York City bouwery, where he died in 1672. After seventeen years in New Netherland as Director-General, entrepreneur, and land speculator, Stuyvesant discovered that the area had become home to him, that his interests centered in America rather than in the Netherlands. And for once, Stuyvesant and the leaders of the commonalty closed ranks, defending together their capitulation to the English before investigating committees of the West India Company and the States-General. The leaders of the commonalty even wrote many letters on behalf of Stuyvesant, supporting the position he had taken and pointing out the impossibility of New Netherland's situation once threatened by the English. Any number attested:

> . . . that the Honble Petrus Stuyvesant, then Director-General
> of New Netherland did, immediately on the arrival and sojurn of
> the English frigates, employ every possible means to encourage
> and animate the Burghers of the City of New Amsterdam and the
> people of the outvillages, especially on Long Island, to all
> possible resistance; certainly, to defend the city and fort of New
> Amsterdam as long as it was capable of defence, but that neither
> the one nor the other could be prevailed on to do so, because
> it was impossible, with any hope of a good result, as appeared
> sufficiently manifest, and was notorious to every one. . . .[2]

To the West India Company the surrender meant merely the loss of one — and by no means the most significant — of its many far-flung enterprises in the New World. There appeared to be little real regret on the company's part. New Netherland had been a financial drain from start to finish and the company had at many times seriously entertained the question of whether or not to dispose of this costly liability. When presented with an opportunity to regain New Netherland during the negotiations of the Treaty of Westminster in 1674, the States-General and the near bankrupt company, with sound business acumen, decided instead on Surinam. In 1664 then, the West India Company simply wrote New Netherland off the books as a failure.

In forty-three years the company had explored a number of approaches to making its North American possession a source of profit. The result was certainly failure. But was the West India Company's failure any different from the failure of a host of similar ventures, such as the Virginia Company, the Bermuda Company, or Colbert's Compagnie des Indês Occidentales? Every commercial company involved in attempts to colonize the New World in the seventeenth century had ultimately ended in failure. Seen from this point of view, the West India Company's experience merely mirrored that of a number of other companies — English, French, and Swedish — which had sought to derive profit from colonizing activities in North America; its failure was nothing more than the failure of a commercial company which had undertaken an impossible task.

Historians and writers on the Dutch period, however, have not seen it in such terms. For them, curiously enough, whether pro-English or pro-Dutch, the failure of the West India Company in New Netherland has somehow come to mean the failure of a conscious effort by the Dutch to create a viable, uniquely Dutch society in North America. The English position, the dominant tradition in colonial American historiography, has attributed this failure to the inability of Dutch institutions to flourish in the "freer" atmosphere of the New World. Andrews, for example, summed up the Dutch period of New York in this fashion:

> *What would have happened in the long run had the English*
> *conquest never taken place cannot even be conjectured. As it was*
> *the English success put an end to the Dutch rule in New Nether-*
> *land; but as long as the province remained a dependency of an*
> *incorporated trading company at home . . . it may well be*
> *doubted, judging from the history of the Dutch administration*
> *in the East, if any elaborate form of self-government would ever*
> *have been produced. Self-administration and self-taxation,*
> *similar to the practices which obtained in the cities of the Nether-*
> *land, might have come, but that anything comparable with the*
> *law making and money appropriating powers of the assemblies*
> *in the English colonies of the eighteenth century should have*
> *evolved is unlikely.*[3]

But, of course, the East was not at all like the West for either the Dutch or the English. And in terms of the commercial origins of New

Netherland an understanding of the tasks to be performed in North America was late in developing, too late for Dutch institutions to be blended with frontier conditions and then to take root.

Defensively articulated as a reply to such intimations, the Dutch position has stoutly maintained that the vitality of New Netherland was worn down between the grasping, intransigent policy of the West India Company on the one hand and the covetous pressures of her English neighbors on the other hand. The Dutch position, too, has overlooked New Netherland's commercial origins, assuming that the company ought to have been engaged in the functions of transplanting a distinctively Dutch society to these shores. The time factor as well has been ignored. The history of New Netherland at least until the 1640's was the history of "beginnings" rather than of continuous development. It seems improbable that a highly differentiated Dutch society could have been established in the forty-three years after 1621:

> Since there was little real settlement in New Netherland until the 1640's, this would reduce even more the time in which a stable society could be established. After nearly twenty years under the Virginia Company only the faintest beginnings of society can be detected in Virginia. And yet, curiously enough, after not much more than the same amount of time both English and Dutch writers have assumed that a thoroughgoing Dutch society ought to have existed in New Netherland.[4]

Thus neither the English nor the Dutch position has shed very much light on the history of New Netherland which, as a result, has become almost unintelligible — a jumble of archetypical heroes, villains, and buffoons whose exploits have been better suited to the art of a Washington Irving or a Kurt Weill than to the art of an historian.

The previous chapters have tried to suggest that the Dutch did not consciously approach New Netherland with a view toward its permanent settlement. Rather, that permanent settlement arose out of commercial experimentation and failure, and that it found acceptance only when the changed conditions of North America in the 1640's indicated its feasibility. But even when the desirability of establishing a Dutch society in North America became more apparent, the commercial origins of New Netherland and the commercial aspirations of both the company and the immigrants to the colony made its realization difficult at best.

As far as the West India Company was concerned, it was largely conducting a holding operation in New Netherland to prevent the area's absorption by the English in North America. The fundamental problem which the company faced, and which the patroons and others stumbled up against, was the attraction of immigrants to New Netherland. However much they tried, Dutchmen seemed simply not interested in emigrating in large numbers. The necessity to recruit emigrants from other nations and in the 1640's and 1650's to permit New Englanders to settle in New Netherland, contributed to the cosmopolitan cast of society there but also weakened the possibility of developing a distinctively Dutch culture in the area. The paucity of numbers, widely spread out over the geographical limits of New Netherland, tended to fragment even further the nature of the emerging society and to impede the development of institutions at all but the local level. By 1664 the population of New Netherland was at most 10,000 and included in that number were the English of Long Island and Westchester County, together with other non-Dutch nationalities which may have constituted 20 to 40 per cent of the total population.

In view of the nature of the population and the commercial origins of New Netherland, it hardly seems surprising that a highly differentiated Dutch society did not develop. Had the Dutch concentrated single-mindedly on this, such a society in New Netherland might well have been created. As it was, the Dutch approach to New Netherland consistently shows that such an aim held little priority throughout the seventeenth century. The roots of Dutch power and wealth in the seventeenth century were many and diverse. Other areas of the New World and the Far East exerted a far greater attractive influence on the interest of Netherlanders. And, as one historian has noted, even the "East Indian trade, which for centuries has fired popular imagination because of the adventurous character of the long sea voyages and of the blunt, open, if somewhat crude narratives left by its principal heroes, was really but one of many branches of Netherland commerce covering a large part of the world. Although the most spectacular, it was not even the most important ramification of Dutch trade." [5]

Much of the writing on American colonial history by an earlier generation of writers has been permeated by an emphasis on sharp differences rather than on broad lines of continuity. While the uniqueness of America has been the blending of a multiplicity of immigrant institutions and a diversity of ethnic groups into a seamless web of national unity, earlier historians have generally concentrated on the distinct elements that went into this process rather than on the process itself. Thus, there have been many works extolling the contribution of the English or the Dutch or the Germans to American history. Individual colonies such as Virginia or the Massachusetts Bay have been singled out for the unique role they played in the development of America. However, beneath these interesting but often superficial differences lies a developing American consensus. The history of New Netherland fits more into the study of consensus than uniqueness.

For forty-three years the West India Company controlled a large tract of real estate which more than a century later became one of the most important states in the new nation. The historical problem has been to show what relationship these forty-three years have had to the later development of New York. Some historians have attempted to link up later development to an earlier dominant Dutch influence. The previous chapters suggest that this is not a very fruitful approach. Others have felt that the application of a regional concept would provide a unifying structure for these years — hence the creation of that vague and rather useless term, the Middle Colonies, distinguished by its mixed population and its aristocratic or feudal institutions. Historians have also tried to demonstrate that the Dutch were as democratic or as religious or as freedom-loving as their English neighbors to the north or south. These Dutch years represent not a unique experience but rather a composite experience that reflects in microcosm what was occurring in the seventeenth century. The end result in New Netherland was a combination of the forms that developed in Virginia and New England, which can be explained by historically conditioned factors rather than by elusive ethnic or regional concepts. This is to suggest that despite a variety of superficial institutional forms, a more fundamental underlying American consensus was developing. This is further to suggest that given the historical conditions of seventeenth-century America, the response in Virginia, New Netherland, and New England to the challenge of creating a society in the wilderness was remarkably similar.

Despite the small numbers in New Netherland, the problem of creating a society was present from the beginning. The men and women who for one reason or another found themselves remaining in New Netherland acquired interests which became more intimately connected with the New World than with the West India Company or the old country. These men and women began with certain assumptions about what could be expected from life in New Netherland and were forced to modify or change these to fit the rapidly changing face of reality in seventeenth-century America. Consistently, and of necessity, these assumptions were at variance with those of the West India Company because in each case their expectations were different. The West India Company initially undertook the settlement of New Netherland not with any grand design in mind to transplant a truly Dutch society there, but in an attempt to make its investment in New Netherland pay off. Once begun, however, and as the numbers in New Netherland slowly mounted up, the societal requirements of the people there grew and, along with these, grew the social, economic, and political problems connected with the ordering of any society. Neither the company nor the inhabitants were really prepared to deal with the problems arising essentially from a new situation.

From this vantage point, the struggles which illustrate this clash of interest between company and inhabitants appear neither silly nor farcical. For it was out of such struggles, and not as a result of the ultimate flowering of preordained forms, as earlier writers have suggested, that the foundations of a well ordered, stable political community were to emerge. Such a clash was by no means peculiar to New York in the Dutch period. Throughout the New World, in Virginia, in Barbadoes, in Plymouth, the same struggle was taking place. Much is owed to these commercial companies that labored strenuously for profit and reaped only financial failure. The historical sociologist Sigmund Diamond, in his study of Virginia, has insightfully stated that debt:

> In 1607 there had been no 'contrey,' only the Virginia Company.
> It was the company's fate to have created a country and to have
> destroyed itself in the process.[6]

As the West India Company withdrew from New Netherland in 1664 it, too, left behind a country.

BIBLIOGRAPHY
PRIMARY SOURCES

PUBLIC DOCUMENTS

Calendar of State Papers, Colonial Series, America and West Indies. 42 vols. London, 1860–   , I.

Calendar of Treasury Books. 26 vols. London, 1904–   . I.

Fernow, Berthold (ed.). *The Records of New Amsterdam from 1653 to 1674.* 7 vols. New York, 1897.

O'Callaghan, Edmund B. (ed.). *Documentary History of the State of New-York.* 4 vols. Albany, 1849–1851.

——— (ed.). *Calendar of Historical Manuscripts in the Office of the Secretary of State.* 2 vols. Albany, 1865–1866.

——— (ed.). *Documents Relative to the Colonial History of the State of New York.* 15 vols. Albany, 1856–1887.

———. *The Register of New Netherland, 1626–1674.* Albany, 1865.

Van Laer, A. J. F. (ed.). "Minutes of the Amsterdam Chamber of the Dutch West India Company, 1635–1636," *New York Genealogical and Biographical Record,* XLIX (1918), 217–28.

OTHER PRIMARY WORKS

Asher, George M. *A Bibliographical and Historical Essay on the Dutch Books and Pamphlets Relating to New-Netherland and the Dutch West India Company.* . . . Amsterdam, 1854–1867.

Bacon, Francis. *The Essays of Francis Bacon.* London: Arthur L. Humphreys, 1900.

Bradford, William. *Of Plymouth Plantation, 1620–1647,* ed. Samuel E. Morison. New York, 1952.

Corwin, Edward T. (ed.). *Ecclesiastical Records of the State of New York.* 7 vols. Albany: James B. Lyon, 1901–1916.

Eekhof, A. *Jonas Michaëlius.* Leyden, 1926.

Harlow, V. T. (ed.). *Colonizing Expeditions to the West Indies and Guiana, 1623–1667.* (The Hakluyt Society, *Works,* Ser. 2, LVI, 1924.) London, 1925.

Hart, Simon. *The Prehistory of the New Netherland Company.* Amsterdam, 1959. Contains excerpts from Amsterdam notarial records.

Jameson, J. Franklin (ed.). *Narratives of New Netherland, 1609–1664.* (*Original Narratives of Early American History.*) New York, 1909.

———. "Willem Usselinx," American Historical Association, *Papers,* II, No. 3 (1887).

Johnson, Amandus (ed. and tr.). *The Instruction for Johan Printz, Governor of New Sweden.* Philadelphia: The Swedish Colonial Society, 1930.

Odhner, C. T. "Account of Willem Usselinx and the South, Ship, and West India Companies of Sweden," *Pennsylvania Magazine of History and Biography* (Gregory B. Keen, tr.), VII (1883), 268–70. Extract only.

———. "The Founding of New Sweden, 1637–1642," *Pennsylvania Magazine of History and Biography,* III (1879), 269–284, 395–411. Translation of *Kolonier Nya Sveriges Grundläggning, 1637–1642.*

Stokes, I. N. P. (ed.). *Iconography of Manhattan Island.* 6 vols. New York, 1915–1928.

Van der Donck, Adriaen. "Description of the New Netherlands," New York Historical Society, *Collections,* Ser. 2, I (1841), 125–242.

Van Laer, A. J. F. (ed.). "Arent van Curler and His Historic Letter to the Patroon," Dutch Settlers Society of Albany, *Yearbook,* III (1927–1928), 11–29.

——— (ed. and tr.). *Documents Relating to New Netherland 1624–1626 in the Henry E. Huntington Library.* San Marino, California, 1924.

——— (ed. and tr.). *New York State Library Van Rensselaer Bowier Manuscripts.* Albany, 1908.

SECONDARY SOURCES

Andrews, Charles, M. *Colonial Period of American History.* 4 vols. New Haven: Yale University Press, 1934–1938.

———. "American Colonial History, 1690–1750," American Historical Association, *Annual Report for the Year 1896,* 42–60.

Asher, George M. *Henry Hudson the Navigator.* (Printed for Hakluyt Society) London, 1860.

Bailyn, Bernard. *The New England Merchants in the Seventeenth Century,"* Cambridge, Mass: Harvard University Press, 1955.

Barbour, Violet. "Capitalism in Amsterdam in the Seventeenth Century," *The Johns Hopkins University Studies in History and Political Science,* LXVII (1949).

――――. "Privateers and Pirates of the West Indies," *American Historical Review,* XVI (1910–11), 529–66.

Bergen, Teunis G. *The Bergen Family: or the Descendants of Hans Hansen Bergen, One of the Early Settlers of New York and Brooklyn, Long Island.* Albany, 1876.

Bensor, Adolph B., and Hedin, Naboth (eds.). *Swedes in America, 1638–1938.* New Haven: Yale University Press, 1938.

Blok, P. J. *History of the People of the Netherlands.* Translated by Ruth Putnam. 4 vols. New York, 1900–1907.

Boeke, J. H. *Economics and Economic Policy of Dual Societies.* New York, 1953.

――――. *The Structure of Netherlands Indian Economy.* New York, 1942.

Bolton, Robert, Jr. *A History of the County of Westchester from Its First Settlement to the Present Time.* 2 vols. New York, 1848.

Bontekoe, Willem Ysbrantsz. *Memorable Description of the East Indian Voyage 1618–25.* Translated by C. B. Bodde-Hodgkinson and Pieter Geyl. London, 1929.

Brodhead, John R. *History of the State of New York.* 2 vols. New York, 1853–71.

Condon, Thomas J. "New York's Dutch Period: an Interpretive Problem," *de Halve Maen* (publication of The Holland Society of New York), XXVI (1961), 7–15.

Craven, Wesley F. *Dissolution of the Virginia Company: The Failure of a Colonial Experiment.* New York, 1932.

Davies, K. G. *The Royal African Company.* London, 1957.

DeForest, Louis E., and Lawrence, Anne. *Captain John Underhill.* New York, 1934.

DeForest, Louis E. *The Settlement of Manhattan in 1624.* Albany, 1935.

DeForest, Mrs. Robert W. *A Walloon Family in America.* 2 vols. Boston, 1914.

DeKlerck, E. S. *History of the Netherlands Indies.* 2 vols. Rotterdam, 1938.

Dexter, Henry M. and Dexter, Morton. *The England and Holland of the Pilgrims.* Boston, 1905.

Diamond, Sigmund, "From Organization to Society: Virginia in the Seventeenth Century," *American Journal of Sociology,* LXII (1958), 457–75.

Driggs, Laurence LaT. "The Two Baxters of New Amsterdam," *New York Genealogical and Biographical Record,* LXX (1939), 3–16.

Edmundson, George. "The Dutch in Western Guiana," *English Historical Review,* XVI (1901), 640–75.

Edmundson, George. "The Dutch Power in Brazil," *English Historical Review,* XI (1899), 238–58.

Evjen, John O. *Scandinavian Immigrants in New York, 1630–1674.* Minneapolis, 1916.

Furnivall, J. S. *Netherlands India: A Study of Plural Economy.* Cambridge, England: Cambridge University Press, 1939.

Geyl, Peter. *The Netherlands Divided, 1609–1648.* Translated by S. A. Bindoff. London, 1936.

Griffis, William E. *The Story of the Walloons: At Home, in Lands of Exile and in America.* Boston: Houghton, Mifflin Co., 1923.

Hansen, Marcus L. *The Atlantic Migration, 1607–1860,* ed. Arthur M. Schlesinger. Cambridge, Mass.: Harvard University Press, 1940.

Haring, Charles H. "The Genesis of Royal Government in the Spanish Indies," *Hispanic American Historical Review,* XII (1927).

Harlow, Vincent T. *A History of Barbados, 1625–1685.* Oxford, 1926.

Hart, Simon. "Dutch Records Tell Story of Hudson Voyage," *de Halve Maen* (publication of The Holland Society of New York), XXXVI (1961), Part I, 7–8, 14.

Hyma, Albert. *The Dutch in the Far East.* Ann Arbor, 1942.

Innes, J. H. *New Amsterdam and its People.* New York, 1902.

Jameson, J. Franklin. "The Origin and Development of the Municipal Government of New York City," *Magazine of American History,* VIII (1882); Part I, "The Dutch Period," 315–330.

Johnson, Amandus. *The Swedes on the Delaware, 1638–1664.* Philadelphia: Swedish Colonial Society, 1915.

Kingsbury, Susan M. "A Comparison of the Virginia Company with Other English Trading Companies of the Sixteenth and Seventeenth Centuries," American Historical Association, *Annual Report for the Year 1906,* 162.

McCormick, Richard P. "The Province of East Jersey, 1609–1702," New Jersey Historical Society, *Proceedings,* LXX (1952).

McKinley, Albert E. "English and Dutch Towns of New Netherlands," *American Historical Review,* VI (1900), 1–18.

————. "The Transition from Dutch to English Rule in New York," *American Historical Review,* VI (1900), 693–724.

Menkman, W. R. *De West-Indische Compagnie.* Amsterdam, 1947.

Murray, Jean E. "The Early Fur Trade in New France and New Netherland," *Canadian Historical Review,* XIX (1938), 365–377.

Newton, Arthur P. *The European Nations in the West Indies, 1493–1688.* London, 1933.

Nissenson, S. G. *The Patroon's Domain.* New York, 1937.

O'Callaghan, Edmund B. *History of New Netherland.* 2 vols. New York, 1855.

Osgood, Herbert L. *The American Colonies in the Seventeenth Century.* 3 vols. New York, 1904–1907.

Paltsits, Victor H. "The Founding of New Amsterdam in 1626," American Antiquarian Society, *Proceedings,* New Series, XXXIV (1924), 39–65.

Pares, Richard. "Merchants and Planters," *Economic History Review Supplement.* No. 4 (1960).

Plooij, D. *The Pilgrim Fathers from a Dutch Point of View.* New York, 1932.

Raesly, Ellis L. *Portrait of New Netherland.* New York, 1945.

Schoolcraft, H. L. "The Capture of New Amsterdam," *English Historical Review,* XXII (1907).

Schrieke, B. *Indonesian Sociological Studies.* The Hague, 1955.

Scott, William R. *The Constitution and Finance of English, Scottish and Irish Joint-Stock Companies to 1720.* 3 vols. Cambridge, England. 1911.

Shelley, Henry C. *John Underhill: Captain of New England and New Netherland.* New York: D. Appleton & Co., 1932.

Shepherd, W. R. *The Story of New Amsterdam.* New York, 1926.

Sluiter, Engel. "The Dutch Archives and American Historical Research," *Pacific Historical Review,* VI (1937), 21–35.

Smith, James M. (ed.). *The Seventeenth Century: Essays in Colonial History.* Chapel Hill: University of North Carolina Press, 1959.

Sprinchorn, Carl K. S. "The History of the Colony of New Sweden," *Pennsylvania Magazine of History and Biography* (Gregory B. Keen, tr.), VII (1883), 395–419.

Thompson, Benjamin F. *History of Long Island.* 3rd ed. 3 vols. New York: Robt. H. Dodd, 1918.

Townsend, Ward. "Augustine Herrman and John Thompson," *Pennsylvania Magazine of History and Biography,* VII (1883), 88–93.

Trelease, Allen W. *Indian Affairs in Colonial New York: The Seventeenth Century.* Ithaca: Cornell University Press, 1960.

Van Brakel, S. *DeHollandsche Handels compagnieen der Zeventiende eeuw.* 'S-Gravenhage, 1908.

Van Winkle, Edward. *Manhattan, 1624–1639.* New York, 1916.

Versteeg, Dingman. *Manhattan in 1628.* New York, 1904.

Vlekke, Bernard H. M. *Evolution of the Dutch Nation.* New York, 1945.

Weise, Arthur J. *The History of the City of Albany, New York. . . .* Albany: E. H. Bender, 1884.

White, Philip L. "Municipal Government Comes to Manhattan," New York Historical Society, *Quarterly,* XXXVII (1953), 146–57.

Wilson, Charles H. *Anglo-Dutch Commerce and Finance in the Eighteenth Century.* Cambridge, England: Cambridge University Press, 1941.

Wright, Louis B. *The Atlantic Frontier: Colonial American Civilization.* New York: A. A. Knopf, 1947.

Zwierlein, Frederick J. *Religion in New Netherland.* Rochester, 1910.

NOTES

CHAPTER I

1 Edmund B. O'Callaghan (ed.), *Documents Relative to the Colonial History of the State of New York* (Albany, 1855–1883), I, 39.

2 The researches of Dr. Simon Hart, Archivist of the City of Amsterdam, in the notarial records of seventeenth-century Amsterdam have provided scholars with invaluable information about the early commercial ventures to the area of New Netherland. These documents represent the first new material to come to light since the publication of the Van Rensselaer-Bowier Manuscripts in 1908 and the so-called Van Rappard Documents in 1923. The notarial documents, together with a brief introduction by Hart, can be found in Simon Hart, *The Pre-history of the New Netherland Company* (Amsterdam, 1959).

3 Murray has incorrectly suggested that the fur trade in New Netherland "originated and developed independently of the fisheries." Cf. Jean E. Murray, "The Early Fur Trade in New France and New Netherland," *Canadian Historical Review*, XIX (1938), 365–67.

4 William Robert Scott, *The Constitution and Finance of English, Scottish and Irish Joint-Stock Companies to 1720* (Cambridge, 1911), II, 300.

5 *Ibid.*, II, 361.

6 Violet Barbour, "Capitalism in Amsterdam in the Seventeenth Century," *The Johns Hopkins University Studies in Historical and Political Science*, LXVII (Baltimore, 1949), 15, 24; *Prehistory*, p. 12.

7 *Prehistory*, pp. 8–12.

8 *Ibid.*, p. 12; Barbour, "Amsterdam Capitalism," pp. 90–91.

9 Charles Henry Wilson, *Anglo-Dutch Commerce and Finance in the Eighteenth Century* (Cambridge, England, 1941), p. 5–6; Barbour, "Amsterdam Capitalism," pp. 18–20.

10 John Romeyn Brodhead, *History of the State of New York* (New York, 1853), I, 16–18; *Prehistory*, pp. 12–13.

11 *Prehistory*, p. 9.

12 *Ibid.*, p. 13.

13 *Ibid.*, pp. 13–14.

14 *Prehistory*, pp. 14, 47.

15 *Ibid.*, pp. 15–16.

16 *Ibid.*, pp. 41–44.

17 J. Franklin Jameson (ed.), *Narratives of New Netherland, 1609–1664* (New York, 1909) (*Original Narratives of Early American History*), p. 3.

18 Simon Hart, "Dutch Records Tell Story of Hudson's Voyage," *de Halve Maen*, XXXVI (April, 1961), 7–8.

19 Cf. *supra*, ch. 6. Le Maire was another Antwerp merchant in exile in Amsterdam. He was an early and heavy investor in the Dutch East India Company. His interests in mercantile ventures were extremely varied. In 1609 he formed a company to speculate in shares of the Dutch East India Company from which he received a somewhat unsavory reputation. Wilson, *Anglo-Dutch Commerce*, p. 14; Barbour, "Amsterdam Capitalism," pp. 24, 77.

20 *Prehistory*, p. 8; Brodhead, *Hist.*, I, 138 n; *NYCD*, I, 27–28.

21 Brodhead, *Hist.*, I, 24–35; *NNN*, pp. 18–23.

22 *NNN*, p. 8. This contrasts strangely with the conduct of the States-General in dealing with two Englishmen in Dutch service: Sir Thomas Gates and Sir Thomas Dale. Both Gates and Dale were captains of Dutch companies who had received permission from the States-General to absent themselves from Dutch service in order to participate in the Virginia Company's experiment in the New World. On the petitions of King James I and Sir Dudley Carleton, English ambassador to the Netherlands, the States-General eventually allowed them full salary during their seven years absence! *NYCD*, I, 1–20, *passim*.

23 Scott, *Joint-Stock Companies*, II, 100.

24 *NNN*, p. 38.

25 *Ibid.*, p. 78.

26 *NYCD*, I, 4; *Prehistory*, pp. 17, 63–65.

27 *Prehistory*, p. 17.

28 *Ibid.*, pp. 62–65.

29 *Ibid.*, p. 20.

30 *Ibid.*, pp. 44–46.

31 Francoys Pelgrom to his wife Barbara, July 30 and August 20, 1613, *ibid.*, p. 74; crew member declarations on August 20, 1613, *ibid.*, p. 75.

32 Jan Kindt, nephew of Francoys Pelgrom accompanied Block on his third and fourth voyages as supercargo and may also have had a financial interest in the company, *ibid.*, pp. 53, 74.

33 In a deed recorded April 29, 1613, Vogel transferred his share in the cargo and ship of Block to the Pelts. *Ibid.*, p. 73.

34 *Ibid.*, pp. 47–48.

35 *Ibid.*, p. 39.

36 *Ibid.*, p. 40. In 1624, David Pietersz. de Vries attempted to circumvent the Dutch West India Company monopoly by associating with the same La Rochelle firm of Jean Macain and Company. His projected trip for them to "New France" was blocked by the Dutch West India Company.

37 *Ibid.*, p. 22.

38 *Ibid.*, pp. 23, 55–56.

39 *Ibid.*, p. 56.

40 *Ibid.*, p. 57.

41 *NNN*, p. 78; *Prehistory*, p. 19.

42 1. Deposition of Simon Willemsz. Nooms, July 28, 1614, *Prehistory*, pp. 91–92. In 1604 Block was skipper of the "Grote Roode Leeuw," one of whose owners was Nooms, *ibid.*, p. 63.

43 *Ibid.*, pp. 39–68, *passim*. In 1617 Van Tweenhuysen, Nicquet, Harencarspel, Pieter Evertse Hulft and Company were engaged in the "celebrated and useful trade and fishery of Terra Nova." *NYCD*, I, 15.

44 *Prehistory*, p. 23.

45 *Ibid.*, p. 92.

46 Receipt signed by Block, September 26, 1613, *ibid.*, p. 76.

47 Notice to the owners of the "Fortuyn," filed October 7, 1613, *ibid.*, pp. 24–25, 77–79.

48 *Ibid.*, p. 25.

49 *Ibid.*, p. 78.

50 *Ibid.*, p. 79.

51 Notice to the owners of Mossel's ship, filed September 30, 1613, Isaac N. P. Stokes (ed.), *The Iconography of Manhattan Island* (New York, 1915–1928), IV, 4.

52 Declarations of two crew members of the "Nachtegael," July 23, 1614, *Prehistory*, p. 84. Cf. also *ibid.*, pp. 27–29.

53 *Ibid.*, pp. 29–30.

54 Cf. *supra*, pp. 13–16.

55 *Prehistory*, pp. 30–31.

56 *Ibid.*, pp. 61–63.

57 *Ibid.*, pp. 91–92.

58 *Ibid.*, p. 32.

59 *Ibid.*, p. 86.

60 *NYCD*, I, 4.

61 Italics mine.

62 *NYCD*, I, 5–6.

63 *Ibid.*, I, 4–5.

64 *Prehistory*, p. 92.

65 *Ibid.*, pp. 31–32.

66 *NYCD*, I, 10–11.

67 I. *Ibid.*, I, 4. In applying for the loan of some Admiralty guns for his voyage in October, 1613, Block stated that "he intended to sail to Virginia, where no Christians had been before him." *Ibid.*, p. 26 n. Although the loaners must have known this to be untrue, Block nonetheless received his guns.

68 *Ibid.*, pp. 95–96; Stokes, *Iconography*, IV, 42.

69 E. S. De Klerck, *History of the Netherlands Indies* (Rotterdam, 1938), I, 202.

70 *Loc. cit.*

71 Willem Ysbrantsz Bontekoe, *Memorable Description of the East Indian Voyage 1618–25*. Trans. by C. B. Bodde-Hudgkinson and Pieter Geyl (London, 1929), p. 8. For accounts of the Dutch in the East Indies consult Albert Hyma, *The Dutch in the Far East* (Ann Arbor, Michigan, 1942); J. S. Furnivall, *Netherlands India; A Study of Plural Economy* (Cambridge, England, 1939); B. Schrieke, *Indonesian Sociological Studies* (The Hague, 1955); and J. H. Boeke, *Economics and Economic Policy of Dual Societies* (New York, 1953).

72 *Prehistory*, pp. 9, 33, 40, 44 n.

73 *NYCD*, I, 12.

74 *Ibid.*, pp. 12–14; Brodhead, *Hist.*, I, 78–81; accounts by de Laet and Wassenaer in *NNN*, pp. 38–39, 47–48, 78, 80–81.

75 *NYCD*, I, 13–15.

76 *Ibid.*, I, 6, 8–9, 21.

77 *Ibid.*, I, 22.

78 *Prehistory*, pp. 37, 40.

79 The nucleus of the second Van Tweenhuysen Company appears to have been

Van Tweenhuysen, Hans Claesz., Vogels, Paulus and Steven Pelgrom, Haren-carspel, Sweers, Samuel Godyn, Nicquet, Hinlopen, and probably Plancius.

80 *NYCD,* I, 22.
81 *Ibid.,* I, 25–27.
82 *Prehistory,* pp. 68–69.
83 *Ibid.,* pp. 54, 60, 69.
84 *Ibid.,* p. 36.
85 *NYCD,* I, 24–25.
86 *Ibid.,* I, 25.
87 *Prehistory,* p. 38 n.
88 Brodhead, *Hist.,* I, 96–97.
89 *Prehistory,* pp. 23, 26–27.
90 *NNN,* 47; Brodhead, *Hist.,* pp. 54–55.
91 *NYCD,* I, 51, 94.
92 *Prehistory,* pp. 26–27.
93 *NYCD,* I, 22–23.
94 William Bradford, *Of Plymouth Plantation,* 1620–1647, ed. S. E. Morison, (New York, 1952), *passim.*
95 *NYCD,* I, 7–29, *passim.*
96 *Ibid.,* I, 22–23.
97 A. J. F. Van Laer (ed. and tr.), *New York State Library Van Rensselaer Bowier Manuscripts* (Albany, 1908), pp. 86–115.
98 *NYCD,* I, 25.
99 *VRB MSS.,* pp. 127–35.
100 *Ibid.,* p. 91; *NYCD,* I, 26.
101 *Prehistory,* p. 38. As late as 1629 the Eelkens Company was still attempting to reach a settlement with the West India Company over claims that dated back to the years of free trade.
102 *NYCD,* I, 30–31; *Prehistory,* p. 38 n.

CHAPTER II

1 Brodhead, *Hist.,* I, 746.
2 T. J. Condon, "New York's Dutch Period: An Interpretive Problem," *de Halve Maen,* XXXVI (Oct., 1961), 7–8, 14–15.
3 *NYCD,* I, 35–36. Many secondary works deal with the West India Company. The best of these is S. G. Nissenson, *The Patroon's Domain* (New York, 1937), pp. 3–20.
4 *VRB MSS,* pp. 117–21.
5 J. Franklin Jameson, "Willem Usselinx," American Historical Association, *Papers,* II (1887), 13–14.
6 Bernard H. M. Vlekke, *Evolution of the Dutch Nation* (New York, 1945), p. 181. See also Barbour, "Amsterdam Capitalism," p. 136.
7 Jameson, "Usselinx," pp. 13–22, 28. Jameson even suggests that Usselinx's ideas were well formed by 1592 or 1593.
8 P. J. Blok, *History of the People of the Netherlands,* trans. by Ruth Putnam (New York, 1900–1907), III, 235–53; Vlekke, *Dutch Nation,* pp. 124–69.
9 De Klerck, *Netherlands Indies,* I, 200–202; Vlekke, *Dutch Nation,* pp. 172–75.
10 Jameson, "Usselinx," p. 28.
11 G. M. Asher, *A Bibliographical and Historical Essay on the Dutch Books and*

Pamphlets Relating to New-Netherland and to the Dutch West India Company. . . . (Amsterdam, 1854) , pp. xiv–xvi.

12 Blok, *History*, III, 303–14.

13 A. P. Newton, *The European Nations in the West Indies, 1493–1688* (London, 1933) , pp. 122–23.

14 Blok, *History*, III, 301–14.

15 See *infra*, pp. 61–62, for the terms Usselinx requested.

16 Cited in Jameson, "Usselinx," p. 31.

17 Cited in *ibid.,* pp. 31–34.

18 Blok, *History*, III, 311–12.

19 Jameson, "Usselinx," p. 46.

20 *Ibid.,* pp. 94–188.

21 *Ibid.,* p. 67.

22 Usselinx compared himself to Columbus at many points in his lifetime. See *ibid.,* pp. 80–81, 89, 151, 196.

23 *Ibid.,* p. 77.

24 *Ibid.,* p. 80. Italics mine.

25 *Ibid.,* pp. 47–53.

26 Cited in *ibid.,* p. 53.

27 *Ibid.,* p. 77.

28 *Ibid.,* p. 84.

29 At one point he suggests that the changes he desired could be accomplished merely by loosely interpreting the charter rather than by formally altering it. *Ibid.,* p. 78.

30 *Ibid.,* pp. 62, 92–93.

31 *Ibid.,* pp. 43–45.

32 Vlekke, *Dutch Nation,* pp. 175.

33 Nissenson, *Patroon's Domain,* p. 4.

34 Blok, *History*, III, 330–31.

35 *NYCD,* I, 6–9.

36 Jameson, "Usselinx," pp. 56–57.

37 See *supra*, p. 30.

38 Vlekke, *Dutch Nation,* p. 212.

39 *NYCD,* I, 39.

40 Jameson, "Usselinx," pp. 58–61.

41 *Ibid.,* p. 59.

42 *Ibid.,* p. 61.

43 See *supra*, pp. 29–31.

44 *VRB MSS,* p. 109.

45 Blok, *History*, IV, 4.

46 *VRB MSS,* pp. 89, 123.

47 Asher, *Bibliography,* pp. xiv–xxx.

48 Wilson, *Anglo-Dutch Commerce,* pp. 13–14, 81–82.

49 Barbour, "Amsterdam Capitalism," p. 77. Italics mine.

50 *NYCD,* I, 39–63.

51 *VRB MSS,* p. 87.

52 *Ibid.,* p. 121.

53 *NYCD,* I, 39.

54 *VRB MSS,* p. 131.

55 *Ibid.,* pp. 129–31.

56 *Ibid.,* p. 133.

57 *Ibid.,* p. 135.

58 *Ibid.*, p. 97.
59 *Ibid.*, p. 99.
60 *Ibid.*, p. 113.
61 George Edmundson, "The Dutch Power in Brazil," *English Historical Review,* XI (1896) , 238–58.
62 *VRB MSS*, pp. 97, 123.
63 *Ibid.*, p. 103.
64 *NYCD*, I, 39.

CHAPTER III

1 *NYCD*, I, 35–37.
2 *Ibid.*, p. 37.
3 *Ibid.*, p. 65.
4 *Loc. cit.*
5 George Edmundson, "The Dutch Power in Brazil," pp. 238–58. See also his "The Dutch in Western Guiana," *English Historical Review,* XVI (1901) and Blok, *History,* IV, 36–38.
6 *NYCD*, I, 66.
7 *Ibid.*, p. 67.
8 *Ibid.*, pp. 66–67.
9 *Ibid.*, p. 64.
10 *Ibid.*, p. 67.
11 *Ibid.*, p. 39.
12 *Ibid.*, p. 61.
13 *Ibid.*, p. 39. In a later reference the trading interest was termed: "those who, in that operation [trade], pretended to have been most clear sighted." *Ibid.*, p. 65.
14 *Ibid.*, p. 34.
15 *Ibid.*, pp. 38, 40, 65.
16 *Ibid.*, pp. 40–42, 62–63.
17 Nissenson, *The Patroon's Domain,* pp. 10–11.
18 Stokes, *Iconography,* IV, 55 and VI, 12.
19 Writing of the year 1628, O'Callaghan noted: "Seven years had now nearly elapsed since the incorporation of the West India Company, and five since that body had been in active operation, yet nothing had been done to carry out that part of the charter which obliged them to advance settlement and encourage population in those fertile counries in North America committed to their charge." *History of New Netherland* (New York, 1845) , I, 110.
20 Jameson, "Usselinx," pp. 71–72. Italics mine. See also his "Origins and Development of the Municipal Government of New York City," *Magazine of American History,* VIII (1882) , 315–30.
21 *NYCD*, II, 228; see also *ibid.*, II, 218.
22 *Ibid.*, I, 40. Italics in original.
23 S. M. Kingsbury, "A Comparison of the Virginia Company with other English Trading Companies of the Seventeenth and Eighteenth Centuries," American Historical Association, *Annual Report for 1906,* p. 161.
24 W. F. Craven, *Dissolution of the Virginia Company* (New York, 1932) , p. 24.
25 *Prehistory,* pp. 33–65, *passim.*
26 *NNN*, pp. 53–54.
27 *VRB MSS*, p. 235.
28 *NNN*, p. 76.

29 *Ibid.,* p. 75.
30 A. J. F. Van Laer (ed. and tr.) , *Documents Relating to New Netherland 1624–1626 in the Henry E. Huntington Library* (San Marino, 1924) , pp. xii–xxv. See also V. H. Paltsitz, "The Founding of New Amsterdam in 1626," American Antiquarian Society, *Proceedings,* New Series, XXXIV (1924), 39–65; W. R. Shepherd, *The Story of New Amsterdam* (New York, 1926) , pp. 6–14; L. F. De Forest, *The Settlement of Manhattan in 1624* (Albany, 1935) , pp. 5–29; Dingman Versteeg, *Manhattan in 1628* (New York, 1904) , pp. 1–38.
31 *Calendar of State Papers.* Colonial Series, America and West Indies, 1574–1660, I, 168.
32 V. T. Harlow (ed.) , *Colonising Expeditions to the West Indies and Guiana, 1623–1667* (London, 1925) , p. 97.
33 M. L. Hansen, *The Atlantic Migration, 1607–1860* (Cambridge, 1940), pp. 25–36.
34 *VRB MSS,* pp. 244–45.
35 *Ibid.,* p. 236.
36 *Ibid.,* pp. 235–36.
37 *Huntington Docs.,* p. 36.
38 *Ibid.,* pp. 38, 64, 82, 86.
39 *Ibid.,* p. 64.
40 *Ibid.,* p. 6.
41 *Ibid.,* p. 82.
42 *Ibid.,* p. 125.
43 *VRB MSS,* pp. 245, 247–48.
44 *Ibid.,* p. 245.
45 *Huntington Docs.,* p. 52.
46 *Ibid.,* p. 55.
47 *VRB MSS,* p. 247.
48 *Huntington Docs.,* p. 5.
49 *Ibid.,* pp. 10, 67.
50 *Ibid.,* p. 10.
51 *Ibid.,* pp. 58–59, 71.
52 *VRB MSS,* p. 235.
53 *NYCD,* I, 65, 39.
54 See *supra,* p. 41.
55 *Huntington Docs.,* pp. 51, 56, 68.
56 *Ibid.,* p. 67.
57 *Ibid.,* pp. 10–13.
58 *Ibid.,* p. 9.
59 *Ibid.,* pp. 9, 72.
60 *Ibid.,* p. 18.
61 *Ibid.,* p. 14.
62 *Loc. cit.*
63 *Ibid.,* pp. 75–94.
64 *Ibid.,* p. 14.
65 *Ibid.,* pp. 15–17. Italics mine.
66 *Ibid.,* p. 10.
67 *Ibid.,* p. 14.
68 *Ibid.,* pp. 132–69.
69 *Ibid.,* p. 168.
70 *Ibid.,* pp. 143–48, 152–67.
71 *Ibid.,* p. 155.
72 *Ibid.,* pp. 143, 160, 163.

73 *Ibid.*, pp. 132–36, 143.
74 *Ibid.*, pp. 143–48.
75 *Ibid.*, p. 168.
76 *Ibid.*, p. 163.
77 *Ibid.*, p. 164.
78 *Ibid.*, pp. 118–21.
79 *Ibid.*, pp. 48, 51.
80 *Ibid.*, p. 106.
81 *Ibid.*, p. 64.
82 *Ibid.*, pp. 48, 51.
83 *NYCD*, I, 37.
84 *VRB MSS*, p. 245.
85 *NNN*, p. 88.
86 *Huntington Docs.*, p. 39.
87 *Ibid.*, pp. 39–40.
88 *Ibid.*, p. 63.
89 *Ibid.*, p. 72.
90 *Ibid.*, p. 90.
91 *Ibid.*, pp. 97–98.

CHAPTER IV

1 *NYCD*, I, 38.
2 *NNN*, pp. 36–60, 67–96.
3 *Ibid.*, p. 64.
4 *Ibid.*, p. 74.
5 A. Eekhof, *Jonas Michaëlius* (Leyden, 1926), pp. 99–139, 62–70. Reprints of three letters by Michaëlius in the years 1628–1630.
6 One letter written in the Netherlands to S. Blomaert after de Rasière's return is in *NNN*, pp. 102–15; a more important letter written in New Netherland in 1626 is contained in *Huntington Docs.*, pp. 171–251.
7 *NNN*, pp. 53–54.
8 *Ibid.*, p. 76. See also Mrs. Robert W. de Forest, *A Walloon Family in America* (Boston, 1914), II, 191. Volume II contains largely "The Journal of a Voyage to Guiana."
9 Stokes, *Iconography*, IV, 53.
10 *NYCD*, III, 9–10.
11 *Ibid.*, III, 26.
12 *Ibid.*, I, 28. Italics in original.
13 De Forest, *Walloon Family*, II, 189.
14 *Ibid.*, I, 40–56.
15 *Ibid.*, I, 17.
16 *NYCD*, III, 9–10.
17 Cited in de Forest, *Walloon Family*, I, 22. Italics mine.
18 *Ibid.*, I, 26.
19 *NNN*, p. 75.
20 Eekhof, *Michaëlius*, p. 130.
21 E. B. O'Callaghan (ed.), *The Documentary History of the State of New-York* (Albany, 1850–1851), III, 49.
22 *NNN*, 79–80. For an excellent discussion of the activities in the first two years in New Netherland, see Paltsits, "The Founding of New Amsterdam in 1626," pp. 39–65.

23 *NNN*, p. 85.
24 *Ibid.*, p. 84.
25 *Ibid.*, p. 86.
26 *Ibid.*
27 *Huntington Docs.*, pp. 208–11.
28 *Ibid.*, p. 6.
29 *Ibid.*, pp. 47–48, 82.
30 *NNN*, pp. 83–84. Italics in original. *Narratives of New Netherland*
31 *VRB MSS*, p. 236.
32 *Ibid.*
33 *Ibid.*, p. 247.
34 *Ibid.*, p. 236.
35 *NNN*, p. 79.
36 Stokes, *Iconography*, VI, 11–12.
37 *VRB MSS*, p. 107.
38 *Ibid.*, pp. 238–39.
39 *NNN*, p. 102.
40 *VRB MSS*, pp. 215, 217.
41 *Ibid.*, p. 236.
42 Eekhof, *Michaëlius*, 111, 135.
43 *Ibid.*, 111, 129.
44 *Huntington Docs.*, p. 236.
45 *Ibid.*, p. 207.
46 *Ibid.*, p. 187.
47 Eekhof, *Michaëlius*, p. 111.
48 *Huntington Docs.*, pp. 235–36.
49 Eekhof, *Michaëlius*, p. 110.
50 *Huntington Docs.*, pp. 207–208.
51 *Ibid.*, pp. 216–19.
52 *Ibid.*, p. 196; Eekhof, *Michaëlius*, p. 136.
53 *Huntington Docs.*, p. 216.
54 *VRB MSS*, pp. 235–46.
55 Eckhof, *Michaëlius*, p. 68.
56 *Huntington Docs.*, pp. 176, 240.
57 *VRB MSS*, p. 244.
58 Eckhof, *Michaëlius*, p. 111.
59 *Huntington Docs.*, p. 216.
60 Eekhof, *Michaëlius*, p. 110.
61 *Ibid.*, p. 138.
62 *NYCD*, I, 181.
63 Eekhof, *Michaëlius*, p. 109.
64 E. T. Corwin (ed.) , *Ecclesiastical Records of the State of New York* (Albany, 1901–1905) , I, 111, 114, 116.
65 Richard Pares, "Merchants and Planters," *Economic History Review Supplement*, No. 4 (1960) , p. 15.
66 *Huntington Docs.*, pp. 199–200; Eekhof, *Michaëlius*, pp. 68–70.
67 *NNN*, p. 85.
68 *Huntington Docs.*, p. 225.
69 Hansen, *Atlantic Migration*, p. 45.
70 Sigmund Diamond, "From Organization to Society: Virginia in the Seventeenth Century," *American Journal of Sociology*, LXIII (1958) , 458.
71 *Huntington Docs.*, pp. 180–83.
72 Eekhof, *Michaëlius*, p. 111.

73   *Ibid.*, p. 69.
74   *Ibid.*
75   *Huntington Docs.*, pp. 114–17.
76   *Ibid.*, p. 114.
77   *Ibid.*, p. 129.
78   *Ibid.*, p. 188.
79   Eekhof, *Michaëlius*, p. 139.
80   *Huntington Docs.*, pp. 184, 188.
81   *Ibid.*, p. 187.
82   Diamond, "Organization to Society," p. 462.
83   Eekhof, *Michaëlius*, p. 131.
84   *Ibid.*
85   *Ibid.*, p. 134.
86   *Ibid.*, p. 131.
87   *Ibid.*, p. 68.
88   *Huntington Docs.*, p. 191.
89   *Ibid.*, p. 187.
90   *Ibid.*, pp. 187–88.
91   *Ibid.*, p. 196.
92   *Ibid.*, pp. 199–200.
93   *Ibid.*, p. 219.
94   *VRB MSS*, p. 270.

CHAPTER V

1   Brodhead, *Hist.*, I, 746.
2   *VRB MSS*, p. 246.
3   *NYCD*, I, 103–104, 126–27, 144–48; *Ecclesiastical Records*, I, 87–88, 127–29.
4   *NYCD*, I, 106.
5   *Ibid.*, I, 91.
6   *Ibid.*, I, 444.
7   *Ibid.*, I, 84.
8   *VRB MSS*, pp. 235–40.
9   *NYCD*, I, 107.
10   *Ibid.*, I, 110–15.
11   *VRB MSS*, pp. 136–53.
12   *NNN*, p. 210.
13   *VRB MSS*, pp. 236–38.
14   Nissenson, *Patroon's Domain*, pp. 28–30.
15   *Ibid.*, p. 26.
16   *VRB MSS*, p. 530.
17   *Ibid.*, pp. 473–74.
18   *Ibid.*, p. 524.
19   *Ibid.*, pp. 197, 541.
20   *Ibid.*, p. 534; Ellis Lawrence Raesly, *Portrait of New Netherland* (New York, 1945), pp. 84–85.
21   *VRB MSS*, pp. 527–28, 539–43.
22   See *supra*, pp. 134–36.
23   *VRB MSS*, pp. 199, 236–37, 248.
24   *Ibid.*, p. 316; Nissenson, *Patroon's Domain*, pp. 28–29, 169–77.
25   *Prehistory*, p. 67.

26 *NYCD,* I, 480; Jameson, "Usselinx," pp. 183–84.
27 Nissenson, *Patroon's Domain,* pp. 12–13.
28 *VRB MSS,* pp. 521–23, 546–47, 553, 670.
29 *Ibid.,* p. 476.
30 *Ibid.,* p. 314.
31 *Ibid.,* pp. 606–608.
32 *Ibid.,* p. 413.
33 *Ibid.,* p. 445.
34 *Ibid.,* p. 430.
35 *Ibid.,* p. 233.
36 *Ibid.,* p. 200.
37 *Ibid.,* pp. 199–200.
38 Nissenson, *Patroon's Domain,* p. 190.
39 *VRB MSS,* p. 233.
40 *Ibid.,* p. 448.
41 *Ibid.,* p. 615.
42 *Ibid.,* pp. 805–22; Arthur James Weise, *The History of the City of Albany.* . . . (Albany, 1884) , pp. 43–44.
43 Cited in Brodhead, *Hist.,* I, 277.
44 *VRB MSS,* pp. 428–429, 647.
45 *Ibid.,* pp. 458, 817.
46 *Ibid.,* pp. 631–37, 642–44.
47 *Ibid.,* p. 335.
48 This was by no means unusual. All promoters of colonies painfully discovered how difficult it was to administer their affairs from afar. Cf. Pares, "Merchants and Planters," pp. 1–13.
49 Nissenson, *Patroon's Domain,* p. 92.
50 *VRB MSS,* pp. 199–200.
51 *Ibid.,* pp. 558–61.
52 Nissenson, *Patroon's Domain,* p. 75.
53 *VRB MSS,* p. 656.
54 *Ibid.,* pp. 428–29.
55 *Ibid.,* p. 487.
56 *Ibid.,* p. 634.
57 E. B. O'Callaghan, *The Register of New Netherland, 1626–1674* (Albany, 1865) . A nonanalytical attempt to show continuity in office holding in New Netherland.
58 Edward van Winkle, *Manhattan, 1624–1639* (New York, 1916) .
59 *VRB MSS,* p. 320.
60 *NYCD,* I, 114.
61 *Ibid.,* I, 110–15, 149–51.
62 *Ibid.,* p. 83.
63 *VRB MSS,* pp. 805–22.
64 Cited in Raesly, *Portrait of New Netherland,* p. 33.
65 Cited in *ibid.,* p. 23; Brodhead, *Hist.,* I, 228–30.
66 *NNN,* p. 191.
67 A. J. F. van Laer (ed.), "Minutes of the Amsterdam Chamber of the Dutch West India Company, 1635–1636," *New York Genealogical and Biographical Record,* XLIX (1918) , 228.
68 Brodhead, *Hist.,* pp. 229–31; *NYCD,* I, 71–81, 93–94.
69 Amandus Johnson, *The Swedes on the Delaware, 1638–1664* (Philadelphia, 1915) .
70 *NYCD,* I, 110.

CHAPTER VI

1 Craven, *Dissolution of the Virginia Company,* p. 334; Pares, "Merchants and Planters," p. 13.
2 C. M. Andrews, *The Colonial Period of American History* (New Haven, 1937), III, 69 n; see also *ibid.,* III, 66–68; IV, 347–48; I, 67–69.
3 *NYCD,* I, 153.
4 *Ibid.,* II, 235.
5 *Ibid.,* I, 111.
6 *Ibid.,* I, 106.
7 *Ibid.,* I, 113, 121.
8 *Ibid.,* I, 422.
9 *Ibid.,* I, 155–56.
10 E. B. O'Callaghan, *History of New Netherland,* I, 178–79.
11 Brodhead, *Hist.,* I, 312.
12 K. G. Davies, *The Royal African Company* (London, 1957), p. 21.
13 *NYCD,* I, 111–12.
14 *Ibid.,* I, 182.
15 *Ibid.,* I, 422.
16 *Ibid.,* I, 135.
17 *Ibid.,* I, 212.
18 *Ibid.,* I, 135, 150, 172, 182, 191. In September, 1648, an ordinance was passed making consecutive residence in New Amsterdam for three years mandatory for all "merchants, Scots, and small traders." It also required such individuals to build a "decent burghers dwelling house, each according to his means." B. Fernow (ed.), *Records of New Amsterdam* (New York, 1897), I, 10.
19 Raesly, *Portrait of New Netherland,* 102–104; *NYCD,* I, 266, 431–32.
20 *NYCD,* I, 297.
21 Raesly, *Portrait of New Netherland,* pp. 84–104, 116, 229.
22 *NYCD,* I, 431–32.
23 *Ibid.; Yearbook of the Holland Society of New York for 1915,* pp. 1–3.
24 *NYCD,* I, 379.
25 Raesly, *Portrait of New Netherland,* pp. 24–35.
26 *Ibid.,* pp. 83–90, 321.
27 *NYCD,* I, 181, 431–32; *VRB MSS,* pp. 401, 416, 412, 431, 518.
28 *NYCD,* I, 432.
29 *NNN,* pp. 258–59.
30 *NYCD,* I, 181, 150.
31 *Ibid.,* I, 185, 415; *NNN,* pp. 211–18, 226–34.
32 A. W. Trelease, *Indian Affairs in Colonial New York: The Seventeenth Century* (Ithaca, New York, 1960), pp. 60–84.
33 *NYCD,* I, 101.
34 *Ibid.,* I, 211.
35 *Ibid.,* I, 213.
36 *Ibid.,* I, 345–46, 425.
37 *Ibid.,* I, 260, 318, 347.
38 *Ibid.,* I, 213, 264–66.
39 *Ibid.,* I, 423.
40 Stokes, *Iconography,* II, 226–27; Raesly, *Portrait of New Netherland,* pp. 34, 83.
41 *NYCD,* XIV, 468.
42 *VRB MSS,* p. 413.

43 *NYCD,* I, 262.
44 *Ibid.,* I, 298.
45 *Ibid.,* I, 296.
46 *Ibid.,* II, 220.
47 *Ibid.,* II, 211.
48 *Ibid.,* I, 260.
49 *Ibid.,* I, 213, 389.
50 *Ibid.,* I, 259; cf. also *ibid.,* I, 332–37. The "Princess" was the name of the ship which sank while carrying back Kieft to the Netherlands. Melyn and Kuyter, as representatives of the commonalty, were also aboard. It became a grievance because, with the sinking of the ship, a number of documents and depositions were supposedly lost. The leaders of the commonalty later claimed these would have conclusively demonstrated their case against the company. Judging from the documents that did survive, such a charge seems most unlikely.
51 *Ibid.,* I, 332–46, *passim.*
52 *Ibid.,* I, 99.
53 Hansen, *Atlantic Migration,* p. 33.
54 *NYCD,* I, 242.
55 *Ibid.,* I, 246.
56 *Ibid.,* I, 246–47, 294.
57 *Ibid.,* I, 313.
58 *Ibid.,* I, 364.
59 *Ibid.,* I, 264, 266.
60 Pares, "Merchants and Planters," p. 6.
61 *NYCD,* I, 265.
62 *Ibid.,* I, 336, 343.
63 Pares, "Merchants and Planters," pp. 10–13.
64 *NYCD,* I, 425.
65 *Ibid.,* pp. 185–89.
66 *Ibid.,* I, 423.
67 *Ibid.,* I, 370.
68 *Ibid.,* I, 423.
69 *Ibid.,* I, 275–318.
70 *Ibid.,* I, 296.
71 *Ibid.,* I, 269.
72 *Ibid.,* I, 388, 422.
73 *Ibid.,* I, 449–50, 453.
74 *Ibid.,* I, 462.
75 *Ibid.,* II, 156.
76 *Ibid.,* I, 199.
77 *Ibid.,* I, 203, 339.
78 *Ibid.,* I, 316.

EPILOGUE

1 *NNN,* p. 453.
2 *NYCD,* II, 474–75.
3 Andrews, *Colonial Period,* III, 92.
4 Condon, "New York's Dutch Period," p. 8.
5 Vlekke, *Dutch Nation,* p. 176.
6 Diamond, "Organization to Society," p. 475.

INDEX

ABOUT THE AUTHOR

THOMAS J. CONDON is Executive Associate at the American Council of Learned Societies in New York. Born in New Haven, Connecticut, he did his undergraduate work at Yale, received his M.A. from Boston College, and his Ph.D. from Harvard University. From 1962 to 1966 he taught history at the University of New Brunswick, Canada, and in 1967–1968 he was Visiting Associate Professor of History at the University of Indiana. He has published a number of articles on American colonial history.